Gerald Heard: The Perennial Philosopher

Writings on Religion and Spirituality

Contemporary and Classic
Gerald Heard
Endorsements

~~~~~~~~~~~~

"Gerald Heard enthusiastically lent his considerable literary and oratorical skills to disseminating the timeless, universal message of Vedanta, significantly furthering the movement started by Swami Vivekananda." (2024 endorsement)
—**Swami Sarvadevananda**, Minister and Spiritual Leader of the Vedanta Society of Southern California

"Gerald Heard was a revolutionary in the only revolution that matters: the revolution of consciousness, freeing us from the delusion of dualism and its violent politics of tribalism, for the realization of nondual reality and its politics of global love of and justice for all life. *Gerald Heard: The Perennial Philosopher* is a clarion call to join the revolution, awaken to truth, and heal the world." (2024 endorsement)
—**Rabbi Rami Shapiro**, spiritual teacher, author of *Perennial Wisdom for the Spiritually Independent*, co-director of the One River Foundation

"Gerald Heard is that rare being—a learned man who makes his mental home on the vacant spaces between the pigeon-holes. He has looked into a score of specialties and, out of what he has seen there, has constructed a comprehensive picture of the world—a picture in which the most diverse elements of reality take their places and are seen in significant relationship."
—**Aldous Huxley**, prominent author, intellectual, notable Vedantist

"Heard's work—and he published a number of insightful books—was one of the ideological sources of the human potential movement and was also instrumental in the spreading of Vedanta in the Western hemisphere." (from Dr. Feuerstein's 2006 review of Heard's book, *Pain, Sex and Time*)
—**Georg Feuerstein, PhD**, noted Indologist, Yoga scholar, prolific author

"Gerald Heard had a brilliant mind ... I can truly say that he broadened my vision of religion and spirituality." (from 2003)
—**Dave Brubeck**, world-renowned jazz composer

"Gerald Heard was unrivaled as a catalyst for the propagation of Vedanta, largely because he sparked the interest of people who would, in turn, reach millions of others. His role in accelerating the evolution of consciousness in the West was huge, thanks to his impact on key movers and shakers in the consciousness movement." (from 2009)
—**Philip Goldberg**, author of *American Veda: From Emerson and the Beatles to Yoga and Meditation – How Indian Spirituality Changed the West*

"By far the person that has influenced me most is the former BBC science commentator and practicing mystic, lecturer, and spiritual advisor, Gerald Heard. ... It was not only his ideas that influenced me but his very *being*, which was distinctly numinous and unlike anything I had previously experienced or have since. ... In Gerald Heard I experienced what I would call the *aura of sanctity*." (from 2002)
—**Dr. (Hon.) Rhea A. White**, founder-director of The Exceptional Human Experience Network

"Gerald Heard is the spiritual godfather of this Western movement [i.e., the Vedanta philosophy during the 1940s]. ... Mr. Heard's controversial books are brilliantly and provocatively written." (from the March 1947 issue of *Ellery Queen's Mystery Magazine*)
—**Ellery Queen** (a pseudonym of Frederic Dannay and Manfred B. Lee)

"Gerald Heard is one of the few who can be properly called philosopher, a man of brilliantly daring theory and devoted practice. I believe he has influenced the thought of our time, directly and indirectly, to an extent which will hardly be appreciated for another fifty years."
—**Christopher Isherwood**, prominent novelist and playwright, notable Vedantist

"To many thoughtful readers of this generation, Gerald Heard's books give the impression of a mind almost uniquely profound, sensitive and original among contemporary writers." (from the 1940s)
—*The New Christianity*

"Gerald Heard—as Huxley's spiritual mentor—must be acknowledged as true grandfather ... of the 'New Age,' the '60's spiritual counterculture ... But I believe Gerald's vision both preceded and transcended the attempted spiritual revolution of the 1960's." (from 2008)
—**Charles E. Vernoff**, Professor Emeritus of Religion at Cornell College, Iowa

Gerald Heard in Hollywood, CA, ca. 1961, cropped from a photo
taken of Gerald Heard with conductor Robert Craft.
(Credit: Jay Michael Barrie)

Gerald Heard: The Perennial Philosopher

Writings on Religion and Spirituality

Gerald Heard

Sky Parlor Publications™ · Nevada City, California

Library of Congress Control Number: 2024941276

ISBN: 979-8-9908834-0-6 (paperback)
ISBN: 979-8-9908834-1-3 (hardcover)
ISBN: 979-8-9908834-2-0 (e-book)

First edition published July 2024.
Second printing, with minor corrections/edits, October 2024.

Cover design and layout by Sky Parlor Publications™.

Sky Parlor Publications™ is a registered trademark in the United States of America.

Sky Parlor Publications™
P.O. Box 252
Nevada City, CA 95959
skyparlorpublications.com

EDITOR'S PREFACE
Spiritual Legacy of Gerald Heard[1]

October 6, 2021, marks the 132nd birth anniversary of influential author-historian-lecturer-philosopher Gerald Heard. The year 2021 also marks the fiftieth year since Gerald's passing. Gerald's contributions to the spiritual legacy of our contemporary Western world are enormous. Following his approximate 1934 conversion to the path of mysticism, Gerald (as he was commonly known) charted a sure and steady course that laid the foundation for others to follow. Beginning with 1937's *The Third Morality*, continuing through 1939's *Pain, Sex and Time*, and blossoming in the 1940s with a series of popular spiritual books, including his quintessential *Training for the Life of the Spirit* (1941), and culminating with his decade-ending compilation, 1949's *Prayers and Meditations*, Gerald's written musings on the spiritual life covered a broad swath of terrain that pointed in one direction: Godward.

In 1941, Gerald founded and directed Trabuco College, a prototype coeducational, interfaith spiritual community in Southern California. Gerald's focus was experiential rather than theoretical. He practiced what he preached, meditating six hours daily in the sublime Trabuco College oratory. Gerald influenced a number of key individuals who would, in their own way, disseminate a spiritual message—Aldous Huxley, Huston Smith, Michael Murphy, and others. The late yoga authority Georg Feuerstein, PhD, wrote, "Heard's work—and he published a number of insightful books—was one of the ideological sources of the human potential movement and was also instrumental in the spreading of Vedanta in the Western hemisphere" (from Dr. Feuerstein's review of *Pain, Sex and Time*).

All spiritual aspirants can benefit from Gerald's message: "There is a purpose in evolution—to evolve consciously, to evolve consciousness. That evolution is achieved only by the skilled, conscious training of our spirits" (*Training for the Life of the Spirit*). And so, on October 6, we commemorate Gerald's life, legacy, and passing. Gerald Heard: October 6, 1889, to August 14, 1971.

~~~~~~~~~~~~~

In this collection, I have assembled a treasury of forty-nine articles by Gerald Heard on the topics of religion and spirituality. The writing that begins this volume, "God Alone Is Pure Being," is a compilation of excerpts from Gerald's three essential spiritual books from the early 1940s: *The Creed of Christ, Training for the Life of the Spirit,* and *The Code of Christ.* These titles are published by Oregon-based Wipf and Stock Publishers, which is releasing first-ever eBook editions of these and additional Gerald Heard titles beginning in November 2024.

Next is reprinted the group of Gerald's writings that first appeared from 1939 through 1963 in the California-based *Voice of India* and *Vedanta and the West* journals. These periodicals served as foundational vehicles for Gerald's cavalcade of ideas and messages, and in these pages, he adroitly navigates numerous spiritual themes and religious topics—from fluent discussions of several Christian mystics, to in-depth studies of Vedanta philosophy, to advancing the practice of kindness long before the message of altruism became popular. The reader will find some writings more interesting than others; several discussions are simply riveting, and numerous spiritual gems can be found throughout. I have, however, omitted 1943's *Vindicæ Flammæ*, a tale of terror set during the Inquisition, which later appeared in the 1947 British edition of *The Great Fog,* and which is decidedly out of place in this collection.

After these writings and rounding out this book are ten articles by Gerald that first appeared in *The Aryan Path, The Christian Century, Christendom, Religion in Life,* and *Faith and Freedom,* from 1938 to 1955. In these articles, Gerald champions nonviolence as a solution to war, the training of skilled spiritual directors, collective contemplation practices, and a theistic method of maintaining moment-by-moment awareness decades before mindfulness became an industry.

Gerald Heard didn't follow trends; he set them. These visionary writings chart the trajectory of an informed spiritual voyager plotting an interreligious route through largely untraversed terrain, leaving a clearly defined trail for those following after.

~~~~~~~~~~~~~

Many of the third-party quotations in this book that also appeared in the original publications have been used without objection ever since. We continue to rely on the Fair Use Doctrine in using these quotations, many of which are formally referenced or otherwise credited to its author.

Reflecting the usage conventions of his time, Gerald almost exclusively uses the then prevalent patriarchal pronouns "man," "he," "him," and similar gender-specific pronouns in nonspecific contexts where he clearly intends a generic application. And so, whenever "man" or "woman," "men" or "women," "he" or "she," "him" or "her," "his" or "hers," or "himself" or "herself" are used as nonspecific pronouns, this usage is not intended to indicate any specific gender.

I have revised certain wording in this collection to reflect inclusive and sensitive language, as I have attempted to strike a balance between Gerald's original writing style and contemporary usage. Toward this end, I have silently incorporated gender-neutral wording in most, but not all, instances throughout the text. For example, "mankind" has typically been replaced with "humanity" or "humankind."

While his observations and insights remain important and influential, in a few places Gerald Heard's prose may strike some contemporary readers as insensitive, off-putting, or simply outdated. The present edition contains some revisions that are meant to address such instances, as well as factual corrections. Wherever the original text has been changed, the change has been made either silently, or else as indicated by ellipses or brackets. A number of passages are accompanied by an explanatory editor's note located within the text or as an endnote.

Similarly, I have broken up long paragraphs (one ran over 1,400 words, another 1,660 words), as well as many of Gerald's trademark run-on, compound sentences (one tallied 116 words) for readability' sake. I've also silently incorporated new punctuation marks as warranted to endow certain sentences with greater clarity. I abridged five articles, omitting some lengthy sections that did not clearly serve the theme or move the article along, as evidenced by his later, less focused essays, "Vision" and "Communication." None of these emendations are intended to change Gerald's meaning but rather to communicate his wealth of ideas in a more readily understandable and readable manner.

Disclaimer: Mention of various meditation, spiritual, and other practices in this book is intended for educational purposes only and does not constitute professional advice or act as a substitute for seeking expert advice from a qualified medical or other professional. The reader is advised to seek expert personal guidance or medical advice as warranted before undertaking any of these practices.

John Roger Barrie
Literary Executor of Gerald Heard
Nevada City, California
July 7, 2024

Photograph of a medal from the Trabuco College of Prayer,
depicting the Crux Orata, or "Praying Cross," which was the primary
symbol associated with Gerald Heard during his Trabuco College years.
(Credit: John Roger Barrie)

ACKNOWLEDGEMENTS

Certain individuals deserve special thanks, as their contributions helped ensure the integrity and accuracy of this work. I am most grateful to noted author and attorney Jonathan Kirsch, Esq., for reviewing and advising on certain sections of the book. I greatly appreciate the skillful work of editor and author Rob Bignell, for reviewing and commenting on selected portions of the book. I extend my deepest gratitude to library technician Leslie Vera of the Nevada County, California Library, for her expert assistance with a number of research matters.

Although our position is that Gerald Heard retained the original copyright in these articles, we nonetheless reached out to various entities, which expressly provided either permission, clearance, approval, or otherwise helped to facilitate the publication of the articles in this collection. We likewise contacted institutions and individuals regarding various additional usages that appear herein. We extend our warmest gratitude to the following entities and persons for the courtesies they extended to us:

- The Vedanta Society of Southern California (VSSC)—(*Voice of India* and *Vedanta and the West* articles; photograph of Swami Prabhavananda and Gerald Heard): Vedanta Press Manager Robert Adjemian, VSSC President Phil Galloway, VSSC volunteer archivist Jon Monday.
- Swami Sarvadevananda (VSSC), Rabbi Rami Shapiro, Brenda Feuerstein, Philip Goldberg, and Paul Edison-Lahm (usage of endorsements or quotations).
- *Prabuddha Bharata* magazine (letter by Gerald Heard to Swami Nikhilananda): Editor Swami Divyakripananda.
- Wipf and Stock Publishers (excerpts from *The Creed of Christ, Training for the Life of the Spirit,* and *The Code of Christ,* which are used by permission of Wipf and Stock Publishers, www.wipfandstock.com): Wipf and Stock Rights and Permissions Manager Jason Robeck.
- *The Christian Century:* Editor-Publisher Rev. Peter W. Marty, Permissions Editor Marie Watson, Director of Finance Maureen C. Gavin.
- The Theosophy Company (India) Pvt. Ltd. (*The Aryan Path*).
- The United Methodist Publishing House (*Religion in Life*): Intellectual Property Support Services Coordinator Lisa Barry.

"If I am to be remembered at all, I hope it would be as an historian of consciousness and its evolution."

—Gerald Heard to Professor Ted Solomon
of Iowa State University, early 1950s

Gerald Heard:
The Perennial Philosopher

CONTENTS

FOREWORD
Gerald Heard and Vedanta[2]
by John Roger Barrie

[Vedanta's] particular blend of empiricism with metaphysic, the width of its cosmology, the vastness of the picture that it gives of human destiny, and the immediate practicalness of its advices and practices—this amalgam seems most suitable to anyone who wants a method which is psychological and a worldview that can match modern knowledge of the cosmos.[3]

–Gerald Heard

The great Hindu saint Sri Ramakrishna (1836–1886) embodied a fathomless spirituality that spread to all lands. Of foremost importance to one of his young, fiery *sadhus* was the land of America. That monk, Swami Vivekananda, imbued with foresight and sanctioned by divine grace, established a number of Vedanta centers throughout the United States, thus anchoring a bedrock of spirituality that flourishes to this day. Guided by generation after generation of Ramakrishna Order sadhus, many a soul has sought refuge in these islands of spiritual power.

One such soul was the British polymath Gerald Heard. Henry Fitzgerald Gerald Heard was born in London in 1889. A precocious child, Gerald, as he was forever known, nonetheless suffered through a childhood "full of stresses and lacking any fundamental peace,"[4] as it was marked by periods of emotional abuse and bouts of physical pain. Both were inflicted by his stern, unyielding father, a fundamentalist minister, who instilled in Gerald "the fear of hell"[5] and subjected the boy to "terrific outbursts of anger"[6] and beatings, and occasionally made him wear a hair shirt; while the physical pain was caused both by Gerald being dropped as an infant by a drunken nursemaid, which broke his back, and his being run over by a carriage at age twelve. Both incidents produced lifelong health issues.

Intelligent, sensitive, and indoctrinated into the Anglican Church by family tradition, Gerald entered Cambridge University in 1908 to pursue ordination as a minister. But his skeptical bent caused him to doubt the doctrines of the very church he aspired to serve. A crisis of faith ensued, and Gerald, having obtained a degree in 1911, left Cambridge in 1913. By 1916, he suffered a nervous breakdown. Recovery came gradually, and the person that emerged favored secular humanism over religion. Still retaining a social idealism, he became involved in liberal causes such as progressive education and social reform.

During this time, Gerald took to secretarial work, first for Lord Robson, then for Sir Horace Plunkett, founder of the Irish Agricultural Cooperative movement. His insatiable intellectual appetite reportedly drove him to read two thousand books a year, a remarkable feat. He published his first book *Narcissus* in 1924, in which the careful reader will find the seeds of his subsequent theories on the evolution of consciousness. His second and more significant book, 1929's *The Ascent of Humanity,* was awarded the prestigious Hertz Prize. In that same year, he met brothers Julian and Aldous Huxley. Shortly thereafter, he became the first science broadcaster for the BBC, which brought him accolades from the likes of H. G. Wells.

In the late 1920s, a significant event occurred. While undertaking his academic researches, he came across the teachings of Buddhism, "the Eightfold Path," as he recalled in a 1953 lecture,[7] which produced a profound effect that stood in stark contrast to his rigid, abusive fundamentalist upbringing. Even though he eventually embraced Vedanta, this encounter motivated him to undertake methods that would enable him to experience firsthand the pure consciousness about which he had theorized. He visited Dartington Hall, an experimental college, and he began practicing yoga. He embraced celibacy in around 1934 and taught yogic breathing exercises to Aldous Huxley in that same year to help Huxley with his poor vision. The would-be Christian minister turned scientific materialist had been bitten by Lord Buddha and was now the victim of an unquenchable thirst, a deep spiritual craving. Gerald had come around full circle.

By the time Gerald and Aldous Huxley left England and arrived in New York City in April 1937, Gerald's renewed love affair with God was in full swing. But it came about through experiential spirituality, not formal religion. Gerald was referencing Hinduism and Buddhism in his philosophically oriented 1930s books, and he advocated spiritual techniques in 1937's *The Third Morality*. Despite its provocative title, 1939's pivotal *Pain, Sex and Time* mentioned yogic practices and advocated meditation and continence in order that one's consciousness may "experience sustained intensity of being."

Although Gerald poured his vast intellect into his newfound avocation, something was still missing. That something was the guidance of a living teacher. Once settled in Los Angeles, by mid-1939 he met Swami Prabhavananda, founder and minister of the Vedanta Society of Southern California (VSSC). Subsequently, and in short order, Gerald persuaded Aldous Huxley and Christopher Isherwood to meet the Swami, and through Gerald's influence, John Van Druten and many others came into the Vedanta fold. Isherwood in particular maintained close contact and involvement with the VSSC over the years, and he acknowledged Gerald's role in his August 1944 inscription in Gerald's copy of *The Song of God*: "Whether you like it or not, you are really responsible for my share in this!" As Ellery Queen aptly noted in the March 1947 issue of *Ellery Queen's Mystery Magazine*, concerning Gerald's impact in spreading Vedanta during the 1940s, "Gerald Heard is the spiritual godfather of this Western movement."

Gerald made his first written appearance in the VSSC's journal, *Voice of India* [*VOI*] (later renamed *Vedanta and the West* [*VATW*]) in the September 1939 issue by virtue of an anonymous contribution, "The Vedanta as the Scientific Approach to Religion." In the very next issue, October 1939, along with Swami Prabhavananda, he was named co-editor, and therein he published his first contribution as Gerald Heard, "Is There Progress?"

Gerald received meditation instructions from Swami Prabhavananda early on. The Swami initiated both Gerald and Huxley before Isherwood took his own initiation on November 8, 1940.[8] In a May 14, 1981, letter to Swami Yogeshananda (d. 2021), who was an American monk of the Ramakrishna Order, Gerald's longtime devoted personal secretary, business manager, and editor Jay Michael Barrie wrote that Gerald was initiated by the Swami in 1939. "Regarding Gerald's dream of Ramakrishna [wherein Gerald was in India with Ramakrishna, and as Gerald walked past him, Ramakrishna pointed to Gerald, saying, "That one belongs to me."] ... he had had the dream in *1939*! He had been asking Swami [Prabhavananda] to initiate him and [Swami] had been putting him off, as was often his wont. Then Gerald had the dream (the account of the dream Chris [Isherwood] gave[9] was correct) and when he told Swami about it, [Swami] was very excited and said, 'You must be initiated at once!'—and he was."[10]

It is not foreign to students of Vedanta to read accounts of disciples questioning their teachers. Gerald expressed such questions in an April 8, 1941, letter that he sent to Swami Prabhavananda. The Swami addressed Gerald's concerns in the May–June 1941 issue of *VATW* without mentioning Gerald by name. Gerald resigned from his editorial post at the time, but the two men never severed ties, and Gerald frequently lectured at the Hollywood Center during the mid-1940s.

"A long-cherished dream of Heard's," writes Jay Michael Barrie, "had been to establish a place where the study of comparative religion, together with research into and practice of the techniques of meditation and prayer as taught by the major religions of the world, might be carried on. In 1941, Heard put the larger part of his financial resources [$100,000 from his inheritance] into building and endowing Trabuco College,"[11] which consisted of "a large complex" of serene Mediterranean-style buildings "situated in the middle of some [nearly] 300 acres, about 75 miles south of Los Angeles, near the remote and small community of Trabuco Canyon."[12] Trabuco College, operated by a non-profit board of directors, was guided by Gerald's visionary direction.

"For the next five years, from one to two dozen revolving students—men and women living under the rule of celibacy—meditated three times daily, studied, worked in the garden, performed arduous chores, prepared and ate vegetarian meals, and listened to lectures on religious life. Gerald penned several religious-themed books during his time in residence,"[13] including his essential *Training for the Life of the Spirit*. A number of eminent or soon-to-be famous individuals visited Trabuco, including Tibetologist W. Y. Evans-Wentz, religion scholar Huston Smith, Zen scholar D. T. Suzuki, Zen philosopher Alan Watts, and AA co-founder Bill Wilson. Gerald spoke regularly, while Swami Prabhavananda, "Aldous Huxley, and others gave talks on occasion."[14]

While Gerald's embrace of interfaith principles was evident in the 1930s, they flourished during the Trabuco era and can readily be found in his *VOI* and *VATW* writings. The term "Philosophia Perennis" was first used by Huxley in his essay "A Note on the Bhagavatam," which appeared in the July–Aug. 1943 issue of *VATW*. Tellingly, the very next issue of *VATW* (Sept.–Oct. 1943) included Gerald's article, "The Philosophia Perennis," in which Heard praised Dr. Ananda Coomaraswamy's studies showing "that the essentials of Christianity, of Buddhism in its two forms, and of Hinduism are one. Here," wrote Gerald, "is the *Philosophia Perennis*, here the Eternal Gospel." It would not be a stretch to conjecture that Gerald's article was inspired by Huxley's intriguing term. Volley back to Huxley.[15]

Indeed, Huxley's *The Perennial Philosophy* was published in September 1945, whereas in August 1946, Gerald published his own *The Eternal Gospel*, which, however, traversed different ground. Yet, the strain of Gerald's common-denominator interreligious approach is already apparent in his November 1939, *VOI* article, "Unknown Indian Influences." As Reinhold Niebuhr wrote in his May 7, 1944, *The New York Times* review of Gerald's *A Preface to Prayer*, "He pleads for a religious syncretism which accepts the scriptures of Vedanta, of Buddhism, Jainism and Taoism together with 'the best in the Bible.'"

[In the present collection, Gerald's main focus is on Vedanta and Christianity. Moreover, he provides brilliant analyses of the human condition, inspired insights into human nature and the inner workings of the mind, intimate details of many spiritual processes, and he knowledgably discusses various spiritual disciplines whereby a person may apply the principles of the *Philosophia Perennis* in order to bring about experiential spiritual realization.]

There is some debate about the reasons why Gerald discontinued Trabuco College. Prof. William H. Forthman, who first met Gerald in 1939 and resided at Trabuco College several times during the 1940s, has written, "He concluded it was not producing the educational and spiritual outcomes he had hoped for."[16] Trabuco College was the first coeducational spiritual community in America to incorporate nonsectarian, interreligious principles and practices. "Thirty years ahead of its time, the Trabuco College experiment was discontinued in [July] 1947,"[17] and Gerald moved out in October of that year.

"The [facility] was made available for several projects during the next two years. None of these ventures measured up to what Heard felt was the *raison d'être* of Trabuco's having been established originally. Consequently, and at his specific request, in 1949, the facilities and property were turned over to The Vedanta Society of Southern California, and subsequently became the Ramakrishna Monastery,"[18] which was formally dedicated on September 7, 1949. For decades, the Ramakrishna Monastery has remained a beacon of spiritual solace to resident monks and lay aspirants alike.

Gerald continued delivering lectures at the VSSC from the late 1940s through 1954, both in Hollywood and Santa Barbara, drawing large crowds because of the spiritual topics he discussed and his scintillating oratorical style. Many of these lectures were published as articles in *VATW*. In 1951, he resumed editorial duties for that same journal as an advisor, a post he held until 1962. Altogether he published thirty-nine articles in *VATW*,[19] many of which were reprinted in Christopher Isherwood's two compilations, *Vedanta for the Western World* (1946), and *Vedanta for Modern Man* (1951). His last article appeared in the July–Aug. 1963 issue, titled "Death," which, ironically and perhaps fittingly, just as his very first article had been, was an anonymous contribution. Gerald also wrote an introduction to 1949's *Towards the Goal Supreme* by Swami Virajananda, the then President of the Ramakrishna Math and Mission, whose book he praised: "Practically any question that might arise in the mind of a seeker is raised and discussed."

Swami Prabhavananda and Gerald maintained their relationship for thirty-two years, until Gerald's passing in 1971. Altogether, Gerald wrote thirty-eight books and numerous articles, delivered hundreds of lectures, and investigated various subjects throughout his lifetime. Naturally, not all of Gerald's topics were of interest to the Swami. While the two men shared some differences in their approaches to spirituality, their relationship could best be characterized as one of mutual respect (Swami typically would address Gerald as "Mr. Heard"), affection, and spiritual love.

During the lengthy five-year illness that preceded Gerald's death, Jay Michael Barrie read to him nightly from *The Gospel of Sri Ramakrishna*. Throughout this time, Swami Prabhavananda solicitously enquired of Gerald's wellbeing and conveyed his blessings to him. At the moment of his passing, Barrie stated that Gerald, already severely incapacitated from the effects of twenty-six minor and five major strokes during the previous five years, suddenly opened his eyes—wide open and crystal clear—as if gazing into some unfathomable Being. In that vivid state of awareness, at the age of eighty-one, Gerald Heard breathed his last breath.

A scholar's scholar and a bohemian's bohemian, Gerald's quest was one of spiritual realization. It was neither an armchair interest nor a passing fad. He maintained a regular and rigorous discipline of meditation for decades. As attested to in general by some,[20] and with specificity both by Isherwood[21] and Trabuco resident Marvin Barrett,[22] he famously meditated six hours daily for many years, beginning in 1939, presumably after he had received initiation and meditation instructions from Swami Prabhavananda,[23] and continuing especially during the Trabuco era. The core of his mature beliefs centered on the intentional evolution of consciousness, and his applied spirituality was intended to affect changes in conduct, character, and consciousness, and to make the human organism a fit vessel for the realization of God. To use Ramakrishna's analogy, he did not come to the mango orchard to count the trees; he wanted to taste the mangos. However, it might be more correctly stated that, accounting for Gerald's unquenchable intellectual curiosity, after he entered the mango orchard and picked a few ripe mangoes, he sat himself down in an elevated area of the orchard so that, while he was eating, he could also count the mango trees.

Gerald was a catalyst for spreading the message of Vedanta and interreligious studies and practices during the middle part of the twentieth century. His passion for experiential spirituality acted like a contagion on those around him. Gerald Heard, the perennial philosopher, made substantial contributions to the Ramakrishna–Vedanta movement, the Vedanta Society of Southern California, and society at large. His massive influence underlies and radically affected the spiritual and consciousness movements of subsequent decades. Gerald's abiding association with Western Vedanta and with Swami Prabhavananda, who himself significantly put Vedanta on the map in this country, have produced profound and lasting legacies that are very much in evidence to this day.

Swami Prabhavananda and Gerald Heard, from July 4, 1948, on the grounds of the Vedanta Society of Southern California, amid new construction then taking place. This date marked the annual commemoration of Swami Vivekananda's *Maha Samadhi*, when, on July 4, 1902, the great Swami left his body and entered nondual spiritual absorption. Photo is cropped and slightly sharpened from the original. Used by kind permission of the Vedanta Society of Southern California.

Gerald Heard: The Perennial Philosopher

Writings on Religion and Spirituality

God Alone is Pure Being

Compilation of spiritual writings from three
early 1940s Gerald Heard books, used by kind permission
of Wipf and Stock Publishers, www.wipfandstock.com.

The Aim of Creation

THE PURPOSE OF THE WORLD is not the establishment of a physical Utopia. ... The aim of creation is the evolution of life; that evolution, when it reaches human level, becomes the evolution of consciousness.[24] That evolution is now achieved and achieved only by the skilled, conscious training of our spirits.[25] We must ourselves deliberately develop ourselves. That evolution which follows will show itself in a threefold development: in growth of conduct, of character and of consciousness itself.[26]

The world exists for people to achieve union with God. The universe and life are the means whereby souls achieve Enlightenment and Liberation.[27] The meaning of all ... the purpose and the end of all is and can only be this one thing, the supreme blessedness, Seeing God.[28]

Prayer is Communion With God

Prayer of the highest quality—contemplation—is literally the creation of an atmosphere, an air in which the soul can begin to breathe, a radiation in which the spirit can mutate. Such intense activity brings the air of eternity into time, and our immortal nature, which is lying drugged and cataleptic within us, stirs and begins to come out of its coma.[29]

Contemplation is the next and necessary step of man's evolution.[30] The mind is making precisely this attempt to enter a general condition of prayer, a general unceasing Sense of Presence and the sufficiency of that Presence. That Sense of Presence is its one and sufficient exercise during its time of prayer. And that same Sense of Presence now begins to frame and permeate all its other times and activities.[31]

This constant recalling at all times, ... during the rest of the day and in all [one's] other activities ... will aid the specific times of meditation and vice versa, for the aim is to attain a state when there is no difference of attention and awareness in the one or the other.[32]

The deeper the prayer—the more the self is lost in [awareness] of the unspeakable One—the deeper is the unity. ... For only in the intense focus of utter Bring can the atomic hardness of our egos be fused. We begin to grow, to transmute.[33] The best prayer being of course complete, unhindered communion with God.[34]

Intentional Living

We come to the provisional conclusion that there is a Reality, an utter and complete Being to be found. ... We pass then to the second step. We reach right resolve. If it is the truth that there is utter Reality then such a Reality should be manifest among us. ... That right resolve leads inevitably to a new and right way of life, a right regime of avowed intentional living. Every activity is now coordinated to that one meaning-making purpose. Thought, word, deed, and livelihood are all integrated in the single all-embracing design.[35]

Heaven Is Being Without an Ego

Sainthood does exist and, quite apart from its goodness, it is a quality of being, a range of consciousness of such intensity, such singleness of spirit, that it may well be estimated as being another species of human creature, as far as character is concerned.[36] But what are saints? They are simply [those] who permit God's forgiveness to come into them so fully that not only are their sins washed out, but also their very selves, their egos, and the root of their self-will.[37]

Heaven is being without an ego. ... [We] must and can get rid of the ego completely. Once we realize that God alone is pure Being then we understand that if only we can be empty of ourselves, ... God does the rest—we are instantaneously filled with the Invisible Reality the moment we get rid of the visible sham. ... You can know the moment you have really and fully gotten rid of the ego. ... You will feel immediately the peace of God, the perfect trust in God, the joy of God. You will know you are in heaven.[38]

The Single-Hearted Do See God

There is a Reality, beside which this world is but a shadow (though a significant and pressing shadow).[39] God is Reality, utterly greater, far more real than anything else. Everything else, everyone else, all objects and persons are merely phenomena, appearances, more or less permanent insofar as they are near or far from that Center. He and He alone is absolutely real.[40]

God is both within us and also ... He utterly transcends the space–time world we experience outwardly.[41] It is that when we see God, as we are transformed, we, as separate self-seeking wills are completely radiated away—we become God. This is not blasphemy. The little ego does not swagger about saying, "I am God." ... We face and are swept by that Incomparable Instantaneity in which every experience of loveliness is gathered up in one overwhelming Present.[42]

The single-hearted—those who free their consciousness from the distortion of greed and fear, from the illusion of self—do see God. ... As God is Reality, seeing Him is not merely obtaining a right view of things as they actually are, it is also a radiation, exposed to which the spirit mutates. We become like what we see.[43]

If we will throw away all our inflammable shams and pretenses, if we will dare seek one thing and one thing only—the sheer presence, the constant and complete reality of God—then desperately seeking we shall find and dying behold we live.[44]

Our Whole Life Must Become Intentional

The mystic[s] [are] those men and women who chose above all else to see whether, not as an abstraction of philosophy, a dogma of religion, a sanction of morality, or a hope after death, but here and now, God might be found, experienced, and known during every minute of every day.[45]

Ordinary events ... must seem to the ordinary person confusing, irrelevant, an endless chapter of accidents. ... The ordinary person's way of living cannot lead to further evolution; on the contrary, it confirms their illusions. ... Our life today is based on the belief that life as a whole has no purpose. ... Our whole life must become intentional and purposive, instead of a series of irrelevant events, adventures, and accidents, happy or unhappy.[46]

The task is nothing less than the shift of the whole being, the entire consciousness, until it alters from self-consciousness to union with the All, to God-consciousness, until the aperture of awareness, the focus of understanding, sees everything, no longer from the standpoint of the self, but from the outlook of eternity.[47] The life of doubt and vacillation then becomes the life of certitude and coordinated purpose; the life of accident turns into the life of meaning, chance into design, the vicious-circled self into the Infinite Being, and time into eternity.[48]

The Kingdom Is Already Here

The Kingdom is already here, around us, within us. ... This full Living Now is true eternity ... always at hand, "closer than breathing, nearer than hands or feet" [Tennyson[49]].[50] The mystic feels that anywhere that God is not unmistakably manifest is hell.[51] Our Lord evidently held that the Kingdom was not an organization but rather a contagion. It is a state of mind which spreads and forms through our being.[52]

We Are Obstacles to the Kingdom

We are obstacles to the Kingdom. We must start without delay on the painful, steep, humiliating path of undoing our busy, deliberately deluded selves. So only will the Kingdom come. ... "The Kingdom of God is within you," yes, but only if we are prepared to let that powerful germ of eternal life grow, until it splits away and consumes this husk, our ego. Unless we, this person with [their] tightly bound triple self-love—love of [their] physical appetites and comforts, of [their] possessions, of [their] place, rank, and recognition—unless that hard

4

and hardening nut is buried and rots and is eaten away by the new life's germ, there is no hope.[53]

Indeed we may say that the whole secret of the spiritual life is just this painful struggle to come awake, to become really conscious. And, conversely, the whole process and technique of evil is to do just the reverse to us: to lull us to sleep; to distract us from what is creeping up within us; to tell us that we are busy workers for the Kingdom when we are absentmindedly (while we daydream of our importance) spreading death, not life; to persuade us that we are wise, practical, creative, when we are sinking daily into a blinder and more fatal automatism.[54]

You are not free. You dream. You flatter yourself that you are free. In point of fact you are an automaton, and every year, indeed by every action, you are becoming more and more of a machine.[55]

Our actions are mainly conditioned reflexes, things which we do without thought, as to either the means or the ends. ... Our deeds, our rushings about, if we review the whole of them at one day's end, have little more purpose about them than the random gesturings and twitchings of St. Vitus' dance. But they serve the one grim purpose of keeping us from seeing ourselves.[56] The very first [step] is to know that I as I am, am an obstacle to the Kingdom. I must start, before anything else, by clearing myself out of the way.[57]

Spiritual Exercises

Petitionary prayer can never be safely used by those in whom any trace of egotism still remains. ... The chief danger lies, not in the fact that I may not be answered, but in the fact that I may, and that which answers may not be God. Spiritual exercises, on the other hand, are what everyone must employ if [they] would not suffocate spiritually. In a phrase, they are the deliberate methods of breathing in the Breath of Life and of exposing the individual consciousness to the radiation of the Eternal. They are the athletic and skilled exertions whereby the soul lays hold, by what is rightly called an act of devotion, and is so raised out of its self-engrossment into God's presence.[58]

Purgation is ... simply the reduction of the ego. Once that swelling is reduced, the individual consciousness becomes free to develop.[59] Purgation in itself is good. For in so far ... as we are emptied of self, ... so far are we freed from accident, from accident in our acts ... of doing what we really do not intend. ... If we go on to Liberation and Enlightenment we can have freedom from accident, not only in our conduct but in our character. Our habit-patterns, our moods, our conditioned reflexes, our natures can be reconditioned, re-freed. ... We will be inwardly re-united, our fissured selves refused. ... Then there is added, to freedom from accident in our conduct and freedom from accident in our character, the final, completing freedom, freedom in our consciousness itself.[60]

That in a phrase is the whole of Meditation and Contemplation: holding the self in the Presence of Reality, of Timeless Being. ... The aim, we have seen, is above all to be able to remain as long as we can in the radiation of the Light Invisible. ... It is that vision and that alone which can radiate away the ineffective ego. Let that be eliminated and *ipso facto* we must be one with Him. ... We gaze, interested, quiet, aware of an immense significance, a tremendous sense of Presence. The swirl of time and space is smoothed out. ... We shall realize that we have been face to face with the Inexpressible.[61]

The Task Is to Bring Peace

Every perfected soul as it attains to the Light of all understanding, as it becomes through the Divine Mercy completely released, turns back and stands incandescent with compassion, to light others on their way home. The freed soul acknowledges in the very discovery of its union with the Highest, its community with the lowest.[62] The perfected worker is now an instrument through which God can express His intentions for humankind. ... The task is to bring Peace.[63]

Peacemaking, according to Christ, alone becomes possible when there has been achieved union with God Himself, with Reality itself, with the source of all power and the foundation behind all appearance.[64] We must be ourselves in heaven before we can bring heaven around us or to a single person around us.[65] All our pain and striving arises from our failure to realize that we are one.[66]

You have to make this grade, achieve this new birth. This is a psychical, a spiritual process. ... You will have to make the grade, somehow, sometime. You had better begin now. Nothing is gained by delay. ... Start now, become wholly free. ... You will begin to enjoy even here the happiness of having found the life eternal and being able to point to others the way.[67]

The Vedanta as the Scientific Approach to Religion

Originally published in *Voice of India*,
Vol. 2, No. 7, September 1939

THE REVIVAL OF INTEREST in religion is perhaps the most significant symptom of our time. For long we have been aware that materialism, whether true or false, is not going to win. There is a vast mass of people—nowhere better represented than in Los Angeles—who, whether their intelligences are able to grasp the arguments of mechanistic science or not, are possessed of wills that are determined not to accept a doctrine which maintains that their lives are futile, their existences mean nothing, and the spirit has no significance.

We are not, however, concerned with this pathetic defiance nor with the childish defenses with which it would protect itself, except insofar as such efforts by their very absurdities prove how profound is the need that can provoke such reactions. We are concerned with far graver symptoms of a great social "deficiency" disease. It would not matter much—save for themselves—if a few millions of oldsters, possessed no longer of livers which will stand drink or nerves which will endure gambling, take to fanciful cults to while away the boredom of retirement and make them forget a future that holds in it no further outstanding event save death.

It is of immediate social concern when the young and highly vigorous start showing similar signs of the lack of spiritual vitamins. For they will not take to cults that only harm themselves nor practice illusions which end in the [sanitarium] or the cult-house. For some time we have dismissed with a superior smile the neurotic vagaries of elderly introverts. With our utterly superficial psychology we have attributed such behavior to balked sex and the death fear. Today the contagion has spread from the dozing [oldsters] to the most athletic and energetic youthful extroverts. As Carl Jung has pointed out, in the fanatical crusading enthusiasms of the young stormtroopers of the Totalitarian States, we have a persecuting dogmatic faith, [which might] be compared with the rise of [certain elements within Islam].

Nationalism today has sprung up as a force capable of destroying civilization because the lack of religion—the lack of a discipline and goal in which the individual might transcend themselves—left a vacuum in people's minds, an emptiness and craving which, being without its right satisfaction, seized upon a false one. Put people adrift at sea in a boat without fresh water, and however much you warn them that to drink sea water is deadly, when the pangs of thirst come upon them and they see the clear delusive liquid near them, they drink it and die mad. Nor is this thirst–madness merely a symptom of "neurotic Europe." Nothing is giving educationalists in the United States greater concern than just this—that there is an immense gap in the national education. In technical education, in making men and women experts and specialists, the United States has nothing to fear. If improvements are required, it is quite easy to see how they may be provided. It is the other side of the educational ledger which is causing a concern so grave that here there is almost a conspiracy of silence, for no one knows how that growing debit may be met.

Lately a questionnaire was circulated among prominent educationalists. It suggested—what is obvious—that American education [has] an increasing list, a list that if not remedied must lead it to capsize. It gave a long series of suggestions as to how this disbalance might be corrected. These ranged from creative drama, through occupational therapeutic hobbies, out to collectivized hiking. Indeed only two activities from the realm of ends were omitted: philosophy and religion. That is significant [as it reveals] the apprehension and the helplessness among progressive and influential educationalists. And while they question and avoid the pressing issue—"Is life possible without a philosophy, without a religion?"—the great public and its government go on their way making the problem more difficult daily. For the person on the street and their [representative] whom they send to Congress have not as yet awakened to the fact that there is any disbalance at all. The people who make public opinion and the laws are still at that pre-psychological condition of mind when it is assumed that, as life in the end must terminate in futility, you can make people content by increasing their means, until they will forget that there are no ends worth living for. As life has no meaning, we shall increase amusements until everyone is so distracted that they won't be able to think even of their own deaths. This is of course pathetic nonsense and, were it not, no rational being could maintain such wishful thinking for a moment.

Here of course is religion's opportunity, yet we see Western religion is helpless to take it. When its hunger for meaning grows unbearable, youth today will turn not to the churches but to those who preach crusading nationalism. Why is Western religion helpless? In the answer to that question there lies, it would seem, the case for Vedanta.

Western religion has made three fundamental mistakes. Taking its cosmology from the rudimentary [Abrahamic religious] worldview, it tied itself to a crude Apocalypticism. By the sixth century, Parousial expectations, long discouraged by the [early] church, were given an ad hoc moral substitute by the invention of the doctrine of Purgatory. This doctrine, leading to ecclesiastical corruption, was repudiated by the Reformation. Henceforward, Protestantism would have no worldview unless it returned to Apocalypticism by becoming Fundamentalist. The Vedanta has a worldview infinitely vaster than the [Abrahamic religions] and one that does not contradict the findings of science. The statement that the physical world is a construction of the human mind from a substratum, a basic unity which our animal senses break up into a manifold, is a statement which modern physics can support. The hypothesis that consciousness is *sui generis* and this particular temporal experience is an event in a series which extends beyond it in both directions, is a hypothesis which research into consciousness tends to establish.

This brings us to the second great mistake of Western religion, and it is even graver than the first. Western religion neglected psychology and psychophysiology. Its concept of deity, fluctuating between a humanized Jehovah (the loving Father of Jesus Christ) and a Trinity in which an anthropomorphized Logos mediates between humans and the inflexible absolute Judge God, made Christianity's one praxis to be simple petitionary prayer. True, Eastern influences introduced a crude asceticism (such as the Thebaid) and an occasional secondhand knowledge of meditation, but psychical and psychophysical knowledge was lacking, and whenever there was any search for these things, the [Catholic] Church ruthlessly persecuted the seekers. In Vedanta, meditation and contemplation are basic and make a complete working psychology, while with this scientific knowledge there is, as a modern [person] would expect and demand, a clear realization of the body–mind relationship, of how individuals may and only may change the aperture of consciousness by a thorough understanding of that relationship. And all this rests not on blind authority, but upon empirical work that any enquirer may repeat (indeed must repeat) and confirm for themselves.

As Dr. Irving Babbitt has said, it is the West that has made experiment and religion seem an impossible combination. But once [we] trust authority blindly and permit authority to rule that deity is arbitrary power only revealing itself in unchangeable dogmas, [then] the Church must first condemn all experiment and then fall into the further, graver error of persecuting and striving to destroy all who differ from orthodoxy's rulings. This was the third and final blunder of Western religion. Tied to an inadequate world-picture, lacking a psychology, fearing experiment, it had to end in the last and worst mistake of brutal intolerance. The Vedanta, having a world-picture that counsels against impatience and rashness, and having a psychology that shows how people may test truth and, further, may change their characters and their consciousness, not only avoids intolerance but has a scientific case for tolerance. Tolerating other religions teaches a person to understand two great truths that the intolerant overlook to their cost. The first and more obvious is that people's characters are not changed by coercion—and yet to change character is the sole aim of religion. You may alter the forms but soon, though your labels may stick, even the forms have gone back to express the unaltered outlook of the so-called converted.

The second and even more important truth that tolerance reveals is that there are not merely higher and lower types in the world, but that people of equal intelligence, integrity, and devotion inherit different methods whereby they must make their initial approaches to the Inexpressible Ultimate. Some are, to borrow Dr. William Sheldon's valuable nomenclatory classification, mainly cerebrotonic, others viscerotonic and a third large class principally somatotonic. The first class will be predominantly intellectual and rational, having little use for symbols or conscious need for psychophysical aids to concentration. The second will be much moved and helped by adequate and progressive symbolism. The third is very dependent on a coordination of mind and body in its religious practices and, obtaining this aid, may often outstep the intellectual who unwisely despises such techniques. The needs of these types are met by the three main yogas: Jnana Yoga for the intellectual, Bhakti for the predominantly devotional, and Raja Yoga for those who combine in their natures the need for a balanced approach—mental, emotional, and physical—to the divine.

Such in brief are some of the outstanding advantages of Vedanta for all interested in religion as a union of truth and goodness. The blend of Hebrew and Greek thought made the "armature" on which was built up that occidental way of life that has been called Christendom. It is today in ruins, and even if it stood, it would be too small an arch to span that diversity of humankind which today physical science brings into contact, though it cannot combine. That can only be done by a psychology, an applied knowledge of the human psyche, as comprehensive and as exact as is today the West's applied knowledge of physical science. It is this that India possesses and at last in the Vedanta Mission has shown an apostolic desire to give to humanity. Here then, and here alone, lies the hope, not of personal salvation (though that is an integral part of the training) but of a new and balanced philosophy and praxis of life that could provide sane and progressive living for a unified humankind.

Is There Progress?

Originally published in *Voice of India*,
Vol. 2, No. 8, October 1939

Werd als ein Kind, werd taub und blind
Dein eignes Icht muss werden Nicht
All Icht, all Nicht treib feme nur
Lass Statt, Lass Zeit, auch Bild lass weit
Geh ohne Weg den Schmalen Steg
So Kommst du auf der Wueste Spur.
O Seele mein, aus Gott geh ein
Sink als ein Icht in Goddes Nicht
Sink in die ungegrundete Fluth
Flieh ich von Dir, Du Kommst zu mir.
Verlass ich mich, So find ich Dich
O ueberwesentliches Gut!

A child become, be deaf, blind, dumb
Thy inmost I must wholly die
All Aye All Nay but drive away
Leave Time, leave Place, e'en Thought efface
Thy way pursue with ne'er a clue
So coms't thou on the Trackless Trace.

> O Soul of mine, through God untwine
> Sink as "I so" in Godhead's "No,"
> Sink in the never-sounded Flood!
> Fly I from Thee, Thou coms't to me:
> Forsake I me so find I Thee,
> O inconceivable Good!

THE ABOVE VERSE, here transliterated into English, was written probably in the thirteenth century somewhere in Western Germany. Perhaps today the consideration of these lines, of their date and place of origin (Statt and Zeit) is as striking a refutation as we could find of our still stubborn illusion of progress. It dies hard, this mistaken belief that just by living we become wise, that "the thoughts of men are widened with the circling of the suns."[68] True, we have all been taught,

> It is not growing like a tree
> In bulk doth make man better be.

But during the nineteenth century, Western people increasingly felt that if only they had more goods, they themselves would become better, [and] that people who lacked machines could be really moral began to be doubted, [and finally] that rapid advances in physics and economics might actually render people proportionately more ignorant of psychology, of their own natures, and [of] vital values. Such notions were considered too absurd, too reactionary, too defeatist to need refutation. Yet such is the conclusion that the history of the last twenty-five years has forced on us.

The first part of the demonstration was purely shocking. We have had rubbed into us the fact that knowledge of means without an equal knowledge of ends leads simply to destruction accelerated by mechanism. If our possible experience stopped there, we should indeed feel rightly hopeless. Here is our age that has patiently and ingeniously built up this vast tower, higher and stronger than that of Babel, to raise us forever above the flood and storm of material accident. Here are we, more cursed and [ignorant] than Babel's builders, not merely in a panic of hopeless misunderstanding, abandoning our prodigious labor, but turning on each other with all our gear and instruments in a frenzy of mutual homicide. There is, however, a second part to this demonstration. It is not as spectacular, but it is as hopeful as the first part is despairing. The essence of this discovery lies in the fact that in the past there have been epochs when people may have been physically ignorant but were psychically highly informed. Although (perhaps, indeed, because) they were without a distracting knowledge of means, they could clearly see their ends.

A few years ago, a couple of Italian archaeologists, anxious to return with artistic spoil from Tibet, entered that land of "fossilized" Mahayana Buddhism. One of them had taken the trouble to learn some Sanskrit. He noted in his diary with naïf surprise that the first lama on whom he tried his knowledge, although the old man had seemed [foolish] and was obviously dirty and poor, suddenly dropped the mask and talked "the subtlest metaphysics" to him.

Those who have suggested that—in a return to a simpler, more intentional, less distracted way of living—we might rebalance our life, have failed to find general support for two reasons. In the first place, until the present international breakdown, it was impossible for the ordinary person to believe that mere increase of technical skills would not cure their discontents. On this were agreed capitalist and communist, materialist and social-service Christian. In the second place, until the psychological knowledge that the past possessed came to light, there could be no assurance that even if we did simplify our life and copy an earlier model, we should acquire a new insight and power. We can face the truth about our own condition because we know there is a way out. Instead of the crude idea of inevitable material progress leading us to a worldly Utopia, we are coming to a true view of human history. We are now beginning to see that whenever people wish, with sufficient singleness of heart, they can come upon the *wüste spur* ["desert trail"]; when they seek, with a determination to give everything, they find.

No doubt the Rhineland, seven centuries ago, would have seemed technically backward compared with all the skills and machines that proliferated there until yesterday—when those trees of crooked knowledge bore their true fruit. Yet in the thirteenth century, those Germans knew more about humanity's nature and its needs than any who speak in Germany today. So, though we must

15

take a grave view of our present [situation], we need not be hopeless. For the ruin of our strength may mean the recovery of our sanity. The self-destruction of our means [may] permit the re-emergence into the vision of humankind of ends worthy of a free people's service and worship, and the disappearance of false knowledge [may] lead to the rediscovery of the true. Whatever the outcome, two facts are clear. The Germany that the world dreads is a phase: underneath, like a spring in the desert, flows that universal song of unity with the whole—a stanza of which heads these paragraphs. And whether it rises again to the surface in our time or not, here under our own feet, the same current of life eternal flows. Whatever the nations do, however humanity may choose, each one of us can in ourselves dig down, find the living stream, and know it "springing in himself to Life Eternal."

Unknown Indian Influences

Originally published in *Voice of India*,
Vol. 2, No. 9, November 1939

NOTHING IS MORE INTERESTING to those who believe that all religions have one source and one goal, than to trace the same ideas and new expressions appearing in religious writings separated in time by thousands of years and in space by continents.

The thirteenth-century hymn of German origin quoted in "Is There Progress?" [see above article] might have been sung by any student of the Vedas in India anytime in the last five thousand years. As Ramakrishna said, all religions lead to God. It is interesting, however, to enquire in this place, where the contribution of India in forming the world's thought in religion is constantly illustrated, how far these parallelisms that we note in all lofty developments of religion are by direct borrowing or by convergence of all spiritual minds on the same goal, so that toward the end their courses lie side by side.

This is of course one of the liveliest controversies in the subject of physical evolution, and in that field will probably never be settled. Does the highest form of bodily life—humans—spring from a single stock or have several blended to produce this astounding creature? Are the great apes like humans because they are their cousins—

common descendants from a single ancestral type, or are they as they are because every animal species and genus must, if it continues and can keep for long enough unspecialized, become humanoid—that is, develop a body that best permits the expression of a rational and exploratory mind?

This very same problem appears again in this subject under discussion [here]: Does the spiritual inheritance of humans flow down one riverbed from which irrigation channels spread to left and right across the earth, or are there many separate streams rising from different springs—though all fed from the same underlying water table and all flowing to mingle in the same sea? Many authorities have felt that in India there is a source land [that is] rich and constant enough in its yield of the Water of Life to have fed all humankind's ecclesiastical channels. Others feel there is no evidence that India directly influenced, for instance, that stream of lofty devotion which arose in the Rhineland in the spring of the Middle Ages and flowed down until it died away (as an uncontaminated source) when late eighteenth-century pietism found itself between a materialistic rationalism claiming to have all the facts and a rationalistic mysticism claiming to have all the immediate contemporary inspiration.

Yet if India's influence on this peculiar Germanic thought (which combines metaphysical subtlety with intense devotionalism) is not direct, there is no doubt that it is indirect. There is no sign of the complete transcendence of anthropomorphism as a goal, and thought and word as a medium, in Christian religion until the introduction into the West of the thought of Bar Sudali—the Syrian monk who called himself by the "ghost name" Dionysius the Areopagite. This profoundly influenced Scotus Erigena, the strange Irishman who in the ninth century is teaching at the court of Charlemagne's descendant Charles the Fat.

Bar Sudali's work is not condemned by the [Catholic] Church because in his book he praises the ecclesiastical hierarchy, saying it is a mirror of the orders of angelic powers in heaven. This made a Church Council specifically praise the treatise, which thereafter naturally becomes sacrosanct. Erigena, however, wrote under his own name and was very unguarded in his theological statements. Hence his work was condemned. Nevertheless, this strain of advanced thought continues to fascinate religious explorers, and we can trace quite clearly the teaching of the Syrian monk of the fifth century shaping the thought of people on the upper Rhine in the fourteenth. Considering how little there is in the Pseudo-Dionysius of traditional Christianity, it is hardly possible to avoid the conclusion that here we have a strain of Indian thought entering the Levant and so spreading to western Europe. It is a fascinating sideline of research to try and discover how lofty a mysticism the Roman Church will accept and where and why it draws the line, calling one mystic anathema and another blessed. As a matter of fact, condemnations seem to alternate with approvals, curses with benedictions. Bar Sudali is almost canonized; his student Erigena [was] cut off from the Church. Erigena's student Richard and other Victorines are treated as little short of being inspired. Their successor Eckhart is condemned; his spiritual sons Tauler and Suso are approved manuals for the devout.

Up in Belgium, Ruysbroeck, using extremes of language that were sufficient to make Eckhart an outcast, is, on the contrary, named Doctor Ecstaticus, while in the south at Ulm in the Danubian basin, Albert, called the Great—Albertus Magnus—not only teaches a thought—Protestant in its severity towards symbols and Indian in its refusal to state the ultimate nature of God, Indian also in its equal statement of God's transcendence of thought and immanence in the mind of man—but is the revered teacher of Thomas Aquinas, the Doctor Angelicus of the Roman Church, the master interpreter of orthodox theology.

As this remarkable man, Albert, was teacher, administrator, Bishop of Ulm, a [re-initiator] of natural science, and [several] years ago was canonized by the late Pope (perhaps more to vex the Nazis than to guide the orthodox), we may take his work as a good example of that Western mysticism that has such strange parallels with the East. Or, it may be, a faraway "runner" of Indian thought—a root planted by the Ganges sprouting a millennium after on the Danube. At the end of his life, during which he had found time to write a whole library of books on an encyclopedic range of subjects, the old man, who had outlived his spectacular pupil Aquinas, decides that he must leave on record one more small volume. It is the most important thing he can say. It is the secret of his life and living. He calls it simply *De Adhaerendo Deo* [*Of Adhering to God*]. Despite all his multifarious activities, he had had one interest and desire—how he might cling to God. Such a type, it might be thought, so combining work with devotion, must surely be following the path of karma yoga by offering all [their] incessant activities to God and so aiming at union. And so in a way this saintly Bishop must have been.

Yet when we read in his remarkable little book, surely here is a spirit that has another path for entering into the Presence, a path which seems closest to Raja Yoga. Consider the following words, remembering that they were written by a Catholic Bishop, now a saint of the Roman Church, whose intercession may therefore be sought by all the faithful when they pray. [Albert] exclaims,

> Happy is the man who by continually effacing all images and who by introversion and the lifting up of his mind to God, at last forgets and leaves behind all images. By this means he works inwardly with a naked, simple, pure intellect and affection about that most pure and simple object, God. See then that your whole exercise about God within you depends wholly and only on your naked intellect, affection and will. For indeed this exercise cannot be discharged by any corporeal organs or the external senses but by that which constitutes (essentially) a man—understanding and love. If you so desire a safe stair and sure path to God, to arrive at the end of true bliss, then with an intent mind earnestly desire and aspire after continual cleanness of heart and purity of mind with a constant calm and tranquility of the senses and recollecting of the affections of the heart, continually fixing them above.
>
> Work to simplify the heart that, being immovable and at peace from any invading vain phantasms, you may always stand fast in the Lord within, to that degree as if your soul had already entered into that always present Now of eternity, that is, of the Deity. To mount to God is to enter into oneself. For he who so mounting and entering goes above and beyond himself, truly mounts up to God. The mind must then rise itself above itself and say, "He whom

20

above all I need is above all I know." And so, carried into the darkness of the mind, gathering itself into that all-sufficient good, the mind learns to stay so at home and with whole affection cleaves and becomes habitually fixed in the supreme good within. So do until you become immutable and arrive at that true life which is God himself: perpetually, without any vicissitude of space or time, reposing in that inward quiet and secret mansion of the Deity.

Here is a pathway of such austere simplicity and directness that it would be hard to attribute it to any specific religion. One can but say this is the essence of all living religion. The austerity of the approach may seem forbidding but, as [St. Albert] remarks after a lifetime of practice and achievement, it is a "sure path and safe stair," as direct as a ladder, as clearly marked—and as steep. And the goal can be seen so clearly even by those on the lower rungs that no one who has glimpsed it would choose to take any route more gently graded but more circuitous. All the direct guides tell us then the same thing. The way is always open for those who wish to climb.

About the less direct approaches—approaches which permit us to postpone the time when we shall reach the clear air and the intense light, spiritual advisers differ and vary their directions. But about the straight way to God for those who want Him only, though the advice may be hard to follow, the path is lit by all the enlightened ones who have found Him. It leads without deviation to Him, and every soul who cares to give all its energy to scale that path may in this life achieve the only end which makes meaning of life, the Eternal Presence.

[Ed. note: St. Albert the Great had long been thought to have written *De Adhaerendo Deo* ("Of Adhering to God" or "On Cleaving to God"). However, modern scholarship has shown that it was likely written in whole or in part by a certain Johannes Von Kastl, a Benedictine monk who died in the fifteenth century, although the work is still often attributed to Albert, especially in Catholic circles.]

Is Mysticism Escapism?

Originally published in *Voice of India*,
Vol. 2, No. 10, December 1939

"MYSTICISM IS SIMPLY ESCAPISM." That little jingle has almost become a slogan of those who occupy most of the key posts in philosophy and religion. Even those who feel that there "may be something in it" shelter the mystics in their congregations or classrooms as though they were [clandestine Communists], or at the very least feebleminded people subject to fits and not to be teased. Now a slogan is a good butt-end of words with which, when the shot of reason misses fire, to bludgeon your opponent, but emotional attacks should have no part in religious or philosophical discussion. First and foremost, philosophy stands for accurate definition of terms, and religion, one used to think, for seeking above all else the Presence of God. We must therefore define these words and discover whether the procedure they describe leads to or away from the goal of our being.

The tremendous word *mysticism* cannot be defined until we have settled with the smaller but perhaps vaguer word *escapism*. Mysticism is a very old word; escapism one judges very new. But the verb "to escape" is clear enough—it means to leave a position that has become impossible. We can then ask: In the history of Christianity, was Benedict an escapist when he refused to become a consul in the dying empire, when he refused to believe there was any future for that bankrupt state and instead founded the order that revived the basic agriculture industry which the empire had ruined, salvaged the culture it could no longer protect, and did these things because and only because he had forged a new psychology or social psychotherapy whereby people of intentional living and goodwill might heal their own neurosis, create a true collectivism, and put first the kingdom of God, then sound economics, and finally the preservation of the intellectual wealth of Western people? To escape is therefore a neutral term. It may be a wrong thing to do, or a right. "When they persecute you in one city flee into another" is an instruction that spread the Christian Church. The person who leaves the ship to attempt to swim to shore with a rope is escaping, but for the sake of the rest on the wrecked ship they are risking their life. Our motive therefore decides whether escape is good or bad. Our motive, again, depends on what we think will happen and what we think the circumstances [are] with which we are confronted.

As a matter of fact, the goal of most of those who charge others with "escapism" is an earthly Utopia. They don't believe in heaven, and God is merely a means, if He is permitted any place, to make people better and happier. Now Utopianism can be called escapism, for it is a wish to live in the future, not in the present, and it certainly is as vague as "otherworldliness" because biologically and meteorologically we know it is impossible for any race of animals to achieve a permanent home, let alone a "heaven on earth" on this planet. As far as hardfisted certainty is concerned, there is then nothing to choose between the two futures that idealists put in front of themselves—neither can be proved to be manifestly evident. The pure idealist is able to retort to the "indefinitely postponed new world-ist" that neither of them can prove their proposition.

When the writer of the letter to the Hebrews remarked of the pioneers whose case he was making, they say openly that they seek another country. He was saying something that certainly today many people would call escapist, but he knew what he was talking about. To escape then may or may not be right. That turns on whither we escape. [And] that brings us to mysticism.

The mystic says that this world is real in a way just as "token coinage" is not to be wasted but its reality depends on its being "quoted" on another currency and security. They do not call this life evil any more than they call an egg evil, but they say, with some common sense, that if an egg stays too long as an egg few things are more bad, more rotten, more evil. The mystic maintains that the only person who is a realist is not the person who pursues imaginary ends, such as happiness by wealth or in some fanciful future—whether for themselves or for others—but the person who, freeing themselves of the delusions of regrets and anticipations, wins the power to see things as they are. Such realists, though their slit of vision was narrow, were the great impressionist painters who threw away livelihood, wealth, respect, [and] who were called fools and knaves, in order that they might just see things as they actually were. Now most people do not believe that there is a reality "closer than breathing, and nearer than hands and feet," a reality quite different from that of common sense. The religious should, however, have known that this was so. Because they lost their vision, its authenticity had to be vouched for by the artists—not by the clerics.

If then there is such a state of being, not in a future life (though there it may be also) but here and now, then the mystic is the realist. [The mystic] maintains that there is such a state, that anyone may experience it who chooses to undergo the arduous training and athleticism of spirit to gain that insight, and that it was to attain that state that humans were created. Or to use our vernacular, the end of evolution is not the creation of bigger and more complicated societies and more elaborate economic structures, but the attainment of a higher and intenser form of consciousness, a consciousness as much above that of the average person today as [theirs] is above the animals'.

Now all high religion has borne witness to this state, to its attainability, and to it as being the goal set for humans by God. It needs, however, a great creative effort to attain it. Creaturely activity, to use the Friends' phrase, may help one to attain this state, or it may hinder; again, it depends on motive and knowledge. "If indeed thou knowest what thou doest, thou art blessed; but if thou knowest not, thou art cursed" [from Adam Clarke's 1831 *Commentary* on Luke 6:4]. The rules whereby the process may be worked are clear—there is nothing soft or vague about them. "But don't they take people away from life?" If by life is meant helping others to follow and not thwart evolution—certainly not. If by life is meant building a more pleasant social order for those who do not wish to follow the stern path of evolution, even then the mystic way is probably the only way of ever getting a more efficient social order than we have today. It is sanction for which our social order waits. Who has the vision to tell us how to act; who can guarantee that "right action is prized at the heart of things"? Only the mystic; all others speak as the scribes. Our social order, as Lincoln Steffens pointed out, has gone as high as people of our characters can carry it—weak bricks can only make small arches, for a larger arch will crush them and all will crash in ruin.

If we want a more effective social order we must produce better people. How? By giving them that training whereby the innate egotism ... is transcended through what the mystic calls the vision of God ... through what we may call an accurate, painstaking, gradual enlargement of consciousness. The ants as they achieved their amazing socialist state found that it could not be done by leaving themselves as they once were. They go through three stages, each individual in its life, before being adequate to carry that fully formed social structure. They hatch out as larvae, then they have to pass into pupas, and only after that second birth and death do they emerge as full adults adequate to sustain the state and not ruin it. The mystics have said the same thing. You must be born again. You begin by being a servant of God, then you must die even to all the things of that life that you may be born a friend of God, and finally you may pass into an even higher state, if so be we suffer together with those who have so attained that we may be glorified with them also. Such a scheme of things is daring, is curiously naturalistic, and is the only adequate answer to our present problem: how [to] find persons adequate in character and powers to the enormous task that our sanctionless society (capsizing because its means have overbalanced its knowledge of ends, its physics, [and] its psychology) now presents. The mystic may be too hopeful, too concerned with an attempt to salvage the unsalvable, but they, put beside the ordinary economically obsessed "secular" or "religious," is a realist and a daring person of action.

[Ed. Note: In this article, Gerald Heard not only provides a convincing *apologia* for the practice of mysticism, but he seemingly presciently anticipated—and preemptively addressed—some criticism he would later receive for espousing his mystical theories about religion, spirituality, and consciousness. Fortunately, history has vindicated Heard, especially in the larger brushstrokes he painted, and in many of the finer details as well.

Heard continues his animated retort in the article immediately below, "The Churches, Humanism and Spirituality," where he unashamedly responds to worldly critics who accuse religion of being "otherworldly." "What in the name of earth and heaven," Heard pointedly asks, "are churches doing if they are not concerned with some other world than that which the person-of-the-world calls the world of common sense?"]

The Churches, Humanism and Spirituality

Originally published in *Voice of India*,
Vol. 3, No. 1, January 1940

THIS IS AN AGE of growing discouragement for all Humanists. The belief that humanity can by amelioration of its circumstances attain to permanent happiness in this world, has been given blow after blow in the last twenty-five years until it is hardly tenable by the least intelligent. The last hope of such [is] that though in the rest of the world this faith had failed, yet in one place, Russia, the light had dawned and was growing. [But] that hope has been dimmed and darkened by a series of "successes" that have been more terrible than failure. The deliberate starving of some two million peasants, the ruthless executions of all who differed with the person at the top, and now the imperialistic lunges against a series of small neighbors—such acts can only be held as proofs of an approaching millennium by people who have ceased to attach any meaning to words or any value to human life.

This failure of Humanism is also reflected in a keen discouragement among many of the [Christian] churches. [Ed. Note: In these opening paragraphs, Heard examines and analyzes some of the reasons why he believes Protestantism abandoned mysticism in favor of adopting some of the principles of secular humanism.] A large number of Protestant communions have increasingly during the last thirty years—especially in this country—come to identify their aims and their methods with those of Humanism. This is historically an interesting development. Ever since the Reformation, when authority was denied to the Pope or the Councils of the Bishops of the Catholic Church, the basis of authority was shifted from the discussions and decisions of humans (who might or not be inspired) to a Book. Authority had to be somewhere, and as, to quote the [Hebrew Bible], there was no longer "open vision," [no longer] the power of contemporary people to have the experience of God. The accounts of vision in the past had to take the place of vision in the present. But once authority is confined to a book, at once that book is bound to be examined critically. If a small arch is to carry such a weight, it must be clear that its bricks and stones are strong enough to do so. ... The examination showed that what the Jews had claimed to be inspired and of unparalleled spiritual majesty showed itself to be of mixed authority and doubtful strength.

The churches would not, however, as the ... heresiarch Marcion pleaded, have the courage to throw over the "bronze age religion of the ... Semites" and cling only to the New Testament. This led to a first falling away of followers. [Ed. Note: Marcion, one of history's most notorious and reviled heretics, was vilified by St. Polycarp as "the firstborn of Satan" for propagating this and similar unacceptable and impermissible Church doctrines, such as maintaining that the God of the Jews and the God of the Christians were different.] But even had the churches abandoned the [Hebrew Bible], the difficulty would not have been surmounted. For a church that attaches all its weight to the historicity of certain accounts of a single life, a church that tries to sanction the spiritual life and prove the reality of God and heaven by the records made two thousand years ago of a small series of none-too-well witnessed events, has to abide by the judgment of the textual critic, and their verdict can hardly fail to be one of "not proven."

This was the position in which the Protestant churches found themselves a generation ago. They had no authority for maintaining that a spiritual or even a moral life could be established against all doubt on the evidence that they could produce. They therefore began a retreat from that untenable position, a retreat all the more serious because it was no longer the open desertion by individuals of the churches they could no longer honestly support, but was a steady lapse of the churches themselves from their own formularies and creeds. Without changing the letter, gradually all spirit was taken out of it. Miracles were dropped first, then the key miracles of Virgin Birth and Resurrection (the latter had been nodal to the first great Western missionary, St. Paul), and finally it was taken for granted that the future life should not be mentioned nor the spiritual world but that the whole energy of the churches should be shifted over to "social duties"—to the improvement of physical conditions in the vague belief that when everyone was comfortable they would then either be able to find heaven for themselves or would find that they did not need it. Heaven would have become unnecessary to people who had such a good time on earth.

So the Protestant churches have found themselves aligned with Humanism, and as Humanism has suffered a slump, the bottom of which no one can yet see, the churches, too, are having a fall which may shake them severely. Yet this shaking may in the end prove to be a very sensible blessing in disguise.

The churches have no real alliance with Humanism. They only took up this line of activity because they were privately or subconsciously convinced by the Humanists' argument that there was nothing in religion save its possible social value, and that if they would drop their "otherworldliness," the practical social workers—the socialists and communists—would see whether they could find some sideline use for the older organizations in the modern world. Now that these so-called realists are lost in a fog of disappointment and acrimonious recrimination, the churches, which, after all, were never very much at home with their new allies, can draw off and think their position out.

That charge of "otherworldliness"—was it after all so shameful an accusation? What in the name of earth and heaven are churches doing if they are not concerned with some other world than that which the person-of-the-world calls the world of common sense and which even they are suspiciously aware is not the whole of the cosmos? The churches should be otherworldly as long as this world

31

means materialism, for materialism is such a lifeless abstraction of even present reality that no society can hold together that tries to make its picture of things in such a perspectiveless fashion. Yet the difficulty remains: granted that materialism is unworkable as a philosophy of life, at least of any social life, [and] granted that even to attain the goal of Humanism there has to be a metaphysic and a way of life that outreaches and underspans the Humanities—just to know that is not enough. I may realize, I may accurately calculate the charge necessary to disrupt the nucleus of the atom and [thus] bring about transmutation. But, unless I can command that charge, the calculations on paper, accurate to a volt though they may be, will bring me no nearer to my practical goal than the recipe for baking bread will feed a starving man.

The first step, no doubt, for the Protestant churches is to realize that Humanism is both in itself stalling and is anyhow none of their business. If it is going to have its funeral, it need not be theirs. But the second step is quite as important. The churches have not merely to remedy a mistake, to dissolve a partnership. They have to take their own initiative, find their own line, and invite people to a new constructive and really progressive fellowship. To do that, they have to begin by remaking their philosophy. That is not to say that what they used to teach is not true. All the working parts of it undoubtedly are. What they have to do, as one of the most active minds in the English Church—the late Dean Inge—has said, is to change from the religion of authority, authority based on far too narrow an evidential basis, to the religion of experience.

Of course, many clergy doubt whether this may be done with any intellectual integrity. Poor as is the quality of the historical evidence on which they base their faith, their fastidious knowledge of the kind of emotionalism which they fear is all that can be called the religion of experience makes them prefer a withered and crumbling archaeological fact to a warm and coarse-smelling gust of conviction. Yet the religion of experience can be scientific, exact, and even cool. If we leave it to the emotional, it will naturally be "enthusiastic." But if the intellectual will explore this avenue, taking all their critical faculties with them, they will find that it is not they who will return empty-handed. On the contrary, their findings will have about them a clarity and even hardness, and a detailed complexity—in short, just those characteristics of true discoveries, those characteristics that the intellectual rightly demands and the emotional can hardly ever supply. This line of advance calls, however, for skill. An accurate technique is needed if accurate results are to follow.

It is here that the Christian churches will have to learn from India. It should not be too great an effort of condescension on their part. After all, in order to be up to date, they prematurely jettisoned miracles, theology, and finally the whole essence of religion: the conviction that the spiritual world is the ultimate reality and this only a significant shadow. Now in order to get back on the rails and to have a true faith, praxis, life, and message, they should not shrink from accepting the assistance of [the] wide and subtle metaphysic and practical psychophysiological technique of training that Vedanta provides.

The Return to Ritual

Originally published in *Voice of India*,
Vol. 3, No. 2, February 1940

THE ATTITUDE OF WESTERN PEOPLE is going through many changes, changes regarding things they took for granted were settled. Most Westerners have no doubt thought that their parents had cleared much rubbish out of their lives, rubbish that their grandparents had somehow tolerated. Whatever happened, we should never again clutter ourselves with superstitions and tabus. The attitude was really not much in advance of the bitter couplet in Butler's "Hudibras":

> He knew what's what; and that's as high
> As metaphysic wit can fly.

Perhaps no subject shows more clearly the way in which casual and hasty rejection of the past is now giving place to reconsideration than what is happening about ritual. In all progressive countries and especially among the democracies, the thought of ritual, of expressing a condition, of creating a state of mind not by words but by behavior, has seemed for long simply ridiculous. All that was a hangover from effete feudalism. Of course you could dress up if you liked, stage a show on the campus, be a self-styled knight of this or that fancy order, or even if you happened to be a Catholic carry on the old forms with a sense that it was just because they were genuine antiques that you liked them. The thought that a "behavior pattern" could actually influence thought, will, and character, could not be entertained for a moment by a rationalist.

Yet it is psychology that has breached the bank of this self-assured belief. Psychology pointed out, first how little we are influenced by argument or oratory. The one method of influencing public opinion to which the democratic rationalist had held, was shown to be almost worthless. That led to the further enquiry: How are people influenced; how is it that change does come about? It became clear that we are influenced by habit formation, by what we do and especially by those particular behaviors that we regularly and precisely repeat. Further, such behaviors are all the more efficacious the less we consciously attempt to interfere with them. Everyone knows that reason will not prevent you falling off a bicycle—however hard you argue with yourself and however clearly you understand the reason why you fall off—if you cross your hands, putting the right hand on the left handle and the left hand on the right handle. There are certain deep motivations that can only be set in motion by physical practices, and when they are in train can be kept going only by obeying rules and not letting the critical intelligence interfere as long as the action is being performed. This fact, of action depending on something deeper than argued thought, is illustrated by the doggerel distich:

> The centipede was happy, until a frog in fun
> Said, which leg, please, comes after which?
> This raised her doubts to such a pitch,
> She fell confounded in the ditch,
> Not knowing how to run.

It is this strange paradox, that we do a thing better by not knowing too much about it, with which ritual deals, and can deal as no other approach permits. For ritual is the recognition of "knack," that an art and craft, if it is in your hand, is all the better for not being in your head, or at least in that part of it that is given over to the describing in words and the criticizing by arguments the processes that go on in the rest of the body–mind.

Once, however, we allow that certain "behavior patterns" are the best and perhaps the only way of getting the whole body–mind to take up a certain attitude and to maintain it, the question arises which of the many patterns we can choose is the best. They cannot all be equally valuable. Some, for instance, have in them much that is purely magical. That is not to discuss what is magic and whether it may not at times work. It is simply to point out that in any rite that includes magical practices, by so much the rite's value as a psycho-physical training is impaired. Military drill is a very efficacious ritual, much more so than any number of orations on patriotism, but drill would be far less efficacious if some of the maneuvers were not intended to set up conditioned reflexes in those drilled but were supposed to cast a spell on the enemy.

Other rituals have combined with them ancient practices that once had point but now have none. For instance, were we thinking of reviving the religious rites of ancient Egypt, we might well find some that were valuable for the purpose we have in view. But we should certainly not be able to take over the full ritual corpus. For example, we should have to omit the Sed Festival, which had to do with the belief that the Pharaoh should and could be rejuvenated. Therefore, when we are considering a scientific revaluation of ritual and the selection of those rites and religious functions that are most effective on the body–mind, we have to consider two main things. The first is use and wont. Certain symbols are familiar to us, [while] others, which as far as we know are "objectively" as efficacious and inoffensive, awake in us misgiving and dislike simply because they are unfamiliar. We find in them associations that those who are used to them do not see.

For example, take the two great rites from the Christian Church. To those who had never heard of baptism, a Baptist service would seem ludicrous. While to those who had never known of Totemism, the sacrament of Communion through bread and wine thought of as flesh and blood would seem revolting. On the other hand, the great puritan revolution that swept the religious life of the Near East—the Nile and the Levant—in the seventh century B.C. has made all those whose religious practices descend from that source unable to understand the sacramental and ritualistic worship of the generative function. To them such symbolism seems simply degraded and disgusting. We have, then, in the first place to choose those symbols that least upset the social heredity to which we belong. It is probably little use trying to teach ourselves to adopt a symbolism that is alien to us. By the time we have made ourselves by reason tolerant of forms that at first sight were puzzling, grotesque, and even repulsive, all natural enthusiasm has gone. Deep devotion is not won by way of indifferent toleration.

Secondly, quite apart from our social heredity, each of us is personally affected to different degrees by different symbols. As the task before all those who would understand is to grasp, or rather to be grasped by, the idea of the Godhead Transcendent and equally Immanent, it follows that Deity is of His Nature inexpressible in our present state of consciousness. Whether, then, we think of Him as with form or as without form, the very fact of our thinking of Him immensely lessens what He is. The puritan, using no forms and feeling themselves superior to the ritualist who uses forms, is not necessarily advanced. Indeed they may find that they have, despite their intentions but because of the limitations of their mind and the immensity of the Mystery they worship, fallen back behind the ritualist.

Many a puritan, as we see with [certain Judeo-Christian denominations] for example, while refusing imagery, nevertheless in the mind relapsed into a crude anthropomorphism that the more elaborate and ritualistic religions avoided. Yet though the puritan must not impose their bareness and emptiness on the ritualist, they may claim a tolerance for themselves and their *via negativa*. Probably also what they are asking for is not a complete banishment of form, but for forms through another sense than through the eye.

There are three great symbolic methods and ritual activities whereby people remind themselves of the Inexpressible. The first is through sight and touch, through relics, sacraments, and functions. The second is through sound. Many puritans are just as much symbolists as any priest, but their symbol is conveyed through the ear. To such, music is the pattern through which Perfection delegates itself; poetry is also another aid. Music, however, is the purest help because in it no word interferes to limit the Limitless, for all definition is limitation. The third great avenue of symbolism is not through the eye or through the ear but through the whole body, that is, the kinesthetic expression of worship that is shown in the dance. We are probably too self-conscious to be able to revive that behavior pattern, and yet there seems little doubt that many of us are predominantly kinesthetic types. Dancing has seldom been more popular than it is today. A false rationalism makes us believe that we can only have a high and advanced experience if we use reason and logic with perhaps a little visual symbolism. The Sufis were not unsubtle thinkers nor unlofty livers, yet they used the dance regularly in worship. It is also of interest to note in this respect that the Sufis, being a branch of Islam, were denied visual symbolism. The line, however, along which ritual might follow up a promising research would be in the direction of music, of symbolism through the ear. Molinos, the Quietist mystic, gave as a formula for approaching the Unnamable: "Silence of the mouth, silence of the mind, silence of the will." That silence, that allaying of the ego's tumult, that stilling of the waves of the mind, is an art that needs every aid. Many to whom visual symbolism is not a medium but a hindrance, not a lens but a thick stained-glass window, would find in carefully applied music an instrument whereby to draw aside the flashing meshes of *maya*.

Dryness and Dark Night

Originally published in *Voice of India*,
Vol. 3, No. 3–4, March–April 1940

ONCE ANYONE REALIZES that real growth of the spirit can be made, they become interested in method. They see that, not only no longer need they leave their life to accident, nor drift and look to amusement to give living whatever meaning it may have. They see that they must set about intentional living, they must undertake training, [and] they must coordinate all their activities and their whole way of life along the path that has appeared and toward the goal at which that path aims.

This insight, or foresight, raises a number of questions. How are they to set about their new task? How much of their past life, which was based upon deliberate distraction and amusement, can remain? When anyone changes over from a way of living in which it was taken for granted that however you lived, the fundamental fact was that life meant nothing and went nowhere, to a way of living in which the meaning of life is [understood] and the place of the individual in that scheme has been discovered, then there must be very considerable modification of the things that are done as well as of the thoughts that are thought.

Right Livelihood, the fifth step in the [Buddhist] Eightfold Path to Liberation and Enlightenment, is something more than abstention from certain debarred occupations and professions such as armament manufacturing or white-slave trafficking. It is even something more than abstaining from gambling in stocks and bonds or from being absorbed in the advertising business. It is getting rid of everything that may distract one's attention from the one end and purpose of living. Many things that are obviously of no particular harm to anyone else have to be put out of the way not because they are harmful in themselves but because they take up too much time and attention when all the time one has and all the attention that one can command is required for the one main purpose which now makes meaning of every moment. Most people think that, as long as what they do harms no one else and is not unhealthy for them, there is no reason why they should not enjoy themselves in that way. This familiar standard of morality cannot, however, satisfy those who have found the meaning of their life. For them, every moment is precious and every ounce of attention is husbanded to bring them as soon as may be to their goal.

But once that is clear to them, and once they have resolved that so alone they can live, they have to ask: How best may I get to my End? Most of us find that the discovery that life has a meaning, a meaning as urgent as it is vast, breaks on us with a shock of surprise and also delight. "So after all that we see about us, the pointless lives of most individuals, the blind clash of classes, the hideous anarchy of the nations, life has a meaning, it goes somewhere, we can go with it." That is the huge wave of relief. The accepted nightmare that drives people to addictions, to possessiveness, to pride and violence and despair, is false.

Then comes also the wave of counter-concern. If that is true, then there is not a moment to be wasted. Already one has wasted so much. "Work while ye have the light; the night cometh when no man may work" [John 9:4]. It is urgent not to waste a moment more of the all too few hours of daylight. So there is a double pressure urging us to use every second. There is the attraction of the goal and there is the rapidly passing opportunity of working on the means to the goal. This sense of stress and attraction undoubtedly sometimes makes beginners suffer from anxiety and a kind of febrile haste. This may be one of the causes of disappointment and that [loss] of interest which is generally called "dryness."

There is much need here, it is obvious, for good teaching and wise guiding. Even if we start young, which is uncommon in the West, we are by nature an impatient lot, and all human beings, whether of the East or the West, seem to have this other factor in common—that their lives are run on what we may call an "alternating" rather than on a "continuous" current. With the best will in the world and with the wisest training, it does not seem possible for them to avoid a certain, and perhaps a necessary fluctuation. Now it is this which is so difficult for the ardent and anxious beginner to endure, and it is here therefore that it is very interesting to try and compare the findings both of the masters of the West and also of the East as to how far this ebb and flow is necessary, and how far the fluctuations—like those of unemployment—may be "flattened out" as the economists say, so as to save the booms and slumps.

The obvious question here is whether the slumps—as in employment—might not be saved by "backpedaling" when the booms are on. Psychologists have taught for a long while [that] those of their patients who have a tendency to too big a fluctuation, and so are honored with the fine frenzied title of Manic-Depressive types, to check the moment of elation and so save themselves from the moment of depression. But, beyond this very natural and practical advice, may we not learn more?

Quite obviously there are a number of rules for the spiritual life that apply to all of us whether we are stolid or excitable. There is a lower limit of observance and practice, which, if we go under it, we shall be simply slothful and not making any real effect on the will and the character. After all, we are like people in a ship that has a leak and which is making for the shore. We must work at a certain pace at the pumps or the water will gain on us, rising in the hold, and we shall founder before we can be safely beached. But there is also a higher limit, a limit above which strain comes on. To use the same simile again: there comes a time when the crew may wear itself out in pumping and so have to abandon their labor before the shore is reached. The leak cannot be wholly stopped. What we have to do (at least we beginners) is to keep the water level down, to keep on pumping out more or at least as much as is coming in. Now our question is, where do those limits lie?

To take another simile, this time from Alpine climbing: when the young go out with an experienced guide, [they] are always surprised at the slow and almost loitering pace at which [the guide] starts. They cannot endure this dilatoriness. They swing off ahead, but when the sun is up and the higher slopes are reached, [the guide] passes them for they have to sit down exhausted in order to get back their strength. [The guide's] set pace is a thought-out balance between fatigue and the distance to be covered and the time for covering that distance. It is significant that all Alpine distances are given not in kilometers but in hours and minutes. It is a well-thought-out race, however slow it looks—a race between the time before the sun will set and the energy at the climber's disposal. Some violent fluctuations would therefore seem to be due to lack of foresight on our part. After all, risks are nearly always taken and accidents nearly always happen because we will not look ahead. We suddenly see an oncoming difficulty and try to get out of it without sufficient time in which to make the necessary change.

But there are deeper rules of fluctuation and of ebb and flow that do not seem due to our present mistakes and carelessness or [that are] under our present control. In learning a language, a golf-swing, the piano—in every skill where knowledge has to combine with knack and blend into skill, there seems a wave–motion, an ebb and flow. There is a period of rapid surface-mind learning and then a disappointing ebb when even that which was thought to have been mastered disappears. It seems possible that during this disappointing time some deeper process is going on, what may perhaps be called a period of storage and profound modification. Again, it may be [that] no new knowledge or knack could safely be taken-in unless first of all the first load had been safely stowed, and room and relationship found for it in the ways and means, the methods and functions of the body–mind. We are probably far more [knowledgeable] than we know, and a new knowledge and power must always mean a modification of old ones. But still again, beyond this recognition of gaps, [pauses], and periods when we seem to "lose way" as sailors say and "hang fire," there are deeper dips. What of those states that the Western saints and contemplatives call the Dark Nights of the Soul? Here a number of difficulties confront the researcher.

First, there is the difficulty of the words themselves. Do all the writers mean the same thing when they use this same title? It seems difficult to think that they do. For example, a textual authority on Western mysticism such as Dr. W. R. Inge gives in his collection of excerpts from various spiritual authorities (*Freedom, Love and Truth*, pp. 160–161) as examples of the Dark Night passages from Ruysbroeck and the *Theologia Germanica*—two sources near one another in date and place. But the Ruysbroeck passage, where he talks of an Autumn of maturing fruits after the lush springing of summer, seems to refer to Dryness, and a fruitful dryness at that, a rich reflection after a high experience, and not to the deep despairs and utter emptying of "Naughting." Ruysbroeck mentions physical losses and hardships as being part of his "Autumn." The desolation of the Night seems in other cases so profound that they would be quite unaware if they were given all the health in the world or lost their closest relations.

The *Theologia Germanica* says the soul is sent to hell, and medievalists did not use that term lightly. The loss of the Presence—that alone counts, and to regain That is the one hope. In these latter cases, then, there does not seem a storage, an autumn harvesting going on. Rather, it would seem, we might say, the very barn itself is being harvested, cut down and taken to pieces. Here we seem past the acquiring of virtues and the abandonment of vices and specific weaknesses. It is the very self itself that is being challenged and attacked. Eckhart, who does not seem to say much about the Dark Night as a specific term— perhaps because he welcomed it—yet teaches a path that certainly with most good people would lead to acute distress. He says that there are three things which keep us from God and, it would seem, three stages whereby we may and do return to Him. The first is by loosing ourselves from our specific sins, the second is by loosening ourselves from all sense of self, and the third by loosening ourselves from Time. Many a Westerner feels a certain chill when they read even those introductory lines of Emerson's:

> The strong gods pine for my abode
> And pine in vain the sacred Seven;
> But thou, meek lover of the good!
> Find me, and turn thy back on heaven.

And certainly Christianity has never been comfortable with what its teachers called Oriental Nihilism, though it is all the more important to note that all the master saints of Christendom, as they climb beyond a certain height, seem to view the same prospect that so daunts those on the lower levels.

Perhaps such high matters should not concern beginners. Perhaps all we on our level have to fear is quite common: laziness; the wish for comfort and excitement; the impatience with the slow assimilation; and the lack of advance, because we will not let fall much, by its weight and back-pull, that [which] makes our advance necessarily slower than it need be, would we abandon more. Still, the problem remains as one of interest to all students of humanity. How much of our difficulties, even the difficulties of the advanced, is due to ignorance, which greater knowledge could remove; and how much is due to the necessities of the case?

An entomologist was particularly anxious to hatch out successfully a valuable moth which had been found in its cocoon stage. The moment came when it began to emerge. It was watched with delighted care. But just when the dangerous emergency seemed safely over, one of the beautiful wings, which made so largely the value of the specimen, remained caught in the husk of the cocoon. In vain [it] seemed to struggle to get free, and at last it seemed quite clear to the anxious watcher that the insect's strength was failing and that it must die in the vain struggle. As it lay helpless and exhausted on its side, trapped and inert, the watcher snipped with sterilized scissors the stiffened edge of the cocoon. The wing was released. The insect crawled out free. But it could not fly; the specimen was ruined. The wing remained curled and shriveled. That final struggle to the limits of life and strength seems to have been necessary. The circulation was not driven into the delicate veins of the wing, and so it could not expand. The agonizing effort was not merely to get free, but to grow whole; [it was] not merely to get out into the new world of winged flight, but to have, full of power and energy, the fully unfolded wings, without which the new and larger life was vain and a mockery. So it may be with our struggles. We may be made not merely to win the larger life, but, through the agony of effort, to attain the powers and capacities and the quality of consciousness to function fully and rightly in that life.

Mysticism in
Theologia Germanica

Originally published in *Voice of India*,
Vol. 3, No. 5–6, May–June 1940

IT IS OF CONSIDERABLE INTEREST to those who today are attempting
to put into current practice the teaching of religion as it has been
most profoundly expressed by India, to see how far the mystics of
the West following the Christian tradition succeeded in rendering in
Western terms thoughts that we today would mainly classify as Oriental. For that purpose, this short essay is [reviewing] one specific
book. This book, however, though it is short and anonymous, nevertheless had a great influence on European religion at the critical time
when the papacy was losing its ascendency and people were daring—
not seldom with unhappy results—to attempt to think for themselves
and to experience religion "on their own." The book in question is
the famous *Theologia Germanica*. Of course, it is no theology in the
usual sense of the word but rather a brief manual for instruction in
living the inner spiritual life. Nevertheless, it is seldom possible—
and certainly at that time and place was certainly not [possible]—to
give people instruction in actual spiritual living and the necessary
exercises without introducing a certain amount of actual theology. If

you are to teach a person to sail, you need not at once teach them to read oceanic maps. But quite soon they will have to master the meaning of charts if they are to handle their ship in any actual seas.

The author's name is unknown, probably at his own wish, for these associates who banded themselves together under the name of the Friends of God cultivated anonymity, dreading that spiritual pretentiousness which is a greater obstacle to enlightenment than physical indulgence or possessions. We know, however, his associates and the scene in which he lived his life.

The Friends of God made a loose association of layfolk, monks, and priests, all of whom were bonded by the practice of spiritual exercises and the tie of secrecy. This author probably lived at that terrible time when humans and nature—nature with the great plague called the Black Death, and humans by a furious, protracted, and unstinted feud between the Pope and the Emperor—were doing their best to make ordinary kindly human living impossible. The reaction of the ordinary person was despair or hideous brutality; the reaction to the same stimuli by these other few, the people who loved God, was for their lives to be raised to an ever more constant and deeper communion with Him.

This book found an immediate answer from such seekers. The author, one may say "of course," is strictly orthodox. Yet the reader today feels that though he is constantly careful to bring his teaching in line with tradition and the [Catholic] Church's rulings, he does not depend on these, and moreover, sometimes his actual findings do not square very well with the tradition. No doubt the author was quite honest in his attempt to combine what may not in fact have been the same conclusions—those of his own soul and those of the Church. He had very good and right reasons for wanting to find that the Church was or should be teaching the loftiest spirituality. The Church was the only channel of grace for the ordinary man. Cut off from that source, muddied though it was, a person would die of spiritual thirst. Nor was that all. The world was already full of people who had so cut themselves off [and] declared the Church to be hopeless—which was all too easy to believe—and that they themselves were the true and full channels of illumination, which was pleasant for themselves to believe but certainly far from easy for anyone who watched their lives to take as true or wise. Against these types—

common enough today—the author turns with sound austerity. If he has to choose between these vain indulgents who see God everywhere and preach the free spirit so that they can live loosely, then (as Ramakrishna said later to another such brother of the free spirit), he spat on such a gospel—and chose the Church with all its mistakes. That in brief is the setting of this important book—a world sick to death, most people despairing, a few using the breakdown of morality as an excuse for grotesque license, and far fewer turning all the more earnestly to find Reality.

Yet the teaching has certain apparent inconsistencies that do not seem to be accounted for by what is said above—the need to back a dying authority against a worse, far worse, anarchy. In the writer's own spiritual thinking, there seem two strains that he himself in his own heart never quite reconciled. One strain is that familiar in the near East and the Eastern Orthodox Church and taken over from those centers by the Western Church. That is mortificatory. The body is "this sack of worms"—a phrase from Luther's last sermon, for Luther never settled accounts with his body either as a monk or after his breaking his vows and marrying. The teaching of the Fathers of the Egyptian deserts is here dominant—a sick body is the greatest health for the soul. They denied Paul's teaching that the body is "the Temple of the Holy Spirit." All life is to be an agony. The author tells us that Christ from the moment he was born till he died on the Cross never had anything but moment after moment of acute pain—a picture certainly not sustained by the Gospels. As Christ always suffered so must we. We must never attempt to attain to that calm which is above all pain. That is not for this life. That is for heaven after death. The thought of illumination here, after which, in a way, this world is heaven, a doctrine that Eckhart actually states (saying he has no wish to die and go to heaven, for heaven will only be more in quantity, not more in quality, from what he has now been given by God's grace).

And yet the author, when he has said these things and given the clear picture of the person who torments themselves body and mind so that after death they may have earned a life of endless joy, says a number of other things which show that, though that was the orthodox picture for those who wished to live the higher life, he and his saintly friends had found something different, something which really did not fit into that picture. He speaks of a person he knows who has attained to what we may all attain, and it is the constant power of going into the presence of God. He speaks of any person as long as they are here "passing from heaven to hell," from banishment from the presence of God to full knowledge of that Presence. In this statement there are two things that refuse to fit into the mortificatory, after-death–heaven design. The first is the obvious fact that when you are in the presence of God you are, as the author allows, in Heaven, and you cannot be said to be in utter wretchedness simply awaiting the release of death. Secondly, he notes that when you are in "hell," even then you would rather be there than "with creatures," for though no person may comfort you nor would you take comfort of any, yet this state is both safe and blessed.

It seems clear that if this means anything, and with an author as honest and as acute as this it must, it means that the soul is then filled with such an intense longing for God that it knows it is separate from Him and so suffers, but the fact which makes this suffering better than any pleasure is that in it is such a vivid conviction of God's Being that one's own loss and damnation matter nothing. GOD IS, and in that fact everything else, oneself of course included, is well lost. It seems rather misguiding to apply to such a state, which most earnest seekers have tasted, if not drunk of, the name Hell. Hell is self-centered despair, if it is anything. In fact a classic description of hell is given by this same great author. Nothing, he tells us with that assurance which we know in ourselves is true the moment we read it—nothing burns in hell save the self and its self-will. The author, then, it seems would have done better had he been able to make use of a freer phraseology and a more exact metaphysic than the rigid theology of his day permitted.

Another point of confusion seems to appear, not when he is trying to describe the state of alert austerity in which the soul must live if it is to travel toward union with God—a union that does not depend on death but upon the degree to which the soul can lose itself in God—but when he is speaking of those upper states of wonderful result into which the soul, by God's grace working on its dedicated will, may enter. He describes the steps of purgation, illumination, and union. But the illumination is not the intense quality we now recognize in the records of the great Oriental saints, and in one or two of the West, while the union seems to fall far short of any *samadhi*. Is this due to the fact that the author has made a ruling which he often repeats, that perfect calm is not and must not be attained in this life? He seems to feel that it would be wrong to attempt to know God in this life.

And yet, when one has said that, on ample evidence, one comes on other passages where he says roundly that a person may "look into eternity" and receive clear foretastes of the eternal blessedness. In fact, it does not seem possible to reconcile this great devotee's findings. We are faced, it would seem, not with a finished treatise of the spiritual life by a proficient master, but the notes of a great seeker and finder who puts down all that he knows and does not try to make it consistent. His picture of Christ's suffering throws a little light on these antinomies that he feels he must somehow preserve and set down in all their self-contradictoriness. He tells us that, though Christ suffered horribly all his life and his Passion was more terrible than human suffering can ever be, nevertheless Christ "had two eyes," and though the one eye looked on the world and suffered in it prodigiously all the time, the other looked upon his Father and never suffered at all.

That picture of the *avatar*—"perfect God in touching His Godhead and perfect Man in touching His Manhood"—is of course the picture the so-called Athanasian Creed gives of Jesus of Nazareth, and it is a picture which Aurobindo Ghose says the Gita renders as Krishna's interpretation of avatarhood. We in the West are now swinging away from the picture of the suffering God–man to the picture and ideal of the serene Buddha, who, though of course he has suffered and still can feel, yet those feelings never disturb his expression, still less the serenity of his mind. He does not weep for a dead friend whom he is about to raise to life nor over a doomed capital of his race because it will not get rid of its overtaking [destiny]. Yet of course it is possible to see that a Son of God could take on humanity so closely that he would share their sorrows with a sympathy that they could understand—when they could not grasp his serenity—while all the time his soul in itself and in its full consciousness looked on, the eye fixed on God translating all the tragedy that came in through the eye fixed on humans.

51

Probably even an authority—which the writer of this [essay] certainly is not—could not make a consistent picture of the spiritual life from the *Theologia Germanica,* but because the spiritual life can probably never be consistent at our level but always somewhat of a paradox and abounding in antinomies, this book is a help to all seekers, with its manifest sincerity, its flashing insights, [and] its deep unbroken devotion. It is also a great challenge to us today, showing how adversity made these people able to become, under the terrible pressure of their days, more and more fit for the great title they took for themselves—the Friends of God.

My Discoveries in Vedanta

Originally published in *Voice of India*,
Vol. 3, No. 7–8, September–October 1940

The Address delivered by Mr. Gerald Heard on the occasion of the [second] Anniversary of the Dedication of the Temple of the Vedanta Society of Los Angeles.

–Original Editor's Note

I HAVE BEEN ASKED by the Swami [i.e., Swami Prabhavananda] again to address you on this anniversary. A year has passed, and in that year much of seeming importance has happened. What the world calls momentous events have taken place. Our reason for taking an interest in the work of this place is, however, due to the fact that we have become convinced that the world never understands what is taking place in it, it never traces consequences to their causes—let alone to their right causes—and that therefore it is always engrossed with accidents and never with the underlying Substance, with Reality. The work of this place is concerned with two things, two supremely important issues: the uncovering of Reality, and the bringing of human life into line with that Reality. We are therefore making the only possible contribution to salvaging an almost derelict civilization when we work at those two is-sues. We are making the most vital of all returns when we attempt, at the completion of another year, to report on this, the one possible pro-gress, the only progress that can outbalance and reverse the world's decline toward chaos.

What progress have we made? We are taught here that the only real progress we can [make] is progress in ourselves. We have to heal ourselves before we can think of healing others—let alone whole na-tions. Otherwise we are simply operating with septic instruments. The patient might recover of themselves if we left them alone, but if we will try our surgery on them and our knives are infected, they must die of poisoning. That is why so-called theocracies and benev-olent tyrannies have been so much more hated and harmful than easy-going laissez-faire democracies and republics. When, then, we would review our progress, we have to keep that fact in mind— growth in spiritual vitality is the only true progress. But that fact compels us to go further. Not only does it warn us first to attain true spirituality in ourselves before we would save the world, it warns each of us who are set on this path and have seen this truth not to judge our fellow seekers and companions-in-training but to attend to our own development.

If then I am to speak to you with any accuracy and truthfulness about the process, if not the progress, of the past year, I must lay before you the type of discovery and the sort of application of dis-covery that one trainee [Ed. Note: the author is referring to himself] has made in the twelve months under review. After all, we are much the same, and, though the self can only speak for the self, nearly all of us go along the same path. Those of you who are ahead will listen with patience to these novice notes.

I believe that the principal discovery I have made is so simple and vast that at times I feel I have always known it and at other times I feel that I shall never quite grasp it. I can put it most familiarly in the words of our own Western *avatar*, Jesus the Christ, [who] seems to have been, like Gautama the Buddha before him, a teacher most anxious to simplify the Way for humankind. With that purpose in view, he reduced the ... Ten Commandments—and indeed, as he said, the whole Law and the Prophets—down to Two. We are, first, to love God unlimitedly and, secondly, we are to love our neighbor as ourselves.

But we in the West thought we could go one better than our Teacher. We have tried to reduce the Two Commandments to one. We have tried to teach that the Second Commandment really included the First and that, as the First meant no more than the Second, the First was really unnecessary, otiose. But Christ was an accurate thinker. The Two Commandments cannot be reduced to one, and further, the Second Commandment cannot be put in front of the First. Unless we begin by knowing and loving God, we cannot love our neighbor. Once we have loved God, we can—and then only—love our neighbor as ourselves. The First Commandment comes first because it alone can make the Second possible. The First Commandment is—and is meant to be—unlimited. We love God without restriction.

But is not that what the Second Commandment says about loving our neighbor? No, and we would never have fallen into this mistake had we ever thought of religion as a subject requiring as much accuracy as chemistry. Our love to our neighbor is both inspired and controlled, fed and restrained, energized and directed by our love toward God. We should not have fallen into the tragedies of persecution had we grasped the precision and accuracy of Christ's teaching on this essential instruction. For once we see that God is infinite being, infinite wisdom, infinite love, then we see that to Him and to Him alone we owe an unlimited devotion and we also see why. Whereas there is no limit to what we may do for Him in accord with His will and being, there is a limit to what we may do for all others and to all others. I may love my neighbor so that, and only so that, they may become what I see from the First Commandment God wishes me—and all His creatures—to become: one with God. I am therefore by the First Commandment guarded from the two tragic mistakes that have ruined so much human love which assumed that there was only one commandment, and that was to love my neighbor as I thought myself to be.

The first mistake is that mistaken love which wishes to give the fellow creature it loves all those physical comforts that arrest the soul's growth. That is the mistake of Humanism. If we aim at making human beings materially so well-off that they find their life good enough in itself, then all we do is to suffocate the soul. The second mistake is a blind reaction from the first: it is to coerce the fellow creature to give up their comforts and to go in the direction in which I say I have found God, or some national or class idolatry that I put in the place of God. Once we have begun to find God, we realize that He is the only real good, so we dare not give to others anything that might distract them from finding the only real happiness. Also, because He is the only real Power and Being, we dare not attempt to drive others to find Him who is the one guide and goal of all. If we have found God, we need not fear that we are not doing enough to help others find Him. As we are taught here, "once the flower has opened to the sun, the bees do not have to be coerced, or preached at, to come to the nectar" [Sri Ramakrishna].

The second thing taught here that has sunk month by month ever more deeply into my mind, may seem at first sight to have little connection with the first. I have found these two things, nevertheless, to be closely connected. The first is the object of devotion—God in Himself, Absolute Reality beside which all the physical universe is only a significant dream. The second is the way of devotion, the method or technique of worship. Increasingly, one has realized how partial and weak much of our Western devotion is because we hardly ever worship with more than one-third of our nature. At the least we are tripartite creatures of body, mind, and spirit. In modern Western religion, the mind is almost the only aspect of consciousness that is used in devotion. Yet the body accompanies us everywhere. We can't leave it outside, parked like our cars. Rather we are like the Scotch countrymen who bring their collie dogs into church. But whereas the dogs behave perfectly, few could claim such sedateness for their bodies. We have not taught them. To learn that the body, too, must worship or it must distract, this is a psychophysical truth that grows in significance the more one practices. And, as the body assists the mind to worship, so does the soul. Further, each has its own approach and utterance: the result is not unison but harmony, a chord, "not three notes but a star."

How is this truth about the method of worship to be linked with that about worship's object? God is Reality; Reality is a Being so intense that, as we are, we cannot see Him. If we would experience Reality, know God, we must draw our entire being together, bring our scattered, dissipated, and distended being into a single-pointed focus. "The single-hearted," those who want only one thing so they have ceased to desire anything else—either appetites, or possessions, or recognitions—they "see God." Unless we correlate our complete being and desire Reality and nothing but Reality with the whole gamut and range of our being, from the highest range of the psyche to the most basic level of the physique, we shall not see God—we shall be devoted to something that is less than Reality and, as a consequence, we shall never be wholly satisfied and we shall never be able convincingly to tell others about God and about the way to find Him.

As l have come to see the connection between these two truths taught here, I have begun to grasp a third which, to use again the simile from music, makes a chord in the teaching. If God is Reality, [and] if that Reality can only be [perceived] when they who would see have dedicated their entire nature to seeing, then it must follow as the day the night that God is not some Being infinitely distant, at best a *post mortem* experience. But if the seer will become single-visioned, [then] God, Reality, may be known here and now. His very nature is Presence; it is only our obliquity of body–mind–spirit that hides from us the Instant, Timeless Splendor.

These then are the three correlated truths that in the past year have grown into a unity of understanding and [have] begun to coordinate the three aspects and levels of one's being. The first is that God alone is wholly Real—all other experiences are sustained on and by that base. The second is that we fail to see Reality, though He is always Present, because we are dissipated. Once we recollect and present our scattered being, bringing the facets into one focus, we cannot but see the Presence. The third is that this transmuting event is not something that we have to wait for till we die, something that we may hope for after death, but which we may have, cannot fail to have, the moment we can ask for it wholly, with spirit, with mind, and with body. Then our self-imposed ignorance vanishes, and we see that God has always been Present, "closer than breathing, and nearer than hands or feet."

That these truths are taught here and that the way to practice them is indicated, is of the greatest value. Here is given a system, when in the

West we have only had fragments of true gnosis. Here is an empirical science in comparison with those happy insights and uncoordinated hints that are all the guidance our own tradition can now yield.

The Future of
Humanity's Religion

Originally published in *Voice of India*,
Vol. 3, No. 9–10, November–December 1940

IF ONE THING CAN BE DISCERNED through the smoke of the present conflagration, it is that the world order, which set the mechanistic
convictions of the West in the forefront of civilization, will have to be
scrapped. Even if fragments survive, the condition of the house of
Western people's spirit will be such that even those parts that endure
will have to be pulled down. What the flames will not have devoured
will be calcined. This disaster may then be the way in which the Divine
Power clears the stage for another and more modern structure. Western people were long warned that they were building a house that was
not fireproof. They would not attend. What was even more serious
was that the East and the Near East—as Europeans call that Slavic and
Turanian belt of peoples that lies between Asia and Europe proper—
(though they should have known that this structure was only outwardly impressive, indeed a firetrap should it ever become ignited),
became so impressed with its size that they were willing to imitate it
and, to do so, to throw aside all their traditional wisdoms.

It is therefore of more than academic interest to enquire what will be the main lines of the practical philosophy that will make the new system in which humanity may find a shelter and a workshop. The first thing that is obvious is that the Indian contribution will be fundamental. Scholarship has now proved as a fact of literature that the specific concepts that gave to Western religion its deepest insights and its most effective techniques were all imported from the Indian areas. In his latest book, *The Flowering of Mysticism*, Dr. Rufus Jones has traced quite clearly [these] sources, coming through from Persia via Baghdad, Alexandria, Cordova, Padua and thence by Paris onto the Rhine, which influenced and formed the thought and practice of the first great schools of Western mysticism. Even before then, it is clear that the Arabian monk, perhaps called Bar Sudali, using the pseudonym Dionysius the Areopagite, had spread a doctrine that was far more Vedantic than "Synoptic."

The writer of this [article] was suddenly surprised the other day in reading *The Mystical Theology* by Dionysius the Areopagite to find it stated, "For we must be in this work as it were men making an image of his naked unbegun nature, which though it be within all creatures is congealed as it were in a cumbrous clog … we must pare [it] away." Here in quaint language is the doctrine of the Atman, which is Brahman residing, hidden at the center of every person and to be realized by discarding the obvious and the outer, the expressed and the expressible, until the Dark Silence is reached. Further, this author adds that this is to be done "in a manner that is unknown how unto all, but only to those who do it, and even to those who have learnt to do it they only know of the result, of the full nature of the experience at the moment that they experience it." In other words, the high and pure state of consciousness and of union cannot be described by even those who have had it, in the words and the thoughts that are all they can use when they come back to us from that tremendous experience.

But apart from the establishment of the literary debt that the East owes to the West, there is the deeper issue as to the form that a world religion might now take and the part that India might play in that new system to embrace humanity. The differences that it is common to say must exist between East and West are not geographical, we now know. They are partly temporal or chronological and partly psychological or temperamental. A medieval scholar would not have found Indian religion, in any of its forms, ridiculous. What they would have said against a number of them was that they were heretical. Indeed it seems that if there had been no Inquisition and the enforcement of a "party-line" in religion, Europe at the close of the Middle Ages would have been very like India—a land of many cults, theories, practices, and hypostases of the Godhead. If all the Christian heresies alone had been allowed to grow—as Christ evidently recommended—"till the harvest," Western religion would have been as rich and complex as India's, showing the full gamut of religious feeling from the austerity of Pali Buddhism to the luxuriousness of the Cult of the Mother in its least restrained developments. Times, however, change and with the change in time comes the change in expression. A child can be unselfconscious as an adult cannot be, and the direct childmind does not find certain expressions and devotions yielding the impression that such things give to the adult, especially if the adult has been brought up in a way of life and morals much influenced by the effects of the puritan revolution.

Nietzsche divided religion into the Apollonian and the Dionysian—the religion of repressed and the religion of expressed feeling. The West is convinced that the latter is the lower and the earlier. The West may not be right. Much of the noncommittal attitude that we find common in the West toward the Holy may be accounted for by two things, neither of which are very superior conditions of soul. The one is that the [average person] feels so little that they have nothing to express, and as they feel little they believe, in their ignorance, that no one can feel more than they can. They do not believe very much in any spiritual reality, and so when they find someone taking the fact of God with the seriousness and the interest that such a fact, were it true, would surely deserve, they feel that so to behave is to be unbalanced or hypocritical.

The other cause of the ordinary person's lack of expression in religion is what has been called the Tabu on Tenderness. People are ashamed to say what they feel. Such a suppression is not we now believe very good for them, and of course it is a form of hypocrisy. Yet though we are likely to see a religion of much fuller expression appear when once more religion as a fact of life is brought back into our conduct, yet it is not necessary that the new forms should preserve exactly the old patterns. If, as there is more than a hope, there is about to arise a religion for humanity, there seems reason to suppose that it will follow the course of development taken by religion when the ... small nation of the Jews combined with the thought of the widely ranging Greeks and gave rise to the philosophy and practice, the ritual and ethics that we call the Christian religion.

The religion of humanity will be syncretistic. Some Shankara of our age or of the oncoming generations will rear a philosophy and deduce a practice which, drawing upon the past, will give a contemporary answer and conduct to the present for its needs and its activities. It is interesting to speculate what in broadest outline that cosmology or theology would be and what its deduced ethic. The most basic thing (at least so it seems to [this] enquirer) would be the working into a world-embracing picture of the doctrine of the *avatar*—the line of Incarnations which eon by eon appear and, dipping into the Time process, make it possible for humanity to "mutate," to take a step further up the ramp of ascent from ignorance to enlightenment. So the [view] of the various higher religions would be brought not into competing rivalry but into harmony.

The next great postulate would, it seems, be the doctrine of God Personal-and-Impersonal, that only in such a polar concept can the fullness of a person's spiritual experience be expressed. The third would be perhaps the doctrine of the evolution of the soul, that this life is only a cross-section in a far larger experience. The ethic that such a doctrine of Godhead, of Incarnation, and of the nature of the soul, would yield would seem to be one which, by the fact that it stressed the *potential* divinity of all people, would teach a respect for life and a reverence for the soul that would be one of the firmest sanctions for good living. It is increasingly clear that no sanction can be found for things of time unless the fulcrum of that sanction is placed outside time—in the timeless, the eternal. We may even speculate and ask whether such a doctrine and practice would not give us a form of society that might be called organic in distinction from the form that we have today, and which may be called atomistic. For if people recover this deep reverence for life, then they need not overlook the matter of inequality. Because a dog is not my equal—it is my superior in power of scent—that does not mean that I wish to exploit it or that it cannot trust me. When we see all humanity as parts of the divine body, then and then only will all, even the humblest, have the one true guaranty of their rights, [especially] the right to be protected and to be helped [to] develop to the highest. Where there is that hope shared by all, there is no hardship in even the lowliest office; there is no pride in the highest. Whatever be the form this religion of the future takes, some such foundation, it seems clear, will underlie it.

Notes on Brother Lawrence's Practice of the Presence of God, Pt. 1

Originally published in *Voice of India*,
Vol. 3, No. 9–10, November–December 1940

As THE SWAMI DREW ATTENTION last year[69] to the fact that Brother Lawrence was one of the modern Western devotees who attained to a definite level of enlightenment, it may be of interest to readers to consider in some detail Brother Lawrence's actual account of his method. As the following lines suggest, that method, though the description of it has been popular, has owed its popularity not to the fact that it is really simple or rudimentary, but because we have felt sentimental about a pretty title and a charming old man.

This book has had uncommon success, awakening trust and response in Catholics and Protestants alike. That is because it is so simple, direct, sincere, and good that no one can doubt the author's bona fides nor fail to wish to imitate his life. The method he suggests is so plain that there are no theological terms over which dispute and confusion could arise nor procedures with which people of different practices might find it difficult to comply. A system that requires only a minimum theology—that God is all-powerful, all-wise, and all-loving—and which dispenses with all method save the constant reminding of ourself of that one fact—that God is always present and only asks for our attention—certainly we can understand its appeal, especially when we learn the results yielded by its practice. And yet if that is so, why, though the book has been so popular and is so simple, have the results not been more striking?

Long before God ceased to be believed in, as Catholic and Protestant believed three generations ago, this little book was being studied, and its practice not practiced. Indeed had its practice been practiced, God would still be believed in as Lawrence believed in Him. People who studied it must have wished to adopt its method, but somehow they failed. They read, admired, they wished to follow [but] they did not arrive, they did not become such as Lawrence. He and those like him say the way is simple and cannot fail. *They* arrived, there is no doubt. Why have we, using their instructions, fallen so far short in result?

The usual answer is that they were inherently gifted. With any method or none, they would have done remarkably well. It is true that many people seem incapable of understanding what the spiritual life is about—they are like colorblind people taken to look at pictures, or the tone-deaf at a concert. But those who care to study such books as Lawrence's, they are not in such a category. ... We cannot then discuss this problem by saying that the world is divided into saints who can attain God's Presence and the rest of us who can't, and that the books the saints write and we read are as little use to us, and indeed as little for the saints themselves, as color charts to help the ... colorblind to see colors. We need teaching—we who study the saints and study our individual and social conditions, [and] we who realize how only by such characters and by our being able to produce such characters, can we salvage ourselves and our civilization. The saints do not start perfect, very far from it, and they did work very hard constantly and pertinaciously as they rose from level to level.

So we can return to Brother Lawrence and his popular booklet. The answer does not lie in "inborn genius"—that is not the reason why his method does not make us into characters like him. It may then be worthwhile examining in some detail this brief book to see if we can discover, as it is a textbook, a book for practical working, [and] why it so seldom works or, perhaps one should say, why it has so many failures. There are of course hundreds, perhaps thousands, of spiritual guidebooks, and this same pressing question might be asked of each of them. But there are very few so simple, so brief, so well-known, so commended, so free of all particular provincialisms of the ecclesiastical or religious world, so directly concerned with the one main issue, so clearly pointing out the essentials of method and the desirability of the End, as this particular book. It is a book that not only any and every Christian can understand and put into practice, but it is one with which most Buddhists and Vedantists could do the same. We may then say that it would be hard to find any other spiritual guide better suited to act as the subject of this pressing enquiry. If we can with its aid and through careful study of it understand why spiritual guidebooks fail to bring interested readers to their goal, we shall have found something that will help us not only to use *The Practice of the Presence* but also these other books, and to use them so as to produce those essential alterations and mutations in our lives which, with these rules, the authors first produced in their own.

The first thing that a careful study of these four conversations and fourteen letters [of Brother Lawrence] discloses is that, though the language is so simple, often even conventional, yet they contain far more specific information than [an] easy rapid reading suggests. The second thing arises from considering and ordering this information. For, that done, we find that this is not at all a beginner's book. Its simplicity of diction, the directness with which the process and the End are described, disguise from us, until we have worked at it, that the system is simple because it is advanced. This is not a spiritual child speaking with unreflective simplicity. This is a man at the end of an intense, never-remitted struggle of a dedicated lifetime, having won to that consummate ease a master's power to extemporize in any mode, which comes only to those who, at the top and climax of their form, having achieved all particular controls, having such perfect command of expression and [understanding] that every event becomes precisely [an] opportunity that allows fresh, inexhaustible creativeness to be exhibited. This opinion is so contrary to that commonly held by readers of Brother Lawrence that it will probably be well to support this analysis not merely by quotations from his well-worn words, but by comparison with other such advisers, to show that, though they are considered advanced and difficult, and he for babes, the reverse is true.

The two who closely resemble his approach, both of them scholars and stylists, are St. Albertus Magnus in his *De Adhaerendo Deo*, and the anonymous master who wrote *The Cloud of Unknowing*. A comparison seems to show unmistakably that their books are complex because they deal with an earlier stage of the dedicated life, of spiritual evolution, than does *The Practice of the Presence*. They are showing how the masterful simplicity, the apparent spontaneity and easy freedom of Lawrence, may be attained and must be [acquired].

The first and simplest thing to note is the actual age of the [aspirants] to whom these three books refer. We know the *Cloud* was specifically written for a man of twenty-four just having completed a novice training and on his choosing to adopt the life of a pure contemplative. Albert is looking back across his immense life; he was a patriarch and an encyclopedist, and [he] resolved as a parting gift to leave the actual instructions whereby anyone who cares to follow the path may find the goal. Lawrence is an old man speaking only and wholly of his own experience without reference to earlier mystics and even doubting whether other people have so found [to be true].

The second thing is that Lawrence himself shows that he was singularly gifted in spiritual character, being converted at eighteen not by concern for himself but by sheer wonder at God's creative power (Plato's "redeeming amazement"). This early, favorable, and unrevoked start did not excuse him from most arduous efforts and mortifying experiences. He went through the severe discipline of an austere Carmelite training, but his real novitiate was the four years in which, in spite of his manifest simple goodness, he remained convinced despite ... kind and wise encouragement, that he must be damned. The Lawrence of twenty-four, yes even of forty-four, would no doubt, if he could have been persuaded to speak, have said things far more wrought with effort and checkered with reflections than did he of old age. Even in the letters, we have a hint of a still-growing freedom and ease. Not only does he tell us in a sort of aside that he has had spiritual sufferings and raptures, which both were keen enough to outweigh any physical pleasures and pains he had ever endured, but we can note the last flush of self-consciousness dying away when, in the first letter, he implores his correspondent not to show to anyone this letter giving his method. So deep are his self-misgivings still, that after prefacing his remarks by telling of the difficulty it gave him to tell, even under importunity, anything of his spiritual way, he adds that if he thought what he had written should be seen by a third party, even his wish for his friend's spiritual advancement could not persuade him to help.

This is strong language for one who believed firmly that to miss your way in this life was to miss it for good and come to a state of endless misery beside which any earthly misfortune was a bagatelle. Nor were the four years of intense self-despair all his purgation, though surely that was a heavy initiation and should dispel from our minds the picture of a charming old innocent who all his life had played alongside his accompanying fancy a God as sunny and as unrealistic as himself. He tells us that the four years were followed by a decade during which he was on tenterhooks and unable to find rest in his vision because he could not reconcile such a marvelous grace—the constant sense of God's Presence—with the inescapable awareness of his own poor despicable nature. Why should he have the supreme comfort and solace when better Christians were denied it? This problem of the acute sense of the self being rendered agonizing just because the sense of God's Presence is perfectly real—that the supreme desire and its satisfaction is accompanied by supreme bafflement and hopelessness, [this] purgatorial paradox of the spiritual life is of course dealt with in the *Cloud*. There the able author has much to say on this stage and how it is to be endured. But he does not speak, save as a distant goal, of the resultant condition and state from which the Lawrence of the letters and the conversations speaks.

Lawrence, it is true, is sometimes considered simple, and even as one comfortably arrested at an early and childlike stage of the mystic ascent, because he uses language in describing his method that uses, with an indifference to detail, anthropomorphic imagery. He declares, in the first letter, that he regards God as his Father, as his King, as his God, [and] that he carries on conversation with Him and goes through an "imaginary" scene of judgment and generous forgiveness. Both Albert and the *Cloud*'s author are careful in this sort of description. They both urge their readers to clear their minds of imagery, and they give good psychological reasons for this procedure in obtaining contact with the Eternal. Is not, then, Lawrence more rudimentary in this respect? I believe his carelessness or conventionality in phraseology and imagery—though no doubt all the more natural in a man of his intellectual simplicity and his time, when the [Catholic] Church was stricter in exacting verbal conformity than in the earlier centuries—also comes from his spiritual maturity and is a sign of his attainment.

His achievement is so complete that under what seems looseness of phrase he is, in fact, and as a matter of actual living, combining these antinomian aspects of ultimate Reality—which all thinkers have to face but few, very few, can blend into a single concept yielding both the power to face things as they actually fall out, and also the ability to act, in the face of such experience—with dynamic sanity and constant initiative. When Lawrence calls God his Father and his King, his God and his judge, he meant as a fact of conduct that he could both love the supreme Reality and yet also face the realization that such Reality could permit him to be tortured and destroyed.

The advanced theological thought of India calls this the confronting of the soul with God as Creator, Sustainer, and Destroyer. It also, with intellectual subtlety, indicates how sanity is to be persevered in and indeed creativeness enhanced by such a revelation, and its solution is Lawrence's—to persevere in facing the fact not with stoical despair but with sublime self-forgetfulness. Then, as Lawrence tells and the [Bhagavad] Gita prophesies, suddenly what has seemed a hideous paradox is in a flash reconciled as a supreme revelation. Under the focal strain, under the blinding jet of the oxygen flame of the divine love and the acetylene blaze of the divine reality—the one seeking the sinner, [and] the other hopelessly desired, incomparably self-sufficient, and unattainable—under this fusing heat the ego melts, for the only thing that burns in hell is self, and the individual by perishing and in the act of voluntary immolation knows themselves to be God. Without any metaphysical aid, Lawrence, by a prodigious love, knew that God was Love when He destroyed, and, by that acceptance, what was destroyed was his separation—intellectual and moral—from God, and God became for him the never-intermitted Presence.

Lawrence was possessed because Nicholas Hermann of Lorraine [i.e., Lawrence's pre-monastic name] had been annihilated. He tells us of this possession in some detail so we can have no doubt about it. The years when as he says he had to work constantly to keep the sense of the Presence may, it seems, most probably be correlated with [his] four years of purgation. There is a large consensus of spiritual opinion both in the East and the West that the period of purgation usually takes from three to four years, during which unremitting and often exhausting and almost hopeless effort is required; and also that during [this] time the soul must desire God ceaselessly and it will be battered between the two rocks—the rock of despair that echoes with the cries, "You will never find Him; He will never reveal Himself" and the rock of despair that countercries, "There He is, and how do you, hopeless flotsam of the seas, think you are going to climb out of the wave troughs up and beyond the unattainable stars?" Then the habit becomes fixed, the weary toiling to raise water from the deep well, to use St. Teresa's simile, is changed, because now the well has become an overflowing fountain. Lawrence was possessed by the Spirit he had dared to go on seeking when he was sure it had damned him. He had not waited. He had thrown all that could burn into hell, and as the Divine is all save that which is able to say *I am I*, when the I was gone, Lawrence was filled for good and all with God.

Besides also telling us of several stages in his spiritual evolution, stages which correspond with that *scala perfectionis* that the systematizing mystics have outlined, Lawrence also refers to his studies in such literature. In the first letter, he notes that he began his intense search to attain union with Reality by reading "many books" on "different methods of going to God and diverse practices of the spiritual life." No doubt these did not come his way when he was a foot soldier or while he was breaking crockery in the Treasurer's house as footman. We can assume he was given such works to study as a Carmelite novice, and we may also feel fairly certain that with the works came adequate verbal instruction. We know from Abbé Henri Brémond (*Histoire Littéraire du Sentiment Religieux en France, de le xvii C*) that the Carmelites had only that decade been introduced into Paris and that their sponsors were men and women of the most remarkable and indeed advanced religious life. Brother Lawrence's instructors must themselves have been saintly persons anxious to advance [themselves] and help others advance in spirituality. This fact probably also accounts for the freedom to follow his bent, [which was] permitted him when he was seeking, and the wide respect shown him when it was recognized that he had found. An unlettered lay brother, a domestic servant of a poor monastery who can say to the inspecting Vicar General of one of the most powerful Cardinals that the great visitor could only come and see him if the Vicar General's one desire was sincerely to serve God, such a cookman, it is clear, is a recognized authority in the aliment of the soul. It was then, after having studied and been instructed, that Lawrence perfected his own simple, masterly, exacting method.

Technically, it is the attainment of uninterrupted monoideism. He tells us that he raised the threshold of attention until he could maintain it constantly at the same height that devout worship at the Sacrament keeps for that time [for] the faithful sacramentalist. He adds the illuminative particular that the rush and noise of the kitchen when at full tide did not lower in any degree this intensity of Other awareness. Nor, he makes it clear, was the concentration attained by a simple rudimentary disassociation through routine, muscular automatism. He could, he says, be continually asked for various things, [and] his mental attention could be constantly summoned by practical demands and could give the right responses. Nor, again, was this state the combination of surface practical awareness and deep attention fixed continually on God, dependent for its right working on familiar surroundings and customary stimuli. When he was sent on journeys to buy wine, though he dreaded the discomforts of travel—being crippled—he found his sense of the Eternal undisturbed.

It is worth noting all he tells us of this state for, because of its simplicity, its profundity may escape us; because of its achieved facility, we may fail to realize the extraordinariness of the condition. He remarks in one place that the business that he had to effect went well, as he had commended himself and it to God, for he found at the conclusion that it had all been managed as it should, though—and this is the phrase worth reflection—he himself recalled no particulars as to how it had been done. From these passages, it is hard to escape the conclusion that this remarkable proficient of the will had so mastered his attention and set it upon the one object of its unceasing desire that he had produced a peculiar and most effective dissociation. By this means, he was rid of all anxiety and strain, all haste and all fatigue. The attention he gave to the task that he was offering momentarily to God, was that quality of intense attention which can only be compared with that attention which the hypnotic subject gives to anything to which their controller tells them to attend. Such attention is so intense that it is without memory or foreboding, as much without boredom as it is free of possessive adhesion, for the ego, with its vibrant self-involvement, continually asking "Do I like [this]; do I dislike [that]?" is absent.

But whereas the hypnotized subject is dependent on the will of his controller and on that, even, to a limited degree, Lawrence was dependent on a Will that he felt to be both infinitely powerful and kind. Nor, though this control was transcendent, did Lawrence feel it to be alien. He tells us he often felt as though God were in him and, had he belonged to a spiritually more outspoken age, no doubt he would have said precisely that, feeling that such a phrase alone was adequate to describe in one term the abolition of his own will and the simultaneous discovery that he was more alive, more conscious, more tirelessly volitional, and full of initiative, response, and uncalculated effectiveness than he had ever been when he was concerned, careful, scrupulous, and self-conscious.

This condition, it is obvious, is very advanced. They who have it, have already entered Eternity, for time is gone. Time is a tension between some regret for the past and apprehension for the future; time is a state of mind created by the ego's characteristics [of] greed and fear. Albertus Magnus in his precise scholarly instruction makes this clear. He tells the student as "a sure path to Bliss" that [the] state of liberation [is] as far beyond pleasure as it is above pain, [and] to "mount up into the dark" or limit "of the mind," [and from] there to accustom themselves to "stand fast in the Lord within you" when, after some practice "in recollecting the emotions and fixing them above," they will find that they have entered the Eternal Now.

Brother Lawrence realized that he had entered Eternity while still in the body. He says, as clearly as Eckhart, the great thinker of mysticism, had said earlier, that "I now see God in such a manner as might make me sometimes say I believe no more but I see." And "In short I am assured beyond all doubt that my soul has been with God above these thirty years." The actual step that brings about this union ends time and passes the soul into Eternity. Lawrence himself describes it in a single sentence that, for its depth, might come from Plotinus. It is a classic description of the act of creative will, the mutation of consciousness. Having said his sole objective had become one thing—"nothing but how to become wholly God's"—he strikes to the heart in the phrase "This made me resolve to give the all for the All." Having seen that the One must be attained by yielding and exchanging the manifold for the One, he let the many go that he might be seized of the One. He succeeded in acting on Eckhart's great cry of prayer, "O Lord God, we beseech Thee to help us escape from the life which is divided into the life which is united." Only those who have completely [misunderstood] *The Practice of the Presence* can, in face of such a phrase, continue to think of Lawrence's method as a gentle, sentimental reverie, a method whereby a wandering-minded monk filled in the longueurs of the conventual day with a theological daydream.

So much for Lawrence's own development and systematization, for the deeply cut steps he hewed to scale the purgatorial mountain and the firm platform he won on its lofty summit. His letters illustrate in still further detail how conscious and defined he had made his specific trail, how little he left to happy chance, how well he remembered and understood the intense effort needed at the start and for a long while, and how shrewd and calculating he was—what a sound practical psychologist in judging every difficulty and in suggesting ingenious and subtle ways of negotiating successive obstacles.

There is no suggestion that he imagined any but proficients would find the way anything but a constant remedying of faults, repairing of slips and mistakes, and indefatigable returning to the climb after bruise, stumble, and fall—in fact, a life of continual restarting after check and arrest. He advises beginners not to trust the stream of their feeling; on the contrary, he specifically tells them "to do themselves violence" in setting themselves at this task of remembering God when it will actually seem "repugnant"—there will be a distinct emotional disgust for the work—and, alternately, it will seem "time lost"—the whole task will seem an illusion, a silly bore. Then the beginner is to tie themselves to the task as a steerer lashes themselves to the wheel when facing contrary seas. They are to bind themselves by the express resolve that, whether they make harbor or not, the ship, even if it sinks, shall be found facing toward port. They are to resolve till death to hold their course. Then, when the will is set—that naked intent of the will, that blind beholding which is the whole teaching of the *Cloud*—then, with that, sure and based, can come a number of subtle devices and advices.

Once the will is really purified in the fire of love and is true metal without alloy, it can be tempered. There is a finer, surer strength than rigidity, and that is suppleness. To revert to voyaging similes: the ship must hold its course, but it must also know, if it is to climb the oncoming waves, how to rise and swing to them. The forces that meet them who would move ahead along an intentional progress are waves as surely as the sea's. There must be give and then go. No one can advance unremittingly until they are reborn and leave the sea for the air. The beginner will find the true criterion of their strength—or rather of the strength given them—not in swift progress, which almost inevitably would lead to pride, but in their humble power of immediate recovery. True, a perfect ship keeps a wonderfully steady keel in all weathers, but for a middlingly built craft its safety lies in its power to roll to the waves. The thoroughly dangerous boat is that which will not roll at all. Suddenly hit by a heavy sea, it reels clean over, never recovers, and founders at one plunge. So are the rigid, self-assured, self-upheld stoics. So Lawrence warns strongly against all rolling in the wave trough of remorse. As Fénelon, the holy Marquis, was pointing out at the same time as this holy scullion, remorse and disgust at the self may be not repentance at all but actually wounded self-importance—mortified, not at having fallen from God, but in being lowered in its own self-esteem.

As soon as the dip is over, the ship must rise. The ship will labor and stagger, rock and sway as we try to keep its masthead steady on the pilot star. The skilled steerer with ready hold does not expect absolute rigidity or throw up their hands when time and again the ship gives and reels. Indefatigably, they bring its head back again to the course. And as they cease to worry and wrench at the helm, not only does their strength hold; the ship also reels less.

Lawrence also notes for his beginners how much the actual impact of the wave may be modified by foresight. That is our peculiar power of mind that gives mind its one but, if employed, decisive supremacy over emotion. We can see the wave bearing down on us and we can handle our craft so that it takes the flood skillfully with its prow well set to it. Lawrence warns that the disturbances in prayer bear a close relation to the thought indulged in when out of prayer. And here we drop the simile of boat, steerer, and waves, for all are one—we are ocean as well as ship and mariner, and so we can decide if the sea is to be rough.

It will be as rough as we care to stir it. We stir it with our constant daily preoccupation with other drives and urges, quite other from the urge to reach and abide in the unchanging eternal dynamic coordinative calm of the Presence and Peace of God.

[Ed. note: Please see the editor's note on page 21 pertaining to the authorship of *De Adhaerendo Deo,* which is no longer attributed to St. Albert the Great.]

Notes on Brother Lawrence's Practice of the Presence of God, Pt. II

Originally published in *Vedanta and the West*,
Vol. 4, No. 1, January–February 1941

LAWRENCE HAD RIGHT TO THINK his system the simplest, best, most thorough, and swiftest. Extend the kingdom of intention and control until there is no province, no quarter of an hour, in which its writ does not run. Then there will be no backwoods where outlaws may gather to attack and pester the camp and the city. Clean out every focus of infection; leave no pocket for flies to breed on its garbage of worry and private concern. The house of the Soul will not need all this screening ... nor its householder always be dashing from their lens and retort to swat the intruding insects. No more than flies can be present if breeding grounds are absent can distracting thoughts, still less worry, disturb the mind that has no concern but God. The Eternal Light sterilizes all these pests.

Again we must remind ourselves that Lawrence did not think this course anything but fatiguing for beginners. If we are seeking immediate comfort, we shall not clean the garbage pit nor drain the puddles. Nearly all of us are seeking something short of the Eternal dynamic peace: we are, all save the saints, beachcombers in soul, though we should feel disgust if we beachcombed in the flesh. Lawrence's recommendation that we should all the time be conscious, or strive to be, every minute, is a short sharp cure—sharp because we are alternating creatures, [and] short because if we stick to it and succeed in switching over into continuous, intentional consciousness—the practice of the Presence—we have done at a stroke and for good what anyhow we must sooner or later do, what is easier done now than when, as must be at any later time, there must be more to undo, and if we stop and start again, we shall take many bites at the one cherry. Our many false starts will amount to a mileage equal to the mileage of the actual crossing if we went ahead and crossed straight away.

Lawrence is too good a psychologist, has too much of actual spiritual experience to expect that one resolve, however keen, will see us through and over. He has warned us of the waves, of the opposing tides we stir up by our forward thrust. He does not expect us to make an unruffled drive and dive to our goal, but he does expect and plan for an ever quicker recovery after each deflection, until what began as a zigzag advance, with pausing and panting at each hooking and crooking, shows less and less fluctuation, [and] ripples forward with a quicker, smoother, straighter flow, till at last, like a streak and a flash, it strikes straight for its goal.

Nothing distracts or delays it now. To change the simile, the perforations in the band of time become incessant, until, instead of a series of punctures, a continuous aperture is pierced through the temporal into the Eternal. Then the Soul has attained; the fog and web of the temporal never has a chance to form. The Light shines uninterruptedly. The hard-working and often fatigued and flustered servant is raised, hears the almost-too-good-to-be-true summons, "Friend, come up higher." They find themselves in the Light, by the source and fount of all energy. Striving is over: the rough water left. With a prodigy of effort, beating and being beaten by waves and water, the swan strikes and batters itself along the sea surface. But suddenly, the pounding pinions no longer buffet the stinging water. They strike, hold, and mount upon the air, and in a moment the agony is over, the huge bird is free in its element, the waves sink down impotently under, the last drops sweep from its feathers, falling to the sea, whose sound even now is waning as the wind currents bear the exultant creature racing upward into the sky.

Yes, there are helpful wind currents to step us up from the sea surface. Lawrence warns us of this also. Be always ready, be alert to mount, but know also that you do not mount solely by that act of will. "You must raise your sail," said Ramakrishna. "The wind of Grace will fill it." Assuredly it will, but we have to learn patience. We must remember we have, all of us, missed many a tide, many a favorable wind. We cannot expect everything to be ready the moment we decide, at long last, that we are. But the waiting, too, has its purpose. There are no accidents in the spiritual life. The waiting shows us whether we are in earnest. We are, as a matter of fact, never kept waiting long, never as long as we ourselves have delayed. Lawrence, then, warns against that beginner's fever which would be immediately at its goal and is peremptory in its demand for instantaneous enlightenment. He uses the interesting phrase that the young hothead he was indirectly counseling was wishing to go "faster than Grace." The wise gardener works indefatigably. They know that, though they must wait on nature's time for fruits, yet there is always something they can be doing to help, and that on the incessancy of their labor will depend the abundance and quality [of the fruits] when [they] appear.

Such then was Brother Lawrence and his method. As for its results, for him we may say that it raised him past all the conflict of purgation to the effortless achievement and unvarying imperturbable happiness that is an authentic manifestation of the Eternal Peace. Circumstances of time and place; conditions of body; limitations of mind; the faults of the particular church to which he belonged [and] of the social system in which he lived; the distresses and diseases of an old, ill-tended, crippled body; the inadequacy of an intelligence long uneducated—of moderate endowment at best and given in the end but little actual instruction: all these handicaps were severe and might have proved arresting. With his single-hearted devotion toward God, to God in his inexpressible perfection, with his magnificent integrity of will, Lawrence surmounted all. Through a system heavily encrusted and opalescent with dogma, with rigid and elaborate ordering, ritual and particularized symbol-ism, he made the pure eternal Light shine as purely and certainly as intensely as any Sufi or Quaker.

In a society where religion had been amalgamated into the state so that when the state collapsed, his church was completely involved in the ruin, he not only kept the witness of the spirit alive in his heart—the Paraclete shone so brightly in this temple cleaned of all but the Supreme Presence—that the worldly wise, as wearily awake to the hysteria of sham religion as they were to the simpler more ruthless hypocrisy of ecclesiastical careerism, nevertheless came to talk with and be roused from their sophisticated despair by this man, who by the simple audacity of simply "giving the all for the All," had found what they with all their endowments had missed. ...

[Many] observers came to study Lawrence. The Jesuits were in the saddle managing the king and his gross sins in order, "A.M.D.G." ["for the greater glory of God"], to manage the State. They had de-nounced the Quietists and imposed a worship that was filled with the images the mystic believes to prove obstacles. They had driven out the gentle saintly Fénelon, accusing him of Quietism. Had Lawrence been even at Fénelon's level, he might have been crushed. After all, he was no Marquis, stylist, scholar, tutor of the heir to the throne, and he could have been silenced by the mere hint of authoritative disapproval. Less exertion, less reflection, than we take to brush aside an ant would have swept him into oblivion. For not only was he personally of complete insignificance, a lay brother of a poor house, he was also of complete humbleness and obedience possibly unattainable by one who has merited the doom to be born to a mar-quisate, and, even when he chooses the [Catholic] Church, to preach with eulogized eloquence, to manage affairs and people of affairs with mastery, to conduct a life of shining spectacular virtue against the terribly effective background of a clever, pretentious, and squalid court.

[When] Fénelon [was] banished—banished to his archbishopric, banished from such a court to his rightful flock that he was vowed to feed spiritually and who did (however frugally he ate) actually feed him—Fénelon submitted with dignity, with true grace but not with cheerfulness. True, he was leaving his beloved pupil whom he had tamed from savagery and trained to affection, a pupil dear to himself as a spiritual son and precious to himself as a loyal son of France, for this child, whom he had broken and reset, was it seemed to be France's sole master. But Lawrence, to whom the Presence of God made for him a light in which all and any conditions were radiant with God's will, love, and marvelous design—Lawrence surely would not have written from the galleys, even still less from the archepiscopal palace of Cambrai, "I am enduring a dry and bitter peace." This is not to underrate the noble Archbishop; it is to elevate or show the true station of the ex-cook.

Lawrence was not silenced. That is the fact, more important than any speculation, however certain, as to how his radiance would have shone unabated had he been exiled. Lawrence might have been accused when passions were running high of certain expressed carelessness about forms when forms were again being advocated as essential by the dominant party, and that party, with the despot behind them, was striking successfully at figures great in rank and station, worthily high in prestige and consummate in expression and defense. Lawrence is inspected—it was the time when anyone of low rank in the Church and showing influence had to be inspected. Surely it may be doubted whether the first visit of the Vicar General of the Cardinal de Noailles was made solely [so] that the busy, and probably harassed, official might talk about his own soul. Yet it is certainly clear that this hardworking man, at work that was probably hardening, this filterer of claims for preferment, this sanitary inspector of moral scandals, this server of tables none-too-clean besieged by the hungry, whose hunger had made them none-too-scrupulous, still found time to come once and again to get spiritual food for himself from the simpleton whom he inspected. He found time to write out for others what he had found, to enter that passage about his being forbidden to come again unless he would give up his life to God, and to urge on the Cardinal (his master) the publication of this pure and lofty Gospel, a request that was granted.

The point disclosed here seems important. Recall that at that precise moment, Lawrence's teaching could so easily, almost inevitably have been regarded as inexpedient. The Church, especially in France, had decided this was of all times the least auspicious in which to teach the laying aside of systems and the Quakerly doctrine that, as all life is sacramental, picking up a straw may and should be done as much for the love of God and in the clear conviction of His Presence as kneeling in adoration before the sacrament. This was what Lawrence taught, and the teaching, advanced though it is, [and] easily misunderstood as it certainly can be, was not only approved but promulgated by the ultra-cautious authorities, hardened with suspicion and hypersensitively nervous over any latitude or toler-ance. Is there not in fact a further and perhaps most important piece of evidence as to the spiritual height Lawrence had attained? Those who spoke with him noted not only his words, but they were also [taken] by his appearance. Like all those few who have become the constant friends of God, he radiated, without the need of expression, the triple charisma: the love, joy, and peace that fills those natures who have lost their egos. They do not have to think and say and act; they *are*, and their still silences bless us more than their arguments, their eloquence, or their good deeds.

Lawrence's words and reasoning could well have been [misun-derstood] and suppressed. They were given [an acceptance] that would have astonished him, not by sectarians anxious by any seces-sion to liberate the Spirit [at a time] when free, pure worship seemed deliberately attacked, but by the highest church authorities, individ-uals charged to err on the side of caution and repression.

That denouement seems to have a moral for us today. It is clear that precisely the same words as Lawrence used would be used by a Quaker, or by any devout schismatic or heretic. The book's success as wide as Christendom has established that. The words themselves therefore would not have assured themselves a welcome; on the con-trary, we should expect them to have been repressed—kindly, maybe, but firmly. What made their issue seem safe and natural was Lawrence himself, or to be precise, his lack of self. Something of an authenticity both so awe-inspiring and so gentle—irresistible in the dread strength of its open tenderness and unsuspecting love—came out from the old man, that those in his presence knew that he was only an open door. Through the incessant beauty of his soul shone the awful meekness of the Paraclete. To doubt that his words could do harm, to feel suspicion that such a spirit might be unsafe and endanger societal security or ecclesiastical arrangements—such doubts and suspicions, in a presence instant with the authenticity of the Eternal, filled the enquirer with shame. He knew, below all argument of caution and reasons of state and church, that nothing but good can flow from the Source of Good.

When we consider this man—his peculiar time of anxious, authoritative repression and his letters and conversations both so free and innocent of the passports of detailed dogmatic compliance, [and] so emphatic that one thing alone matters above sins and sacraments: the constant communion with God—the question must rise in our minds: "How often have the martyrs, by failing in profound incessant charity for those who opposed them in their desire to throw at their persecutor's feet the challenge of their lives, failed to see that they were themselves debarring the spread of their message?" "The blood of the martyrs is the Seed of the Church."

What church? Certainly the implicit violence and hostility of not a few such witnesses were seed from which sprang a church as ruthlessly cruel in persecution as ever its persecutors. The message of the Sermon on the Mount was never carried by such martyrs. Today the world is in a desperate pass. People of great courage and devotion and with a great cause to serve are resolved that the other side must be crushed beyond recovery and they themselves are ready to die and wreck the world if only their enemy may be totally destroyed. Each side maintains that there is not the slightest use expecting any decent or lasting settlement as long as the other is free to live. The enemy is one who is incapable of understanding the right. We have to go back to the wars of religion to find such a fatal implacability. And it is there, on the shore of that deadly sea of the mutual blind hatred of two intense devoted convictions, of the death duel of the champions of the Spirit of Freedom and the Spirit of Authority, that we find Brother Lawrence.

He spoke in the camp of Authority for freedom, and because of the love he felt for [all people], through the love he had won to and from God, the authoritarians listened and published his message. He succeeded in speaking of real religious liberty, that incessant service which is the only perfect freedom, to those obsessed with the need of order, because he never felt these people to be at heart different from himself. He knew that we all need God. That is our one peremptory overwhelming need, but in spite of our awful thirst we cannot stoop and drink because we are masked in our prejudices and prides.

Because he spoke with absolute simplicity and with living proof of what he had found, he knew he had nothing to fear from people whose need was as great as his. When we are dying of thirst, we do not strike or silence one—however fanatical—whom we see is coming to lead us to a well from which they have drunk and lived. His examiners therefore also knew they had nothing to fear from him. That is the one foundation of all peacemaking: the assurance that from this man, at least, I have nothing to fear. Suspicion and its dim father, recoiling caution, could find no [foothold] in this man's innocent humility, because, in a deeper sense than we say it, Lawrence never stood in his own light. In the light that streamed over him, he strove to be perfectly transparent. He gave no personal or temporal tinge to his profoundly simple message. For that reason, his anxious authorities passed it and published it, and precisely for that reason those who have most loved God and cared least for anything else, even for the forms in which people have spoken of God, these saints of every race and sect, as well as those particular executives of his day, have loved and prized his words.

Here is a true bridgebuilder, a *pontifex maximus*, spanning the gulf between the devotees of freedom and those of authority, and his power to span and embrace and hold these two extremes, who [otherwise] must destroy each other, is not [due to] ingenuity of compromising phrase or eloquence or appeal to reason. No, it is that gigantic gentleness—that irresistible authenticity which sees in all the same vast universal need it has felt in itself, and which sees that need can only be satisfied by the same simple solution. Because Lawrence really did give the all for the All, he received back from the All, [and] all his [fellow creatures], now seen as part of that All and only needing to recognize their part in that All by giving all [of] themselves to it, to become one with the All. This and this only is the faith that overcomes the world, for it reunites all humanity by making it one communion with the Eternal. Those only, but they infallibly, who are so filled with the Presence of God may and must draw all people, none of whom they can think of as alien, into that incessantly practiced communion.

This is Lawrence's particular message to our day and hour: be filled until you are nothing but the All, and then you will discover that because He is indeed the All, you do indeed embrace and draw out of the ignorance and illusion of separateness every other human soul. For there can be no boundaries, no limitations, no exclusions toward any. However much any may feel that they are separate, the higher Knowledge, the true gnosis of charity won in the Presence of God, knows that this is illusion that must vanish when it meets the challenge of truth in Love. This gnosis also knows that God's presence waits to descend fully to recreate people, until the last person shall consent to wish for that presence and, so attaining the power to see it in their neighbor, will be united with God in humanity. Finally, the gnosis in the power of its endless life knows that, as each individual becomes aware of their real nature in God, their enlightenment gives them the power to kindle the same illumination in others.

On Ramakrishna

Originally published in *Vedanta and the West*,
Vol. 4, No. 2, March–April 1941

On March 2 [1941], we celebrated the birthday anniversary of Sri Ramakrishna. The speakers were Swami Prabhavananda and Mr. Gerald Heard. The substance of their addresses is given below. [Ed. Note: Only Heard's address is included here.]
–Original Editor's Note

WE HAVE HEARD from Swami [Prabhavananda] what Ramakrishna has meant for those who have been brought up in the tradition of his direct teaching and under those who were his personal disciples. What does this Teacher mean to us as Westerners?

There are certainly three features that stand out in this life, features which for us make the life of religion appear with a vividness that it lacks in our own environment and which it certainly has not had in Europe for the last three hundred years or more. The first outstanding characteristic is the totality with which the life of religion, the dedication to God, was pursued by this saint. Once Ramakrishna had decided that God was to be found, for him that was the one goal, this was the pearl of great price for which everything else is sold.

There remained no other interest in his life, and any other concern that he had was simply to help others so that they, too, might attain to the vision which he had seen.

With this totality there went, naturally, an attitude toward what Buddha calls "livelihood." This, too, was forced to a degree that in the West we should consider unbalanced. The saint felt such a deep repugnance toward money, because of all it stood for, that he could not be induced even to touch a coin.

Such features, such reactions, are of course not uncommon in the religious life. In the West, when the vows of a monk were taken seriously, the idea that a person who had chosen the life of religion should have any other interest was treated as scandalous, and the ideal of holy poverty was driven to its logical extreme. Those who trust God should trust Him wholly, those who had found the Source of all Being should give earnest of their sincerity by depending on Him and not on their financial resources for their economic supplies, supplies that of course would be of the simplest, for the demands of the body are scant if the soul itself is fully fed: "Athirst for Thee, All craving dies."

This brings us to perhaps the oddest feature of the religious life as illustrated by a great saint. That is hard to express in our modern language. Perhaps the simplest way we can put it is to say that saintliness is something other and beyond merely "being good." That is not to say that saints are not, from the point of view of the conventional person, scrupulously good. But it is to point out that when goodness goes beyond a certain point, it passes, as we might say, out of the visible spectrum into the invisible, into the ultraviolet. That, however, is not to say that we are faced with something as dubious as the invisible clothes that the false weavers pretended to put upon the king in the fairy story. On the contrary, the interesting thing about total saintliness is the strange, almost uncanny effect that such intense dedication gives those who [permit] it to work. We are beginning to learn that it is no use trying to make out that the first-magnitude saints are at all like us. Their strange practices, their intense powers of devotion and concentration, not only alter their conduct and so make them intensely good, and not only alter their characters, giving them a strength of will, an integrity and a coordination that we never attain,

[but] their actual bodies are changed. They function differently from us. As they would say, the body itself becomes the temple of the Holy Spirit, the physical frame can be kindled by *sattvic* power.

We think that the life of the holy is mainly being moral, and we are right insofar as we are thinking of the first step. But if we want to be really encouraged, if we wish to have the energy to attain a life of selfless devotion, then we should be wise to look ahead and see to what heights of intensity, to what transforming conditions of consciousness the spirit of people can mount if they seek only to be combined with the spirit of the Eternal. Of course it is common in the West to say that such intensity is simply a blankness, an emptiness. That is a mistake which we make because we do not understand the upper ranges of human consciousness. To the child, when the adult sits still, poring over a mathematical problem, the elder seems lazy, inactive. So with us and the saints—their still intensity of contemplation seems to us to be mere laziness. The sleeping top is nevertheless revolving far faster than the top that has begun to wobble and is making violent movements. Indeed we may question whether we shall ever really alter the world unless we learn to be less active and gain the power of dynamic stillness.

Excerpt of a Letter from Gerald Heard to Swami Nikhilananda

from *Prabuddha Bharata*, Vol. 53, No. 3, March 1948
(facilitated through the courtesy of *Prabuddha Bharata*)

The particular importance of Ramakrishna for the West seems threefold, to me. First, that he shows religion "in its own right," secondly, he himself is a contemporary saint, and thirdly, that his message was and is contemporary. ...

The refreshing fact about Indian religion is that it is "neat." It does not think of God, as William James is supposed to have said, as "a useful ally of my social conscience." It knows that He is Reality, and this world has such reality as a shadow may have cast by the sun. Ramakrishna had that as part of his inheritance.

He added to that the fact that he could keep that faith alight in a world which was increasingly denying such a fact. And ... he did not have to do so—as so many of the modern Catholic saints have had to do so—by becoming increasingly narrow as the world became increasingly "educated." Ramakrishna is an apostle to the world and not merely to India, because he was able to say that "all roads lead to God," and that devotion to Him in whatever form will lead the devotee to enlightenment.

[Ed. Note: Swami Nikhilananda translated and published *The Gospel of Sri Ramakrishna* in 1942.]

The Cloud of Unknowing

Originally published in *Vedanta and the West*,
Vol. 6, No. 3, May–June 1943

HUMAN KNOWLEDGE is always getting into trouble by naming new things in the wrong way. Science has not avoided this difficulty. Joseph Priestley, the discoverer of oxygen, did not realize that he had found it, [and he] insisted on calling it by a wrong name, and thereby caused a great deal of confusion in chemistry. In the next century, Darwin's name became associated both with the hypothesis of evolution—which is certainly a very fruitful one, but which as certainly he did not originate—and also with the hypothesis of a cause of evolution, "Natural Selection," which he [quite] certainly did originate but which has not proved very fruitful.

But of all the names for important branches of knowledge, none perhaps has proved so persistently unhappy as "mysticism." The Catholic Church, which has always had an admirable desire for order, has divided the knowledge that humans may have of God into three categories: natural theology, the evidence of God working in nature; and dogmatic theology, the evidence of God working in history, are the first two of these three divisions. But a third one is obvious. Science [is divided] into three great sectors—the study of the inorganic, the organic, and consciousness itself, [or] the material, the living, and the mind. Besides the study of the evidence of God's working in the world and in life, there must be a third branch of research, the study of God's working directly on the soul itself, the religion of personal experience. This the Church acknowledged fully and studied pertinaciously. It was named the third great theology. But its specific title was unhappy. It was called "mystical theology." This was an accident for which the Church itself was not directly responsible. The naming had been done before Christianity arose.

"Mysticism," most historical and etymological authorities seem to agree, is derived from the Greek root *muō*, and probably means silence [or hidden, secret]. Certainly the Greek initiates were sworn to secrecy and silence about their initiatory experiences and certainly they kept their secret well, for no account of the procedures has survived. Certainly, too, silence was wise advice. Much talk about spiritual experience always seems to do harm. But, on the other hand, a certain sense of occult superiority is also a danger. It would seem that, at the beginning the Mysteries were not meant to be exclusive, [but] only to set a standard of restraint for those who applied for training—you were not to talk about details that the outsider was too lazy to study for themselves. But you might, as did Plato, Plutarch, and Aristophanes, openly state that you had found a way of life, a way over death and fear, and that the way was open to all who would walk it.

The Christian Church took over this attitude [toward] the religion of direct experience. It also taught that, though the public and those only in early training must withdraw when the actual "Mystery" was performed, yet everyone might apply for training and for admission as an initiate. Why, then, has mysticism become so unfortunate a word, a word with an almost invariable epithet of contempt—"mere Mysticism"? The fact that, by an unfortunate assonance in the English tongue, it sounds like *misty-ism*, something vague, damp, weak and thin, would not account for its poor standing, had any clear meaning been originally attached to it. And yet it should, of all the theologies, have been the most distinct. Natural theology has always had a hard time, though it has much more to say for itself than people now imagine. Historical theology has also lately had some heavy hammering, but mainly because it would confine itself to the single and precarious line of historical witness given by Hebrew thought with a small admixture of Greek philosophy. But, even at their heyday, the two "'exterior" theologies, the rational and the historical, were never so firmly situated as was the theology of experience. That is why the great Carmelite authorities on prayer call mysticism, often quite briefly, *science*—the direct, experimental, and skilled knowledge of God.

Science is quite the last word that a modern person would choose as a synonym for mysticism. It is possible that the third theology was starved out by the other two. Certainly, dogmatic theology soon began to rule what mystical theology might or might not discover. Such a censorship always checks research. When, therefore, dogmatic theology got into difficulties, mystical theology, long [upheld] and restricted, could no longer stand on its own feet. Once dogmatic theology is defeated, people think the issue of religion is settled. Mysticism is only a shadow thrown by certain historical events. Disprove the events and the shadow will vanish. As an actual fact, no Protestant seminary has a chair of mystical theology. These centers of study only cling on under the protection of dogmatic theology. But this need not be so, and should not be so. Mysticism is in itself a valid approach to Reality, perhaps the most valid, and although it should seek confirmation of its findings in the other theologies, its findings can stand on their own feet.

That is not to say that whatever notions may come into anyone's mind when they are praying or contemplating are inspirations—far from it. It is to say that, using the mystical experience of the past, and translating into our present terms the researches of other generations into this science, we also may have the experience they had, and may state it in our own vernacular. For the volume of such experience is great. Even in Western Europe right down to the last three hundred years, there has never been a generation throughout the Christian era that did not produce works of actual research on this subject. The trouble is that these treatises are naturally couched in the terms of their times and, further, with a caution that the dominance of dogmatic theology compelled. It is therefore necessary to take these statements out of their local phraseology and see if we can put them in our vernacular. It is then generally found that they are perfectly consistent with all the findings of mystical theology of any age or country, and that they also show an independence of dogmatics in any narrow sense and a psychological knowledge in the deep sense, which are as surprising as they are refreshing.

The volume of such writing is, as has been said, very great. Perhaps, then, the best way of illustrating the fact that "mysticism" is really experimental religion worked out as a scientific system, is to take one treatise, a treatise written in our own language by a brilliant writer who lived toward the close of the great epoch of mysticism, the close of what Pitirim Sorokin calls the last ideational age, and a writer, also, who shared quite a number of our Western predispositions.

The Cloud of Unknowing has become a popular book. New editions of the text are regularly issued. Commentaries, from the Catholic to the Humanist point of view, have been published. It is not hard to understand this interest. A long prose work of Chaucer's date, written with more wit and liveliness than appears in Chaucer's own prose, must have a literary appeal. Add to this that the author is an enthusiastic authority on mysticism, and another topical taste is met. Witty religion is the counterreformation technique of our day. We like saints, provided they never cease being humorous. Someone who can practice the Presence of God and yet never fail to be good company is the present *beau ideal* of the person who has really succeeded, really made "the best of both worlds."

But the *Cloud* only superficially belongs to the "Chester-Belloc" school of propaganda. The author evidently could not help being witty. He was far from being proud of the fact, indeed he was frightened of it, realizing how easily it could do harm. The Abbé Brémond has said the poetic mystic is the spoilt mystic—*a fortiori*, the humorous. The *Cloud's* author did not therefore intend to commend himself by his power to entertain. His text may make amusing reading once, but if it is studied it will be seen that it is as exact and sober as a textbook. Indeed it is a textbook—a specialist writing for specialists and, further, writing on a specific point in the great specialty called mysticism.

The *Cloud* is unsuited for general devotional reading because it does not deal with the whole of the life of union with God, but at most with one third of it. To take the classic division of St. John of the Cross, the spiritual life divides broadly into three great areas. One aspect of each of these areas is the particular phase of renunciation—or deliverance—through which the soul goes at that particular level. These so-called nights are "of the senses," "of faith," and "of the spirit." The *Cloud* is devoted to the study of the second "night," and to defending the right of those who wish to go so far, and to leave all to advance up that path. This second "night" divides the deeper mysticism from the more general. Both nature mystics and all moralists know something of the first "night" and of the necessity for it. The person who has refused to control their senses will never see "with wondering eyes and clean, / the world through all the gray disguise / of sleep and custom in between."[70]

But the second "night" is so much beyond the first that there is as much controversy between the nature mystics and moralists of the first night and those who choose the second night, as there is between the nature mystics and the average sensual man. For in the second night, all the beauty of nature and all the [aids] of "religion-with-form" are abandoned. What had helped is now shunned. Nor is this all. Up to that point moralists and mystics are one. The life of athletic self-control is practiced and commended by both. So living, a person becomes permanently mobilized. But for what? "For the social service of his fellow humans," answer the moralists, "to commend a rational and disciplined life whereby humanity may become healthy, peaceful, successful, progressive." This answer, however, the mystic would not give for themselves, though they would not deny its validity for others. They would say that they practiced self-control not in order that they and their [companions] might enjoy more efficiently the present life, but in order that they and all others might enter into quite another life. In brief, they are not concerned with the life of action, but with the life of *being*; they are not looking for more powers to tidy up the world, but for a new consciousness whereby they may see it as God sees it.

Here then is a split between those who see religion as an aid to social amelioration and those who see it as an end in itself. A great deal of the *Cloud* is taken up with this defense, defending contemplatives from the charge that they are useless creatures who discredit religion.

The remainder is given to explaining four things: (1) the type of person who may attempt this work; (2) the preliminaries they must have gone through to qualify for it; (3) the techniques that aid this "blind beholding"; and (4) the mistakes and dangers that should be guarded against.

In an attempt to get as close as possible to the author's meaning, the present writer made for himself a rendering of the *Cloud's* text, based on the Father Augustine Baker/Dom Justin McCann edition of the *Cloud*, into the commonest, most colloquial English he could find. The whole text is of course far too long to be given here, but it has been suggested that a few passages illustrating the author's graphic teaching on some points might be of help. About the first division—who should attempt this work—it need only be said that the author believes that it can only be undertaken by those who can follow the "Life of Perfection," i.e., who can practice poverty, chastity, and obedience, and further, [who] have a special calling to pure contemplation, a life that is not engaged even in good works.

As to the second part—the necessary preparations—he does not think that contemplatives are born. Though an aptitude is given, it will never blossom unless a great deal of preliminary cultivation and pruning has been undergone. Contemplatives, according to this authority, are religious people who began like all religious people: they renounced the world, the flesh and the devil; they strove hard to let their natures become anonymous, chaste, charitable; [and] they learnt prayer and worship as even the busiest good person must learn them. The difference between them and the actives is that when the actives stopped acquiring and turned to producing, the contemplatives went on. They would not cash out. Like old-fashioned businesspeople, instead of distributing profits in dividends, they put the profits back into the business. Nor does the contemplative do this merely on the ethical level. For example, they do not merely abstain from healing the sick. They abstain in what they take from God quite as much as in what they venture to offer people. They ask God as little for consolations as for powers. They deny themselves heaven as the ordinary, sincere good person denies themselves the world. As the *Cloud* says, "he loves God and none of His works." Or to use Fénelon's rendering of the same pure devotion, "we learn to love God without fear and without hope."

There is no need to give quotations from this author on these points. He expresses himself tellingly, but what he has to say on these first two particulars are "the eternal commonplaces" of the mystical life, of those who dare believe that God may be known in this life and dare hope that they themselves might attain that supreme fulfilment. It is in the two latter divisions of his work—the discussion of techniques and of the mistakes—that the writer's originality is most marked. Here then are a series of excerpts illustrating his teachings.

First, as to the objective. The contemplative is to think of God without form. Hence, they must realize that God is hidden from them by the darkness of their own mind. "That," says our author, "is why I call this ignorance a 'cloud of unknowing'" (page 21). But how is anyone to work in such darkness? Are they to sit still in a quietest vacancy? "No," he says, "you must understand this technique, and the extraordinary way it works in your consciousness. For if it is properly understood, it is no more than a sudden involuntary impulse, a 'stirring' to God, just as a spark will flash out from a live coal. It is amazing how many such 'stirrings' can take place in a single hour, if the mind in which they take place is really willing to let them happen. And (though each of them lasts only a moment), while it lasts it obliterates all consciousness of this world. But each such impulse is followed straightway by a slump. We find our mind taken up with some thought or with some memory or anticipation. That's due to the body" (pages 18–19).

The author therefore goes on to advise how such slumps, such distractions, may best be avoided. His main advice is, "just as you have to realize that you have a 'cloud of unknowing' between you and God, so you must put a 'cloud of forgetting' below you and the whole creation. Probably you think that this cloud of unknowing, this complete ignorance, keeps you quite far enough away from God. But if you really understood your situation, you'd see that as long as you can be conscious of any created thing, so long as you haven't a cloud of forgetting between you and the whole creation, you are even further away from him" (page 21).

(Compare this teaching with that of the *Theologica Germanica*, how that a person is safe "when he is in Heaven," i.e., has the sense of God's presence, and safe "when he is in Hell," i.e., when they know that they have lost that sense; but they are in deadly danger "when he is with creatures," i.e., has lost the vision of the One in the confusion of the manifold.)

The disciple then asks his teacher how he is to think of God and is answered paradoxically, "I can only answer that question by saying I don't know." This is explained further by pointing out that the human mind can grasp created things but not the Uncreated: "nobody can *think* of God." "So I'd abandon everything that can be thought about and devote myself to what I can't think of. Why? Because He can certainly be loved but never imagined. You may reach Him and hold Him by love—never by thought" (page 23).

Then follow the particular advices as to how this thought-less intention, "this naked intent" is to be maintained against the mind's incessant tendency to break down into reflections and reveries. "So when you intend to undertake this exercise ... turn to God with a humble impulse of devotion. ... A simple intention aimed at God without any further definition, is quite sufficient. If you need to have this intention held in a single word, so you can keep it from slipping, choose a short, single-syllabled word. The briefer the word the better it fits this kind of spiritual exercise. Try the word 'God' or 'Love' or any other one-syllabled word that you find best suits you. Fasten this word in your heart so that you never let it slip on any account. With this word you are to beat on the 'Cloud' above you and with it also you are to drive down, under 'the cloud of forgetting,' every thought that rises up" (pages 26–27). (It is worth comparing this advice with the use of the *mantra*.)

But what is the pupil to do when right through the "song word" distractions succeed in interfering? "If they keep on rising, keep on repressing them. If the labor seems hard, find out methods and tricks to dodge distractions. ... Here are some. Try them and improve on them if you can. As much as you can, carry on as if you were unaware that the distractions were pressing between you and God. As it were, try to look over their shoulders, searching for something else. If you do this, I give my word for it, your effort will grow less in a little time. ... Here's another method. When you feel that you simply can't repress distractions, then surrender to them as a coward and weakling goes down in battle; conclude that it's simply silly to struggle any longer with them and so yield yourself to God in your enemies' hands. Feel that you are defeated for good. I beg you to attend to this advice particularly, for I believe if you will try it, you'll melt all (opposition) [into] water. Because if this method is really understood, it is nothing but a true self-knowledge—an experience of your true self, a thing far worse than nothing, and this knowledge and experience is true humility. And this humility deserves that God Himself should descend in His power to counterattack your enemies" (pages 79–81).

These methods of dealing indirectly with distractions have been approved by almost all masters of prayer. As to the second method, de Caussade in his study on *Holy Abandonment* often repeats the advice that we should say to God, that if it should be His wish that at this moment we be distracted, desolate, weak, [and] yes, even worrying, we are willing to accept these degradations for as long as He wills. Then often, as soon as we accept, the burden is raised.

Besides these methods for dealing with distractions, the *Cloud's* author also gives a number of chapters to warning against dangers into which rash people may fall—[those] who would follow his method without understanding it and without having a competent adviser. He is particularly concerned that pupils should not do themselves psychological damage by thinking that the movements of the will, which he advises, are bodily movements. "I believe," he says, "that it is very necessary to be cautious in understanding language which is meant spiritually for fear it should be taken physiologically. In particular, care should be taken with the words 'in' and 'up'" (pages 121–122).

He then goes on to explain how beginners can disturb their physique by this mistaken concentration. "So they give up humble prayer and contrition too soon out of rash pride caused by their intellectual curiosity and (as is their notion) concentrate on complete contemplation. But this activity of theirs, if it is properly understood, is neither a physical nor a spiritual process. It is simply an unnatural activity and the devil is the chief cause of it. Indeed it's the quickest way to destroy body and soul, for it's madness and has no sense in it and indeed it will turn a man mad. And it comes about in this way: they turn their physical senses inward ... trying to see, hear, smell, taste and feel inwardly. ... So they reverse their senses contrary to what is natural ... at last they derange their minds and, as soon as that happens, the devil has power to delude them with hallucinations. They see lights, hear sounds, smell fragrant scents, taste delicious flavors, and experience a number of odd heats and inflammations in chest and abdomen, across the shoulders, in their kidneys and nates" (pages 123–124). He goes on to describe the extravagant behavior into which such people are led. "They stare as though they were out of their minds and grimace as though they saw the devil. ... They squint and roll up their eyes like a stunned sheep. Others hang their heads on one side as though they had a maggot in their ear" (page 125).

The author develops this point at some length. He is very much of an Englishman and he would have had no sympathy with violent *bhakti* expressions of devotion. He declares that the contemplative method he teaches actually makes for seemly deportment. "Anyone who has achieved this method, it will condition their behavior not merely mentally but physically. Their appearance will prepossess anyone who sees them. Indeed, if a boorish man could undertake this exercise, his whole appearance would undergo so rapid an improvement that the best people would want his company" (page 128). "His looks and his conversation would be full of spiritual insight. His tone would be one of quiet assurance" (page 129).

The author's entire discussion of the dangers that can befall young contemplatives who give full rein to their emotions and concentrate on physical exercises, is of unusual interest. He seems aware that changes in consciousness can be produced by concentrating on areas of the body. Beyond that, he does not seem to know anything about any physical exercises that might help concentration. Nor does his method require such knowledge. To make use of Nietzsche's old distinction, the *Cloud's* author is Apollonian in his religion, not Dionysian. Quietness is all; any violence is mistaken. The rule may not be universal, but it is interesting to see how many supporters it has among the great Western teachers of prayer. The author of *The Mirror of Simple Souls*, writing perhaps one hundred and fifty years before the *Cloud's* author, advises the same quiet "abstraction." Louis of Blois (Blosius), a successor of the *Cloud*; Father Augustine

Baker, a commentator on the *Cloud* in the sixteenth and seventeenth centuries; John of the Cross; Lallement and Surin, Jesuit teachers of contemplation in the seventeenth century; de Caussade—all these authorities advise avoiding any excitement. Do everything quietly, advises that great teacher, François de Sales; depart even from your sins quietly for fear while bolting in panic you may trip up, fail, and be overtaken.

Yet in this quietness there is of course no lack of fervor. Father Baker, the *Cloud's* most thorough commentator, can find no harsher word for a contemplative than "tepid." He strongly advises the pupil, however moved, not to give way to emotions, to check tears and exultations, but this is not to get rid of devotion, but to generate it at pressures that the easy release of emotional expression would have dissipated. In this he is undoubtedly following the *Cloud's* intention. "I bid you," he writes to his pupil, "do all you can to hide from God Himself the stirring of your desire for Him. Why? Because any spiritual desire is less spiritual (and so further from God), the more it has about it any physical expression" (pages 113–114).

The aim then is an intensity of experience that goes utterly beyond any possibility of bodily response, [just] as light, when it becomes intense, vanishes into the invisibility of the ultraviolet wavebands. It is to that "purity and depth of spiritual feeling" to which this author points. The aim is to reach a "circulation of current" between the human and divine so complete that, as there is no longer any resistance, so is there no longer any physical manifestation. "I wish," he sums up his teaching, "to help you tie the spiritual knot of burning love between you and your God in spiritual union and agreement of will."

[Ed. Note: The ellipses that occur in the citations quoted from *The Cloud of Unknowing* above, indicating omissions in the text, were made by Gerald Heard in his original article.]

The Mirror of Simple Souls

Originally published in *Vedanta and the West*,
Vol. 6, No. 4, July–August 1943

IN THE FOREGOING ESSAY on *The Cloud of Unknowing*, there was mentioned an earlier treatise that follows much the same path. A few remarks on this text may serve as a sequel to those on the *Cloud*. It will be seen that the *Mirror*, too, has a telling title, but it is far from being a book of the same caliber, at least in style, as the *Cloud*. To start with the title, before plunging into the text—before, one might almost say, going through the Looking Glass—the name given the work is difficult. The *Cloud* is clearly obscure; the *Mirror* is speciously clear. For the author does not mean that his text is meant for children—far from it. Perhaps a better translation—for the book was not originally written in English, and, to add to the puzzle, the original is lost—would be to call it *The Reflection or the Image of the Single-Hearted or the Pure in Heart*, those who, by authoritative definition, see God.

Yet the book is, one might say, in the same category as the *Cloud*. Indeed it would not be inapposite to issue a trilogy, beginning with this *Mirror*, having as its middle volume the *Cloud*, and concluding with Walter Hilton's well-known *Scale of Perfection*. The last two are English classics, but the first matches them because it, too, has about it a certain meiosis, a certain dread of too much effervescent sweetness. These northern wines of the spirit are dry and still. Even with Bernard there is often too much sugar; the famous sermons on the Canticle push the imagery of that erotic love–cycle as far as it will go. The sweet wines are the commonest and the more general taste, and perhaps the public is right. But some of the greatest masters of Western mysticism have been "dry." When the Spanish Carmelites restart the empirical study of prayer or orison, St. Teresa, who certainly is not *sec* ["dry"] is the novices' fancy, [though] a maturer palate turns to John of the Cross, who is as "dry" as the *Cloud*.

Another connection between the *Mirror* and the *Cloud* and the *Scale* is that the three works "plot a curve"; they show a spiritual sequence—the dry school might even say a descent. It is certain that the school of pure contemplation and imageless worship gains its impetus, if it has not its origin, from the Pseudo-Dionysius. Then, after the Dark Ages had kept these strange texts in cold storage (though a Latin text had existed, Erigena, who made it, was condemned for pantheism), between the poles of Paris and Cologne, the Dominican masters and the Victorines develop the implications of this accepted metaphysic to a great height of actual experience. There is a phrase from the *De Adhaerendo Deo*, [formerly] attributed to St. Albertus Magnus, "Him Whom I need above all things is above all things that I know" and so "I am carried into the Darkness of the Mind." Such a definition is of course the whole proposition of the *Cloud*, and it is exactly that Dark Light which the *Mirror* is intended to catch and reflect.

The *Mirror* is indeed far freer than the *Cloud*. Already with the English classic, a touch of caution has clouded the bright defiance that is clear in the *Mirror*. Sides are being taken, something like the dawn of Lollardy is abroad, and, if sides must be accepted, the *Cloud* is going to settle with the old school and its hardening outlines instead of with the new with its empty phrases. But with the *Mirror*, there is no thought but of the goodness of liberty, the joy of being able to attain liberation. Probably the Franciscans had not begun their *bhakti* drive for the sole worship of the crucified Manhood, that cult which, as Père Poulain points out, was to give rise to the stigmata, this form of bodily damage not being known before the rise of the Friars Minor. When we reach the *Scale*, there is a further "contraction of orthodoxy," or even a retreat into sub-orthodoxy, for Hilton continually uses "Jesus" as though in the name of the Manhood was included the full Godhead, a position that the strictest theologians would call "temerarious."

It may be asked, if these three Northern [European] classics are grouped together, why not add that other product of devotional thought from the "banks of the narrow sea"? Why not include the most famous of all the Western books of devotion, the *Imitatio*? The answer is given by strictly orthodox writers: the *Imitatio* is not a work of mystical theology but is one of ascetical theology; it has turned from attempting to render and describe the highest states of the soul to giving advice on the preliminary training required before that or any of the higher conditions of the spiritual life can be attained.

To return, then, to the *Mirror*, we may say that this important work is of such value because it shows the mind of European people before the intensification of the feeling of guilt had made them despair of their own efforts and of the love of God to aid those efforts before, to use theological language, the Second Person of the Trinity (God in His aspect of Forgiver) not only became solely connected with Jesus of Nazareth, but completely eclipsed the other two aspects of the Deity—God as Creator and God as Sanctifier. This predominance of the idea of Redemption had, we know, two unfortunate results. On the tough and lazy it had the effect, well-known in Protestantism, of leaving everything to God: grace did everything and works were not required—a doctrine that goes far to account for the poverty of high sainthood in the "reformed churches." On the tender and nervous the results were the reverse, but hardly happier. As nothing the soul could do would make God forgive it, it remained often in a frenzy of doubt as to whether such an awful Being, who had exacted the unutterable torture of His Son as the price of overlooking man's offense against Him, had really forgiven this particular soul, considering that this soul not only was damned because of its original sin, but had also committed sins on its own.

The *Mirror* is little concerned with this obsession. Its author knows that the way to God is a stiff climb, but he knows that it is his Father's home to which he is clambering, and that his Father is waiting to welcome him. It is in his description of this scaling of the mountain of perfection that this author is uniquely interesting. Many critics have remarked that it is interesting to find in the *Cloud* John of the Cross' famous ascent through the "nights of the soul" described two hundred years before the Spanish mystic. But in the *Mirror,* we have an even more definite, if not more vivid, description of these "nights," and the *Mirror* is [likely] certainly a century earlier than the *Cloud.*

Perhaps the mention of dates should call us back for a moment to the actual textual question, for in itself it is interesting enough and has some bearing on the problem of the development of religious thought and mystical practices in particular. There is little doubt that the *Mirror* is—or was originally—a Flemish work of the middle of the thirteenth century, for the author (though himself anonymous, as was natural for such writers) names the three censors to whom he sent his work to see whether it were sound. They were all Flemings. None, it would seem, were individuals specifically appointed to "vet" theological works. They were simply persons of high spiritual standing. Their advices are given, and these, too, show us what a comparatively free theological world of thought existed in the thirteenth century. The work is exceedingly free in its handling of religious mysteries, but all the censors say is that they wouldn't advise the author to circularize too widely among the ignorant what was undoubtedly a very high point of view. Their advice was probably taken, for, as said above, the Flemish original has disappeared, though English, Italian, and Latin versions have come to light. The book must therefore have been popular in its time and probably circulated among contemplative houses, such as the Carthusians. The first English translator is unknown, but we undoubtedly owe a Latin translation to a Carthusian, Richard Methley of Mount Grace Priory in Yorkshire. He gives a number of comments and, as he is a century later, it is significant to see how he tries to modify his author's boldness of phrase and point of view.

The chief interest of the *Mirror* is not, however, the author's cheerful rashness about theological particulars and generous trustfulness toward God, as of a child toward a parent, but his precision when he comes to describe processes whereby the soul attains its freedom. Though he is cheerful, that is not to say that he is not earnest. If ever there was a devotee, this author is that. He is determined to go to the utmost limit that the soul may attain in this life, and he clearly believes that this can mean the Unitive Life.

It is in describing this process that he uses the simile of "nights" to divide up the process into its stages. Whether he made the precise distinctions with which John of the Cross has made us familiar—the Night of the Senses, the Night of Faith, and the Night of the Spirit—is not, I think, clear. His book is not a textbook, and indeed, as anyone who has studied the Spaniard knows, he too did not write a book of rules but a series of lyrics on which he later comments—a charming but hardly a scientific way of teaching psychology.

The author of the *Mirror* seems to have written his book partly for himself, partly for God, as an act of thankfulness and praise—it ends in an almost incoherent outburst of gratitude to God simply because He is—and only almost as an afterthought, for us. But what is indubitable is that he knew of these "denudations" and considered them unavoidable. The question then arises: In what sense does he use the word "night"? Is it an utter desolation, the "great dereliction," or is it simply a loss, a stripping? There is little doubt that John of the Cross does not always speak of the nights as painful. Sometimes it would seem as though he thought of them as being like an anaesthetic—the loss of normal consciousness is inevitable. Whether that loss will be painful or not will depend largely upon whether the patient struggles against the deprivation or accepts it.

The *Cloud* is even less inclined to describe the entering into the darkness as a pain. It is a loss of a pictorial certainty for an intuitive conviction of Something so intense and intimate that any picture of It would simply rob It of Its fullness and drive It further away. When we get back still further, to the *Mirror* itself, the certainty that the nights are not losses of a valued experience, but a gain so great that the recording apparatus goes out of action becomes quite clear. The process is one of withdrawal, not of the soul from God or God from the soul, but of the soul from the world, the body, from all the manifold, from all images of God and reasoning about God—a withdrawal not of God, but by Him and into Him.

This extraction is no doubt a long and extensive withdrawal, for this author calls it "the gentle, far night" and he is certain that not only has the world of sense to be left wholly behind, but the world of rational thought—indeed, as he has not the advantage of the later psychological vocabulary, he spends a good deal of time setting up love against intelligence, which he identifies with the rational, analytical capacity of the mind. The phrase (a very necessary one that saves mystical feeling from the charge of emotionalism), "the intellectual love of God," had not yet come into currency. Yet, it must be repeated, though the process is long and demands of the soul everything, there is no necessity that it should be an agony. Indeed it may be asked whether the great dereliction may not be due to an intense attachment to God with form, an attachment that grew steadily throughout the later Middle Ages and through the Modern Age in all Christian thought and feeling. Then, when this attachment has to be abandoned, the soul does not feel nearer to God but as though it had lost Him. The *Mirror* was written by a man who apparently never felt this exclusive attachment to Jesus of Nazareth and so was able to complete his psychological evolution without an acute emotional crisis.

The book is certainly not easy reading. For one thing, the author likes using a form of dialogue—a debate between personified virtues—which at the time was considered extremely telling, and like most fancy modes is now a considerable nuisance to a modern reader. But anyone interested in mysticism not as a literary subject but as a practice will find in its many chapters—it is a bigger book than the *Cloud*—frequent insights of great value and problems which, if they are not solved by the author, stir the reader to ask themselves whether they are making use of all the technical information available. Important as these elements are, perhaps the chief value of the book is the sense of authenticity that it gives. Here is a man who sold all that he had, bought the Pearl, and found that it was the priceless, the incomparable.

Closing his essay, most people must ask themselves three questions: Is there anything or anyone more necessary to know than God? Do I know enough of Him? Am I doing all I could to know all I might? The answer to these three questions is no. To the first, it will always be no. To the second, it will be no until the soul has lost itself in Him. Until yes can be said to the third, life can have no rest.

[Ed. Note: Three years after Heard penned this article, it was discovered that the author of *The Mirror of Simple Souls* was not a man, as Heard had assumed, but rather Marguerite Porete, a Beguine, who was condemned for heresy during the Inquisition and burnt at the stake on June 1, 1310.]

The Philosophia Perennis

Originally published in *Vedanta and the West*,
Vol. 6, No. 5, September–October 1943

THOSE WHO ARE INTERESTED in Vedanta and the West are naturally always on the lookout for the rising of one more of those bridges that must, in this generation of birth and death, make possible a new understanding between people of goodwill in East and West. For, speaking as a Westerner—and it is a judgment with which an Oriental would doubtless agree—the state of our Occidental culture today much resembles that critical path into which the older West found itself precipitated in the second century of the Christian era. Then, an Oriental religion, the last of many Oriental competitors for the prize of the Roman Empire, had begun to win converts in a surprising way. The Imperial Court was interested; a possible heir to the throne was found to be involved. Neither patrician nor slave was safe from the contagion of the new faith. But faith without a frame of reference is always a wine without a bottle. As we know, the frame of reference for Christianity, the form in which that faith became the philosophy and culture known as Christendom, was found in Greek thought. With that amalgam, the world in the West remains content until today. Now in our generation, that system has reached exhaustion, no longer answering the intellectual questions of people nor giving a sanction to their propriety. Hence our crisis. And, once again, at the moment of crisis, out of the East has come a light and a faith—or perhaps we should say that, though the light is one, it has come and is coming to us like a rainbow, a thing not only of hope but of many colors.

This brief [writing] is to draw the attention of others similarly interested, who may not have come across this particular thinker, to the work of Dr. Ananda Coomaraswamy. For some time, thoughtful people have been gathering the articles of this writer. They reveal an immense scholarship that is not only thoroughly at home in our Western religious and philosophical thought, but which shows its relevance and illumination through the Light from Asia. Dr. Coomaraswamy is the curator of Oriental art at the Boston Museum of Fine Arts. He has, therefore, the entree to minds that would not otherwise listen to his words about religion—for culture can still command respect in our decadent West where cultus is despised. Dr. Coomaraswamy has used this approach to show us of the West that we cannot really understand art, still less hope to produce it, until we understand that it can only spring from a profoundly religious point of view. In his searching essay, "Am I My Brother's Keeper?" which appeared in the magazine *Asia,* he points out that when we collect works of art, we kill what we would preserve, like uneducated children tearing up wildflowers. And he points out that we ourselves really know this, for ... the demand of the tourist was to find a place that they called "unspoiled"—viz., a place where their own "culture" had not yet penetrated. He adds that the words "to spoil" mean not only *to ruin* but also *to loot.*

But it is to an essay that has lately appeared in book form that the rest of these remarks must be devoted. This small booklet is called *Hinduism and Buddhism* (by Dr. A. Coomaraswamy, The Library of Philosophy, 15 East 40th St. New York City). The point of view is that of the Hinayana school of philosophy. But the author, by taking that position, does not wish to oppose it to the Mahayana form.

The Greater and the Lesser vehicles can both travel along the Noble Eightfold Path. What he is concerned to show is that Buddhism and Hinduism are not in conflict; the one is a development out of the massive foundation of the other. Still further, Dr. Coomaraswamy wishes to show—and certainly his scholarship would seem to sustain it—that the essentials of Christianity, of Buddhism in its two forms, and of Hinduism are one. Here is the *Philosophia Perennis*, here the Eternal Gospel.

History does not repeat itself, but it does recapitulate, and the themes sounded earlier are found in the vast orchestration of life coming back time and again with new and fuller harmonization. So is it with East and West in this matter of religion. Today we shall not repeat in any detail the great syncretistic effort of the second century. But, on a larger scale, we shall see another blending of East and West. The original element in this new blending will be, as Dr. Coomaraswamy has pointed out, not a borrowing, indeed not a real syncretism, but a recognition of a common thought manifesting its power under different forms. As he says, the great religions do not so much borrow from each other as all draw from a basic philosophy, a way of life, an [understanding] of reality that has been there all the while but which we have forgotten. This realization that ignorance is our greatest mistake and fault is of course a thought that the East has stressed more than the West, but, if it is true, then what the East can do for the West is not so much to convert it, still less to make it adopt its forms, as to remind it of the truth that it knows but has forgotten and let drop to the back of its mind.

It is here that we return to the thought of such perennial teaching—that it is in the life lived, in the fruit of the tree of religion which its power of propaganda resides. Religions may appeal because they are strange and subtle in their philosophy or rich and colorful in their rituals. [But] they will only last if they can alter the quality of character. The practical person makes that their test. It is also the test given by Christ and by Buddha. Dr. Coomaraswamy points out how this Eternal Gospel has a stark simplicity and a total demand. He quotes repeatedly that telling statement of Eckhart, as summing up all the truth: "The Kingdom of God belongs only to the thoroughly dead." The doctrine of being born again by dying to the self—the teaching of the story of the pearl of great price, that everything must be given for it—this to him is the perennial philosophy. It is always being overlaid and mistaken.

So, when we have let it be lost, the East comes to us again to remind us that there is a commandment greater even than the
commandment to love your neighbor—which we have thought to be
the last word of morality. The first commandment comes first not
only because it is first by its very nature, but because, unless it is
practiced first, the second can never be fulfilled. Otherwise, our love
for our neighbor will remain only a slogan, and when we try to put it
into practice, we shall in fact start liquidating them—because, in the
form in which they actually appear, we really detest them. The first
commandment is, then, the guarantee, the only possible sanction
for the second, the only possible power that can give "The Social Gospel" any virtue to redeem humankind. Some may say: "Why do we
need yet another voice to tell us that; why do we require the same
light thrown from another angle?" The fact remains that a new voice
often awakes us when we are drowsing under the repetition of the
truth spoken to us in familiar terms. Further, Hinduism is also teaching the West that, since "All roads lead to God" people have to find
that road which best suits their nature. Catholicism helps some, hinders others, Vedanta likewise. Here in Dr. Coomaraswamy's
rendering of Hinayana is still another way of reaching the same goal.

Thomas Kelly

Originally published in *Vedanta and the West*,
Vol. 7, No. 1, January–February 1944

WE ARE BEGINNING to discover that William James' description of conversion does not cover all the facts. There can be a conversion not from sin to godliness nor from indifference to zeal but from goodness to God-consciousness. Thomas Kelly is a case in point. He was, as so many Quakers, a very good man—useful, respected, charged with "concerns." The Society of Friends produces a large number of men and women who, if they do not quite come up to the standard of conduct attributed to Bonaventura (i.e., that he was born without original sin), at least do not seem to need to be better; they can safely spend their time in improving the world. There is no doubt about the world's need, so little doubt that it is hard for anyone of goodwill—let alone the members of a Society whose "concerns" have so signally benefitted humanity—not to leave perfection alone and give their lives to [saving others]. As has been said, Thomas Kelly felt that need. He went to Germany. He saw German Quakers living under such constant peril that the immediate reaction of even the most tepid lover of humanity would be to vow themselves to perpetual practical rescue work.

Yet that experience in Germany was part of the pressure which drove Thomas Kelly to the extreme spiritual attitude that he took in his last few years and which has made him known since his death through the small collection of addresses called *A Testament of Devotion*. Why was this his reaction? "Man's extremity is God's opportunity." Certain situations, when they are suddenly seen with full seriousness, can make any ordinary human goodwill reaction appear grotesquely futile. There are only three choices left to the onlooker: turn your back on them, go mad, or turn to God. There is enough evidence to show that Thomas Kelly felt when he saw Europe under the shadow of death that "morality tinged with emotion" was no answer. He had also experienced a personal disappointment that had brought home to him with perhaps equal fierceness the vanity of professional ambition. Yet people have been confronted with horror and become fanatic revolutionaries and have reacted to the loss of their individual hopes by becoming embittered. These things are occasions, not causes.

Of course the only real cause is the Grace of God, the direct and adequate cause of all spiritual growth. Thomas Kelly had reached that age when both good and bad tend to repeat themselves: the curve of growth "flattens out"; there is a rut of righteousness as well as of wrongdoing, and as criminals after a certain age tend to become recidivist, repeating with automatic monotony the same kind of crime, so there are recidivists of rectitude. It is at the beginning of that stage that a person may suddenly mutate spiritually. It is what Carl Jung calls second adolescence, with the promise of second adulthood if the patient has the power to endure it. "The dangerous age" is far more dangerous than [is realized by] those who usually employ the term. The danger is not of a ridiculous reversion to youth but of the second birth.

Thomas Kelly had all the symptoms of oncoming success. Life had dealt well with him. Marriage, parenthood, academic authority, the power to influence and shape the young, the opportunity to counsel with the authoritative—these things, which combine personal satisfaction with moral commendation as few other things do, had come to him. He had been brought to the center of Quakerism. Every year he was becoming a weightier Friend. Then came the stroke of seeing what was come to birth in Europe and the touch of feeling how much he had wanted personal success. He saw humanity's need and his own suddenly together. He saw his own life—had it gone exactly as he had planned it (and it nearly had)—and the life of Western peoples, with an instant realism. He realized that even if he had succeeded in the particular way he had desired, even if success should come to him (as well it might) in considerably more influential form, such success would be utterly inadequate to the crisis that had come upon civilization. Such knowledge can of course lead to a species of desperation. Tolstoy, for instance, appears to have been driven by it almost to suicide. Thomas Kelly, however, had not the artist's hypersensitiveness; he was able to add a certain stoutness of psychophysique to a robust faith in God. It is some advantage to have hold of a strong working religion, practical and homely—a religion both strongly moral and on friendly terms with its God, when the moment comes at which, through that form and phase of the Godhead, the Creator increases the God-knowledge of His creature.

Consequently, Thomas Kelly rebounded under the shock into violent joy. Of the four choices* that Ramakrishna says are open to a person to whom God reveals Himself, Thomas Kelly seems to have chosen a very presentable mixture of the child and the merry madman. He certainly showed no sign of the "stone" or the "ghoul." His was an innocent happiness, an obsessional interest, [which was] a little disconcerting to people whose religion was Apollonian, but with it plenty of social concern. He was not going to seek the desert so as to find time to learn more of God: he was, on the contrary, coming back to tell the world.

A Testament of Devotion, being only a few addresses with a short biographical introduction, cannot of course give us a full contour of a spiritual life. The note of intense high spirits and an active and intense advocacy is sustained throughout. Did he never have any "lows" any "aridities," any questionings? Surely, he must. A sermon on *De Profundis* would have been informative. The language is also very specifically Christocentric and redemptorist—there is a passage about the world being seen by the newly enlightened person as marked with cruciform marks and bloodstained. Did he know that others could have as intense an experience of the love of God as he

115

had had, and not have it in the terms he uses? For this reason alone one could have wished that he had lived. He died suddenly—while washing dishes after a meal. Perhaps, after all, the experience he had had, took more from him than he realized.

The success of the book shows at least one thing. A book that describes religion as a way of life and as an end in itself can interest more readers than we suspected. It may be only armchair interest in traveler's tales, but it may also be the beginning of a wish to see for oneself.

*Original Editor's Note: "'A man who has realized God shows certain characteristics. He becomes like a child or a madman or an inert thing or a ghoul' [from *The Gospel of Sri Ramakrishna*]. The actual meaning of the word 'ghoul' in Bengali is a creature which does not distinguish between what is clean and what is filthy."

Three Key Answers to Three Key Questions: How Can I Love God? (Pt.1)

Originally published in *Vedanta and the West*,
Vol. 11, No. 3, May–June 1948

THERE IS NO MORE STRIKING WAY in which the teaching of the saints reaches our hearts than in their sudden answers to really searching questions. Three of such answers are given in the following lines. It should be possible to make a collection of such pointers as might be of great value to souls who happen to have reached some turning point in their lives. The three authorities here quoted are very different, yet their replies all give the sense of authenticity and applicability—they are wide and at the same time instant.

The first to be quoted is Thomas Aquinas. He is thought of as the supreme [scholastic]—the strange medieval brain that could best play that odd form of verbal chess whereby you mated each other with syllogisms and gave much display of allowing your opponent to be answered, but in matter of fact never yielded him the slightest concession on any of the issues debated. The whole thing was a foregone conclusion. But Thomas was, despite his occupation—which included that of a diplomat—a saint, one who was always breathless spiritually because he never could breathe in deeply enough of the atmosphere of the soul for lack of which we are always suffocating and most of us in coma. Thomas at the end of the Mass in St. Nicholas Church in Naples on St. Nicholas' Day, as he celebrated, *saw*, and after a silence of days was at last willing to say why he had ceased to write his *Summa*: "Because what I have seen makes all that 1 have written mere chaff." And when he had said that, he was silent again and after a few weeks he was released. The veil, the membrane of the mindbody through which the soul can at best but breathe with pain, was at last removed.

We are told that once he was asked, "How can I love God?" He replied, "*Will* to love Him." The answer is as searching as it is simple. The problem of loving God is very real. The soul knows that it must do so, if ever it is to escape its deadly captivity to the self. But the love of God is different from any other love. The two loves we know are of persons and things. We love things by interest, which means by so penetrating their nature that we understand them. We cannot take that kind of interest in God for we can never hope to understand Him. There is the intellectual love of God, but that has nothing to do with the analytic method that has yielded such remarkable results in our handling of inanimate nature and such ludicrous results in theology—the sad pretense [of] a science, which produces only greater confusion of the mind and enmity in the heart. We cannot then love God as we love things.

Our only other method of human love is our love for persons. Again we love very largely because we think we understand our friend. Most affection is little lasting because we find that our knowledge was inaccurate. But we have, if we are patient and have a real need for affection—and not merely wish to have someone listen to us—quite extensive opportunities of understanding one another. We are very much the same—much more than our egotism lets us allow. And being gregarious creatures, we have to depend largely on one another. Though then affection is always [breaking up], it is always being spun again—we are like spiders in that respect. And of course in all human affection there is some wish for return. Motherlove, which used to be thought so selfless, has now won and worn for some time the explanatory working title [of] "smother love."

Of course, because the [love of people and things] are our only two ways of human loving, we cannot begin by loving God except from motives in which these two urges are paramount—we hope to gain a return; we hope to understand. Yet everyone realizes the hard truth in Spinoza's famous saying: "He who would love God must not expect God to love him." There is, however, a third faculty in humans besides the two others of interest and affection—there is the will. True, you cannot ever wholly separate the three basic faculties. But it is possible to recognize that one or the other does take the lead in any enterprise of behavior. As we may be first touched by a person and then become interested in them and, contrariwise, we may be interested in a thing—an art or science—and then become devoted to it, so the will may be the starter. True, the will very seldom is the initiator in anything that has to do with our life in this world; it comes in afterwards to give us persistence. We start because, as we say, our interest was caught or we were touched. In fact, we were passive at the beginning. Only after, and to keep us going, did the will take over.

But as God is not to be understood—as our minds can understand—or to be loved in the possessive way that our hearts naturally like to love, there is then only one way to love Him truly and that is, as Thomas says, through the will, by willing it. That is of course not an irrational act. As the Christian Church has held, the existence of God can be deduced. By the balance of probabilities—which is the basis of all our rational acts—it is more likely than not that the Supreme Being does exist. But it is hard to love a deduction or indeed to have any devotion toward a plus balance of probability. But that again does not mean that one ought not. One may experience rightly some guilt because of one's inability to feel either affection or vivid interest in the Being Who, though He be incomprehensible and is not for our convenience, can nevertheless be argued to be worthy of adoration. We may know we ought to love Bach's Mass in B Minor, but because our musical taste is very poor, we may only feel boredom, yet not ashamedly. Therefore, after we have discovered first about God that His existence can be deduced, and next about ourselves that we cannot love in any human way a deduction, we find out thirdly that we have a faculty that just fits our very awkward need—we have the will.

We don't like using the will for two reasons. In the first place, it is tiring; and in the second, when we use it, we don't seem—at least for a long while—to get any results, either outward or inward. The will is, always, for us (not for God and that is another grave difference between us) in the future tense. While inwardly, when we use the will, we don't get that warm sensation (which actually can make failure melodramatic) that rises from the movement of the feelings. We have little or no sensation when the will works, and often when we do have a sensation it is far from pleasant—we feel we are committed, that we have foolishly trapped ourselves. Nevertheless, we know that acts of the will are our supreme human endowment—the one way we ever get control over ourselves or our environment.

In a piece of doggerel that shows better than worthy verse a great Victorian poet's real conviction and probably acute regret, Tennyson wrote:

> O well for him whose will is strong!
> He suffers, but he will not suffer long.

The way to enlightenment and liberation is through acts of the will—there is no other. We find ourselves a mass of fantasy and wishful thinking—and so we shall end in the anecdotage of senescence unless we have painfully compacted that mush, by acts of will, into a firm one-pointed consciousness by the time we are old. For whether there is a God or not, or whether we can love Him or not, there is no escaping the fact that this world is so made that we can will, and out of our will a consistent consciousness can be made. But if we try to get our wish, we shall end at best disillusioned, at worst in complete fantasy.

The *bardo* [i.e., plane of existence] of the Mahayana seems a terribly convincing attempt to show people into what headlong delirium the soul must be plunged that leaves the anchorage of the body before it has transmuted all the pandemonic force of fantasy, which should by acts of the will have been shaped into the one-pointed devotion to the Supreme Will. The human will is then the specific faculty whereby a person gets in touch with the Supreme Being. "Thy will be done," as Eckhart says, is the one complete and all-powerful prayer. "But I can't go on saying that" is the usual answer and a fair one. If we think that we are simply saying "encore" to the

Infinite, our part becomes a little otiose. He does not need our aid, still less our applause to encourage Him to do what He is always intending and can never be turned from.

It is here that faith comes in—the naked faith of which the masters of prayer so often speak. We make an act of faith that, when we exercise our will and intend that—we shall will only what God wills—something actually does happen. We will and thereafter don't feel or speak or behave a whit the better. "Nothing has happened," says the ordinary consciousness. "Had anything taken place, I should have felt the effect." Yet we know that when the high non-sensuous consciousness works, our everyday consciousness is utterly unaware of it. That has been proved is all work on Extra Sensory Perception. The cards used for the scoring will show after that you have been exercising this power. But while you are actually doing it, you will have no feeling of any sort to guide you when you have "hit" right and when you have missed.

We know that God is regarding us and that we can regard Him. When then we bring ourselves into an act of relationship with Him by willing that His will be ours, we are like a patient who puts themselves into the focus of an X-ray. They will feel nothing or see nothing while the operation is on. And they will not for some days experience any improvement. They might say, even when the improvement comes, "As I saw nothing to account for it when being given the so-called treatment, what beneficial effects I now experience may just as likely be due to some natural improvement and have nothing to do with this theory of invisible radiation."

But this illustration makes the relationship easier than it actually is. We know that God is confronting us; we know by deduction that as He exists, we do come into relationship with Him whenever we make an act of the will to do so. But that is all. As to how He will act, when and where, we are of course always in the dark—the dark of blind faith. T. H. Huxley used to speak of life being played by each of us being confronted by a "veiled antagonist" [on] the other side of the board. The simile is a telling one—one that none with even the slightest experience of prayer but knows to be descriptive of much of the time spent in prayer. In chess, the greater the [expert] with which one is confronted, the more certain one may be that their moves will leave one in the dark. One may be sure only of two things—that every time I move, without exception a move of reply will be made, and secondly, every one of those moves is directed to take away all my freedom to move. Yet even here the analogy is far too feeble. For the best chess [expert] has a finite mind and must play a game confined within the simple rules of the game, a game that is to end with one of the antagonists unable to move. The game the soul plays with its Maker is not only played with an infinite opponent, whose resources are inexhaustible, but also the aim of His "play" is not to take away the soul's freedom but to restore that freedom to it and to keep on doing so until at length the soul has won the power to retain it. Even if we were allowed to view the entire "board"—instead of through the slit aperture of what we call the present moment— how could we hope to understand at each move, or a whole lifetime of moves, the strategy of the Master?

We are therefore confined to the one exercise that is germane to our attempt—our intention to love God, if we only knew how. We can and must keep on making these "blind acts of the will," knowing that to each of these "openings of the soul by the soul" God responds by a reply of infinite inscrutable aptitude. Of course this is not easy— perhaps it is the hardest thing in the whole of our lives. For it means that we must never complain, which is with us even a stronger passion than our appetite to enjoy. It means in the end we shall know that there is no chance or accident because we can now practice the constant Presence of God. And that end is far off, not because it is not rationally obvious, but because the nearer we get to really willing to do God's will, the purer the opportunities He can and will give us by so doing.

At the beginning, He mixes the satisfaction of our desires with the performance of His intention. So, [we] feel we are something of a success—of course a very nice one, but we *are* lucky and religion is something that the ordinary person might well invest in—it pays. Then that goes and we fall back on a less obvious aim—we have to comfort ourselves that at least we are resigned and are growing in virtue through the way we accept our failure. And then that goes too. Like Job, the soul has to yield its last desperate cry, "I will not let mine integrity go from me" [Job 27:5] and can only mutter, "Yea, though He slay me, yet will I trust in Him" [Job 13:15]. For at the worst in the deepest darkness, the polar facts remain. God *is*, and nothing that can happen to my fortunes alters the facts which show deductively that the Supreme Being exists.

And the other fact is that I have a will. Though that will may produce no results, I can keep on making acts with it. My holding on to my intention or my surrender of my intention—those two facts have really no more to do with whether I succeed in carrying out my will than has the existence of God to do with whether He comes to my aid at the time and in the way that would soothe my feelings.

It seems clear then that Thomas Aquinas' saying is true and apt. It is hard, but it is the precise answer to the pressing question, the most pressing question in the whole of life: "How shall I love God?"

In the following two articles, the two other questions are, "How shall I find God when I have lost Him?" and ["How could I endure the ruin of my life work?"]

How Shall I Find God
When I Have Lost Him? (Pt. II)

Originally published in *Vedanta and the West*,
Vol. 11, No. 4, July–August 1948

THIS IS THE SECOND of the three key questions asked of masters of spirituality. This question—"How shall I find God when I have lost Him?"—naturally follows the first, which was, "How can I love God?" We have been told that we love Him by wishing it, by the will. This advice when it is followed leads inevitably to our "getting results." We find that something has begun to happen. It may be what we hoped and wished; it may not be. But it will be something that intensely interests us. We may be able to describe it by the terms others have used; we may not be able to describe it at all.

One thing, however, is so probable that (though it is not so certain as the fact that we shall find that something of strange importance has happened), it may be said to be almost as certain as that. We shall begin to think that what we have found, however dim and odd it is and however hard to tell anyone else of, is something that we have gained for good. We may say that we are converted for life—"have a new heart" was the old phrase—or we may say we have found the autotherapy that suits us at last, that we do know ourselves and have penetrated down to self-knowledge and interior peace. One thing we are sure of is that we shall never lose this state and go back to what we were before, any more than we shall once again become an adolescent. Indeed, one of the surest symptoms of this state is that we feel very mature, really grown up, rather solemn, quietly assuredly rational, [and] patient with others who seem to be curiously unsure. In short, we are in a state of self-contained discreet self-satisfaction.

Then it goes. We may do something that accounts for this. We may have done nothing in particular. Just being comfortable in the way described above seems enough—and certainly it should be—to lose us our modest complacency. Then the discomfort may well be intense. We had become used to a certain experience, and that experience not only freed us from a lot of rather silly and some harmful ways we had of killing time and soothing our sense of futility, before we found this other way. That experience made us able to entertain ourselves and not be frightened or disgusted at ourselves, as we had never been able to do and to be before. If religion is, as Dr. Alfred North Whitehead used to say, "what the individual does with his own solitariness," this new exercise of using the will to make acts of comprehensive interior attention certainly made loneliness more interesting than most company. But now we have to own that we are in a terrible muddle because, having thought we have found God for good, we now have to own that we have lost Him.

If we have been having feelings—however quiet and refined—the glow has gone out of them. If we have been enjoying thoughts that seemed to clinch matters, we find that the neat bindings have become loose. After a time we find that this losing is, if not a "Night of the Soul," at least part of its spiritual exercising—painful but helpful—if we know what to do about it.

Eckhart gave the answer to the question, "What am I to do when I find that I have lost God?"—Go back to where you last had Him. Eckhart does not seem to have blamed the person who asked. He seems to have taken for granted that this losing was part of the process of learning—as the lung has to empty to take a new breath, as the mind when learning a language seems to have phases of forgetting before going on to a new and wider grasp of remembering. The author of *The Imitation of Christ* certainly thought these fluctuations were unavoidable, and the author of *The Cloud of Unknowing* in one of his shorter works likens them to the tidal and wave conditions that a voyager on the sea must be prepared to find and in which they must learn to handle their ship.

The Desert Fathers held strongly that "short prayer pierces Heaven." As sustained pressure of unwavering attention is impossible [for] most of us, we must and can, by a series of blows or lance thrusts as the *Cloud of Unknowing* calls the process, pierce for moments into that upper atmosphere where we could not sustain ourselves. And, though we cannot stay there, we can bring back something that makes us more resolved to continue striving to cause what has still to be only an instant, to become eternal.

Certainly the time when anyone never loses hold of God would seem to be equated with the time when they have attained constant practice of the Presence, and surely that must be very close to the unitive state. Father Augustine Baker notes, with that curiously pleasant diagnostic detail he employs, that the soul was bound in the twenty-four hours to go through a series of such dislocations, interruptions of its current from its source. He thought that for twenty minutes after a meal it was not possible to retain the awareness of the Presence of God, and that sleep generally "de-ordinated" the attention. Perhaps some people would deny that—but he certainly had much experience, and the state that he was referring to was probably a very distinct and clear condition of recollectedness, or to use a favorite word of his, "abstraction." (That point will come up again— the point of the degree of "abstraction" or detachment that the soul has attained—when the third question and answer is being discussed in the third article [in this series].)

Here it seems interesting to note that a human would appear to be a creature whose consciousness is an "alternating current" rather than a continuous one. We are tidal creatures. There seem to be in the daily cycle three such rhythms, and each one of them may— maybe should—strain, and if we are not ready, detach our hold on the unseen Eternal. There is the tide of sleep–waking, the wave of the diet–nutritional rhythm, and the ripple of the breath. Perhaps behind that again is the heartbeat. Each of these sways and swings the frame of mind, angle of thought, and base of feeling out of its position and throw it into another. May it not be that this is a necessary part of our training in achieving constancy of consciousness? Even if we let go, we are free to catch hold again before we have been swept too far from our moorings. And if we do not let go, the strain, like the gentle pull on the thread when it is being spun, gives us tensile strength.

Consciousness has continually to be reminded that it must keep conscious or it ceases to be so. Of course, at the beginning we all know how slow we are to wake up to the fact that we have fallen asleep. That is the great value of following a rule of life. For then, when we have fallen to sleep comes a duty, an "office," a call to prayer and, though we feel as disinclined to it as we feel disinclined to get up out of a warm bed at two o'clock in the morning, we have to do it whether we like it or not. However badly we do it is better than letting the whole thing slide because "one does not feel in the mood." Of course one does not—the mood has gone and it is for us to [create] the next one.

The spiritual life is then for all beginners and perhaps for all the middling lot that the Western mystics call "proficients" and we might term "professionals," a constant and ever-more rapid Recollection—another word much used by Occidental religions. We are continually pulling ourselves together because we have, in the stream and fluctuation of time and under the wash of events, begun to fall to pieces and to become completely unraveled. Progress in the spiritual life, one supposes, might be gauged by the speed with which one gets on to the unraveling before too many stitches have been dropped and unknitted. Most people find that they are getting a little handier at the task as the years go by, if they really think the matter is as important as thought would seem to show that it is. Of course, if one lets oneself become badly "de-ordinated," engrossed in some addiction of the body, some anxiety of possessions, some desire for social approval, then that is as though one's knitting had been caught in the paws of an extremely agile and ill-willed monkey. Before the remnants can be recovered, little may be left of long periods of patient work. François de Sales himself said he might easily lose what had taken him many years to work in a quarter of an hour: one outburst of hastiness or of what the world would call "righteous anger" might prove fatal to the endeavor of a large part of a lifetime. It appears that our knitting is always done till we are out of the body, and perhaps long after, by "chain stitch" and not "lock stitch."

Yet however far we have become unraveled, there is always this sovereign advice to help us back. We have lost God, but once we had Him, not of course in actuality or we would never have lost Him, but in potentiality, we were on the way, on the trail. All we have to do is to trace back to that moment and there start again. Of course, though the advice is clear, it is hard. Discouragement keeps on tempting us to cheat and advises us to try and start where we are. That will not do. Recollection is, in one of its meanings, remembering. We have, like [certain cognitively impaired] people in their talking, wandered, and we must go back to the last time we were coherent. We must trace back to where the deviation and the dissipation began.

But as we continue, we do find that, each time we slip, we do not have to go quite so far back as we had to do earlier. That does not mean that the task gets easier. For the goal is constant recollectedness—each act performed in the sight of God and then discharged and left with contrition but not with remorse or even regret. We have to work up the whole series of approaches that lead to perfect instantaneity. When we are past being swept away by passions, then we have to learn to correct the tidal displacement of mood and consciousness made by the tide of sleep. Some Sufis say that it takes several years before the sleep–mind will accept the attitude of the waking–mind. And even when it does, most of us know that it is still very capricious.

Sometimes in sleep we can control the dream; sometimes we can detach ourselves from it, knowing that both dream and earthly waking are dreams. But most of the time we are its object and not it ours. Then there is becoming aware of the optimum psychophysical lucidity that appears somewhere in the alimentary cycle. Swami Brahmananda [a disciple of Sri Ramakrishna] thought that the best condition for meditation was when the stomach was partly filled. Sir John Woodruff quotes a Tantric authority saying that the stomach should not be wholly empty because this produces a slight but definitely distracting tension in the mind. And of course, [this awareness applies to] the care of the breath so that the lucidity which opens between each inhalation and exhalation may be caught—Sanskrit authorities have told us much about this. Every one of these dips after a crest will tend to "ebb us out" until we lose touch with the shore [that] we should hold to, and [instead we] find ourselves adrift. But Eckhart seems to teach, and experience would seem to confirm, that if we would have the courage to trace back the moment we discovered our loss, we should be able to find the spot where it began and, once there, we could start anew.

Again, of course, the temptation [of] discouragement appears. We feel we cannot go on this hindsight search time and again. We fear we are making no progress if we spend nearly all our time going back. But this may be a complete [misunderstanding] of our process and progress. For each of these returns is really far more like a zig-zag ascent in which, it is true, after going right we then turn left, but always the traverse, whether to the right or left, goes up, and each drive is on a higher level than the one before. By this going back we are learning two essential things: (1) self-knowledge—the structure of the human mind and the kind of things that throw it off its rational attentions; and (2) further, we are learning humility. This humility is the real stuff, for it leads to true discrimination so that at last we can make the distinction between ourselves and the thing that is always straying. When we reach that stage, it would appear we discover that the straying part of ourselves loses its power to wander. We begin to make the final recollection; we at last "come to ourselves." We remember who we are. And once we do that, the journey is over. For the whole notion that we were far away from our Source and Goal was the illusion, and the distance we were from God was never more than the depth of our illusory self-love.

How Could I Endure the Ruin of My Life Work? (Pt. III)

Originally published in *Vedanta and the West*,
Vol. 11, No. 5, September–October 1948

THE FIRST OF THE THREE basic questions that we have been asking [in this series of three articles] is the question of a devotionalist. And the answer is given by a devotionalist. For, in spite of all his scholastic rationalism, Aquinas was a spiritual lover, devoted to his *ishtam*, Christ Jesus. Besides this first question, the second is psychological. For Eckhart was perhaps the most *jnana* of all the Western mystics of whom we have adequate record. The first question tells us how to love God—when we have made up our mind that it is this that we would rather do than anything else. The second tells us what we may do when we find that, despite our intention to "adhere," we have lost contact with the Eternal Being who is our life. The third question is practical. It is then, as should be, answered by a man who was the most practically successful of all the saints canonized by the Church of Rome.

By founding the Jesuits, Ignatius Loyola gave back to the Roman Church half the territory and all the intellectual prestige that Rome had lost to Protestantism. The non-Christian world was re-assaulted with a vigor that none of the other founders of the Orders had been able to mobilize. Indeed, the missionary attack compared with that which the Church had not been able to summon since it made peace through Constantine with the Imperial power. After Ignatius' work took shape, to be a scholar and a devout Christian no longer became a paradox, but something of a commonplace. Jesuits made a new architecture for Europe, [which was] tired of medieval gothic and Renaissance pedantry. They captured the teaching profession and, in a little while, were makers of astronomic instruments for the emperor of China—who was therefore not unimpressed with their metaphysics—and founders of a communist paradise for the pre-agriculturists of the Paraná, who were captivated by their teachers' wonderful skill in music.

Ignatius knew what he had done and what was growing from the plan he had laid down. Working up from his psychological instrument, the *Exercises,* by the selection of lieutenants who could supplement his genius by adopting the techniques of militarism to the needs of ecclesiasticism, he had already made a company whose head he named The General—and whose headship he accepted for himself—a Generalship commanding such complete obedience over individuals of outstanding ability that the Jesuit general was soon called the Black Pope.

The actual Pope, however, was as capable as Ignatius of perceiving what a mixed blessing such an offer of service could prove to be. Ignatius himself was far too capably complex a character not to have many enemies. One of them was elected Pope when the Society was yet young, yet had shown its mettle. When Ignatius heard of the election, he said (and it is obvious he was no more a rhetorician than a coward) his "bones became like water." The self-control of this man had become so complete that his closest associates bore witness that when he was merry, they never knew whether he felt cheerful; when he showed [dark] anger, [they never knew] if he was inwardly the slightest disturbed; when he was peaceful, [they never knew] that there might not be despair or bitter pain in his heart. This self-statement of his condition is therefore valuable and need not be doubted. The destruction of the Order was probably the one thing that could really affect this utterly mortified nature.

Yet when someone with more psychological curiosity than consideration asked, "What will you do if the Pope dissolves the Order?" he replied, "One quarter of an hour in orison and it would then be all the same." Again, it does not seem possible to doubt his word. And when we examine the reply, we see there is about it a realism and definitude which makes it not only convincing—carrying its own authenticity in the very style of it—but also arresting and informative. For in the first place it is an answer to a question so general and so grim—and yet so specifically aimed at those who have tried to be of service—that nearly everyone has heard it asked—if not of themselves, of someone they have admired—and hardly anyone dare face it. Even the good too often take refuge in the plea, so little substantiated by history, "God could not let His work (which of course I have been doing) come to naught!"

What would you do, what could you do, if your life work—in which you had sublimated your passions, sunk your possessions, and exchanged your pretensions—should be put to death and you, poor pointless thing, left to live on? It is possible that the good confront this issue at its sharpest point. But every person of energy must know how helpless they are, should their work—the meaning of their social, economic, and physical being—be taken utterly from them and they become an unwanted failure. And in the second place, the answer is an exact, diagnostic reply. Ignatius knows what is at stake, what the failure of the Society will mean for him, because of what it will mean to his loyalist friends and for the Church that he adored and which was still fighting an undecided counterattack. Ignatius was not a contemplative. His vocation was action—[a] call to save his communion.

Ignatius does not, then, play the stoic or any of the roles of the superior person. He does not dismiss the painfully apt curiosity telling the enquirer not to be inquisitive and so wrap up his wound in the mantle of offended dignity. Nor does he make light of it all. He might have carried conviction if he had laughed it off. He had proved his toughness, yes, and his capacity for humor, so that he might have felt it wise to say that it would really make no difference. Or he might have said, "God will never let it happen." Again he had shown his belief that he was doing God's will was rigid enough to have made such a statement credible. He does not use any of the great clichés—*Fiat Voluntas Tua: Laus Deo: Deo Gratias* ["Thy Will be done, Praise be to God, Thanks be to God."]. He gives a timetable. And that is characteristic of him. For like all moderns he was interested in time in a way that the medieval was not.

His *Exercises* show that—so many weeks to have acquired this attitude toward Hell, so many to gain that toward Heaven.

So when he says "one quarter of an hour," there can be little doubt he means exactly what he says. Ignatius prayed by the clock. He was making a careful estimate and calculation between two things and the distance between them. He knew he loved his work and the extent and weight of the hopes he had for its success. He knew it was his life as far as he, an individual, had any reason for living. But he also knew how he was involved, engrossed. This was a certain degree of real discrimination—the power to see the two things—the work and the person who worked: Ignatius Loyola. And the Being that looked on and saw both the Society of Jesus and its founder with an equal detachment—that Being it was who could see what to do with Ignatius, what must be done with the busy passionate Spaniard, if that creature's reason for living was suddenly taken from it.

Ignatius never quite lost touch with that central Being; though he evidently by his own words did not always keep in close contact with Him. In fact, the distance that Ignatius found was separating the two sides of himself at the crisis in his life was precisely fifteen minutes. He was out from the shore, away from his base a quarter of an hour. Give him that time and he would know what to do with it. In that little space he would be able—he had evidently done so before—to [draw] in the slack of the line that kept him and the Atman [his innermost soul] within apart. Then, once that contact was really made, once the eternal life had absorbed the temporal, the fluctuations in the waves of circumstance would make no more difference to him than billows of mist sweeping past a walker can make them sway.

"Orison" was for Ignatius what we should probably call induced contemplation—that total awareness of Reality which many who have practiced meditation can after some time summon by an act of the will. In Ignatius' case, it was not an instantaneous act. We may venture to think that in Ruysbroeck—to mention another Westerner—it would have been if not instantaneous, at least a matter of seconds. Ignatius lived too busy a life to be in immediate contact, but—and in this he differs from many of our busy church people of today—he did not neglect to keep in mind the time it would take him to recover the essential contact. And, of course, he was aware that each day, by his contemplative prayer—which we are told he never neglected—he brought himself back to that distance. Had he found that his distance was increasing, then there is little doubt he would have put himself into "retreat." Ignatius had no intention of "gaining the whole world and losing his own soul" [Matt. 6:26]. The quarter of an hour was as much free play or "slack line" as he allowed himself.

Ignatius' reply is then very germane for those—the vast majority who feel that they must live active lives but find, in Father Augustine Baker's phrase, that that life does "de-ordinate" them. Not only would the total miscarriage of their effort throw then into something like despair—the little *contretemps* of dealing everyday with people [that] make them irritable, depressed, patently unspiritual, uncharitable, un-peaceful. And they often wonder with gloom how they could take any major disaster—and pray God that He will not try them. Does not the answer to this very common state we have all experienced lie in Ignatius' advice? "Know how far you are out; take care never to be beyond where you can recollect yourself. Day by day—three times a day—make at least an honest checkup, and if you find the distance between you and your anchorage is increasing, take more time till you are once more within sufficient distance to make yourself fast and secure should the wind come down and the sea rise." This checkup Ignatius calls the "examin." It does not take long—one honest glance will show how much one has drifted in the three or four hours one has been attending to surface things. Of course, the necessary rehauling may take considerable time and exertion.

A similar illustration of this practical power in an "active" is given at the beginning of a Japanese monk's account of his penetration into Tibet, when that country was closed to outsiders. A Tibetan abbot, whose big monastery lay near the frontier, had permitted a foreign pilgrim to enter. The Lhasa government, learning this, not only degraded the abbot—which meant that he lost a powerful and dignified position—but condemned him to be drowned in the almost freezing waters of the source stream of the Brahmaputra River. He was taken in his criminal garb to be drowned. When they arrived where he was to be bound and sunk in the stream, he made the Ignatian statement, "Permit me to read over slowly to myself three times the *Diamond Sutra* and then it will be all right." The time was permitted him. He then with complete composure let himself be lowered with a heavy stone round him into the stream. After some time the body was raised. He came to life again. He quietly submitted to be once more immersed. A second time he was raised, only to be found once more alive. Only at the third time was his release completed.

[Ed. Note: Heard's appalling but dramatically instructive tale was adapted from a book published in 1909 by Ekai Kawaguchi (1866–1945) titled *Three Years in Tibet*. Kawaguchi wrote that a certain Lama Shabdung narrated to him the foregoing account of the execution of a high lama named Sengchen Dorjechan, which took place in June 1887.]

So many people today talk of Brother Lawrence and the continual practice of the Presence of God, and when they do so, [they] often disparage any regular times of prayer and meditation. They say to spend all one's time with exercises, or even a good part of it, is both pretentious and unnecessary. And yet we know that when many such good social workers meet disaster, their conduct does not differ—for it cannot—very much from that of the most casual [person]. They are still desiring the fruit of their works and have not achieved karma yoga. But they may be right that they cannot give their lives to trying to achieve a constant contemplative state. They must also realize, if they read Brother Lawrence with the slightest real care, that the state he reached was very advanced and [that he] had taken a life of austerity, which they would consider unhealthy.

May not the middle step between that Carmelite perfection and the way that most of us feel compelled to live, lie in the Ignatian advice, "Know how far you are out; never let it be more than a quarter of an hour; and see daily that you keep that distance—see that it is not growing!" Then, when ruin and death come to complete our detachment, they will serve this, their intended purpose, and we, too, shall be able to add to the authentic record of essential advice, "Fifteen minutes in prayer and it will be all the same. The One remains; the many change and pass."

[Ed. Note: This article, with its candid title, was published one year after Gerald Heard discontinued his Trabuco College experiment, which unquestionably stood out as a major part of his own life work.]

Return to Religion

Originally published in *Vedanta and the West*,
Volume 11, No. 6, November–December 1948

[This is] an Introduction to Swami Virajananda's book of aphorisms on the Spiritual Life, *Towards the Goal Supreme*, scheduled for publication by Harper & Brothers some time in 1949.   –Original Editor's Note

THERE IS A GROWING DEMAND TODAY for books on the spiritual life. But it is one that is easier to make than to supply. Religious books are still being printed by the thousands. Yet it is hard to draw up even a small list that would meet the present enquirers' need. Why? Partly because most religious books are written by professionals in the language, and to support the cause, of their specific sect. True, they do wish to bring comfort and self-understanding to the reader, but they also have the obligation to prove that their religion is true and often that it alone is true.

This was always a grave handicap for those religions—till lately the only ones known in the West—which were and still mainly are exclusive. A large number of those people who today are wishing to enquire about the spiritual life actually left the religion in which they were brought up, or their parents did so, because that religion seemed grossly careless about the truth of many of the statements that it made and even more grossly uncharitable to those who dared raise this grave question of truthfulness. Hence to offer them spiritual information in the terms of such theology is not merely not to attract them but to repel them. It is very hard for ministers and clergy to realize that "the return to religion" is not a return to orthodoxy, [but] that it is a return to an interest in the spiritual not because the interpretation of certain historic events has become any more credible. The contrary is true. The reason why today so many people want to hear from experts about spirituality is simply because the economic revolution has failed and is over; the Psychological Revolution has begun.

Not through creeds or rites but through anthropology, psychology, and psychical research, are free minds today exploring a new empire of the mind. These are the people who are asking the real practitioners—not the purveyors—of religion to give them not dogmas or closed systems, but data. What the world today needs, and an increasing number of pioneers are seeking out, is the psychologist who has gone beyond the limited findings of the psychophysicist [and] the restricted techniques of the psychoanalyst, [and] who can also arrange the data of psychical research and finally—and this is the real proof of the adequacy of the process—bring about a coordination of their life that can henceforward interpret and embrace, explain and include all experience. That is the reason why Protestants today increasingly tend to read such masters of spirituality as François de Sales and Fénelon. These writers are felt at once to be experts. They speak very little of dogma and much of method. Though both of them [are] masterly men of affairs, they are interested in specific advice and counseling; they employ organization, but only when it is a convenient matrix in which to work upon the development of individual consciousness and character.

Another advantage that the reader finds is their style. When we go to a doctor, we do not ask of them eloquence or the gift of a pretty way with words. We want neither rhetoric nor poetry; we want a diagnosis and a prescription. The two standard methods of Protestant instruction and edification have been hymns and the weekly sermon. The great Catholic directors owe their popularity both in-side and outside their Communion to the fact that they are always precise, always great diagnostic psychologists and, even when their Letters are found for centuries to be applicable to thousands of souls, they seem like all great physicians actually prescribing for a specific, individual case.

Instruction is in fact of very little use unless it is a reply to a ques-tion, and indeed its use is in the same ratio to the intensity with which the questioner puts their problem. Though the Western mas-ters of spirituality are unfailing aids to those who would survey the problem of their own souls—though they show clearly that path of hope which lies between the glib rationalism that falsely promises self-control by an act of the will and the despairing emotionalism that declares "Human nature never learns nor can be taught"—still we keenly need something more. With this they would agree—they would say without sacraments and the graces of God that come through the [Catholic] Church, decay may be arrested but progress can really not be made. A person may be "returned to normalcy" and may come to accept society and society to accept them, and may even come to accept the universe with a resignation that may pass for peace. But they may never attain to that understanding of them-selves, their [companions], and nature, without which this world and this life remain an enigma only to be sustained with courage.

It is at that point that the student who has benefited from the instructions of the Western directors has to ask themselves: "Should I not, must I not, join their communion if I am to attain to any kind of completeness?" This problem, this issue (i.e., "Shall I for the sake of profound psychological knowledge join a communion that ex-communicates all others, that claims the right to persecute because it alone, it believes, has the truth?") tortured sixth-century Western-ers. "Madman or slave, must man be one?" cried Matthew Arnold. On the one hand was a materialistic rationalism that managed the outer world so as to obtain increasing power and was helpless to pro-duce rational conduct from human beings. On the other hand was a church having great psychological insight and able to transform cer-tain characters, but apparently [was] as indifferent to historic truth or scientific demonstration as it was disregardful of the rights of people.

That dilemma has now ended, and it may be that historians looking back on our age will take this change to be more momentous to human society than the discovery of atomic energy or the fixation of chlorophyll. For now we see with our growing knowledge of Vedanta not only that we may have all that Catholicism could give of method in spiritual training, and may have it without yielding one iota of truth, [and] further may have it and keep the widest charity toward all other religions and systems, but that we may hope to have a far deeper and wider psychological knowledge than Western spirituality has so far attained.

Two brief illustrations may be given of this. First, the attitude of the Occidental masters of spirituality toward psychic phenomena. Lacking the vast cosmology and subtle psychology of Vedanta, visions and all manner of psychic powers have either been thought to authenticate the dogmas of the [Christian] Church—and so give those who experienced them a certain height of spiritual rank and authority. Or, if they did not support the Church's theories, then they were diabolic. True, a great master such as John of the Cross allows there is a third source: the unknown parts of the human mind itself. But even he has only the vaguest notion of the vastness of this subject, of its importance as a correlate in the development of spirituality and the expert care that is therefore needed in guiding all who would advance any distance in the life of prayer.

The second illustration is akin to the above. Owing to the West's ignorance of psychophysiology, the methods of training the mind-body were very crude and indeed dangerous. When we reflect on the "discipline"—the whip is still regularly used in all "enclosed" orders—[and] when we study physical mortification as understood in Catholicism and when we compare the dangerous crudity of such methods with the subtlety, thoroughness, and variety of methods used by Vedanta and Mahayana [Buddhism], and indeed by Hinayana [Buddhism]—we see the incomparable superiority of the methods of the East. Indeed, as we have looked on Asia as a huge fringe area into which our physical science is only now penetrating, so now we must look upon our West as a penumbral belt into which the true psychology and psychophysiology of the East is infiltrating at last.

Finally, the frame of reference of Vedanta—and its children Mahayana and Hinayana—is so much vaster and at the same time more rational than that narrow and hasty picture which Catholicism took from ... the Jews and [according to the heretic Marcion] never had the moral courage to reconstruct and enlarge. [For example,] the doctrine of eternal punishment—a grotesque amalgam made from [Judeo-Christian] emotionalism alloyed with Hellenic speculation—has always haunted and hindered the minds of the spiritual in the West. With its great metaphysics, Vedanta has been able to preserve justice and ally it with mercy. On this count alone—and it is a big one—the Eternal Gospel as interpreted by the Orient is a surer guide to ultimate understanding than anything the West has till the present provided. Yet most people when they pick up some Oriental text—such for example as *The Crest-Jewel of Discrimination* of Shankara or the [Yoga] Sutras of Patanjali—are daunted by the subtlety and gnomic elaboration of the system. That is why they should start with works written by modem masters of Indian spirituality. Swami Prabhavananda's *The Eternal Companion,* the actual conversations of a great spiritual trainer, is such a book.

This new volume of aphorisms on the spiritual life, *Towards the Goal Supreme* by Swami Virajananda, will prove to many readers a sequel to *The Eternal Companion.* The volume can be started almost anywhere, and there is hardly a phase of the spiritual life that is not touched upon and illuminated. Practically any question that might arise in the mind of a seeker is raised and discussed.

Indeed, it is hard to think of two books that could prove better helps to any enquirer who wished to see whether the thought of India could not help them toward an understanding of their own life and a mastery of their own nature. [These books] should prove the kind of standard religious reading that for so long we have only been able to obtain from such authors as François de Sales, Fénelon, Jean Grou, and Dom John Chapman.

God Is Shy

Originally published in *Vedanta and the West*,
Volume 12, No. 2, March–April 1949

WORSHIP IS SOMETHING that the West finds hard in its modern mood to justify. God does not need to be praised we say, and certainly we find it hard to understand Pope Pius X's special commendation of the … one hundred and fifty Psalms on the ground that these are peculiarly pleasing to Him because He wrote them Himself to show us how He wished to be praised.

But worship is not so hard to understand if we see that it is in fact an act of criticism. "Your Worship" addressed to a mayor—"The Worshipful Company of Cutlers"—such titles do not mean that the chief citizen is adorable or that the incorporated masters of a trade were hoping for divine honors. Both addresses declare only that these people are "worthies." They have been adjudged and found worthy of respect. So worship, even when offered to the Supreme, is an estimate. We then have to ask: Worth how much? Worth for what? A good boat is called seaworthy. It will stand up to the tests of its element. It is not land-worthy. So with all special works. But with people, because they are the supreme generalized creatures, when we say they are worthy, we mean that they are worthwhile anywhere, always.

We use as a synonym of their worth that they are "sterling." Sterling, in origin, means a currency that, because of its purity, is everywhere valid.

A person's worthiness is then the criterion whereby we rate and quote all other more partial worths. Christ made that clear with his question: "What shall a man be given in exchange for his soul?" A person's price (their wage) may fluctuate economically and often hovers on the elimination line. They fail to make themselves worth their keep. Morally, too, they can become a drug in the market. But if a person has an eternal soul, then they can be the one constant standard of worth throughout time. If they sustain their spiritual integrity, then the world in the end must not only tolerate them but demand them.

The goldsmiths were the first bankers. That seemed natural. They had the stuff. But they themselves lacked worth. They had sterling but weren't. They were always going bankrupt under dubious conditions. People were at a loss to find someone who wouldn't lose their money. An [odd] little sect had arisen then. They used to feel God's presence so vibrantly that when they sat together silently thinking of Him, they quaked. So keen a sense of His Presence naturally had a lag. When the next day they did their business, they still felt that He was there. Why then swear and vow, seal and bind? Your word given in that Presence made all other guaranty otiose. Business so done prospered. Growing business can take capital. People invested with the Quakers. As a consequence, four of the great banking houses of London, when that city led the financial market, had Quaker origins. This is not a success story. Indeed it may well be a failure tale. Holiness, "wholeness," is power—at its very lowest it will make you money. Had the rise of big business been the end of the Quaker story, then as Ramakrishna no doubt would have told us, so the *siddhis* lure people from *samadhi*. But the Quakers have held out for higher recognition. They studied their scriptures and saw that their *avatar* had said that a child of God may be recognized because they are a peacemaker. The Quakers made themselves more widely recognized and deeply trusted as peacemakers than as bankers.

So, glancing at the story of this one small and far-from-occult sect, we have discovered two things about the worth of a person's soul. When it is upright, it can make more money than all the crooks. When it is devoted, it can make more peace than any army. In short, the nearer it comes to God the more powerful it is. Isn't this then, after all, going to end as a success [story]? Find God and humans will find you everything else. If you want money, then cool clean millions. If you want fame (and the average person wants that generally more than cash), then you can have steady high-grade admiration, "worth-ship."

The spirit of humanity is the candle of the Lord. From watching the spirit of people can we understand, estimate, [and "value"] the spirit of God? Yes, in a way, but mostly not. There is a principle now recognized in psychology called by its definer, Dr. Charles Baudouin, "the law of reversed effort"—the more you try, the less you can repeat your first spontaneous achievement. There would seem to be a similar law in theology, a "law of increasing ignorance," we might call it. Even in the successful religions we can see it. The first wonderful "hits"—of prophecy, psychotherapy, healing, or what have you—are not sustained. People thought they knew God and His [designs]. "He means me to be happy, to be healthy, to be a success, to help others, for our side to win, for us to know His intentions." And for a little while they seem to show they are right, and then it is clear they weren't.

That brings us to the odd title, "God is Shy," borrowed for these lines. The term was coined by a devout Jesuit who for years with great success, but apparently with equally humble misgivings counseled seekers. It would seem that what he was trying to startle his hearers into understanding was simultaneously their need for and their ignorance of God. Here was a knife-edge, up onto which he would try and make them mount with the prod of this *koan*. [Ed. Note: A koan is a terse, illogical phrase used in Zen Buddhism to implode the rational mind.] For either they would mumble a lot of unworthy ... praise-phrases about His Highness, or else they would fall off the other side into a sentimental or "cupboard-love" false intimacy.

"God is Shy" startles us—and a moment after, it rouses our curiosity. We need that. In the West, [the] religious and irreligious share a fatal ignorance. They both feel that God is found: found and used ... by the believer, found out by the atheists. The conception of God as

Mysterium tremendum et fascinans ["majestic and fascinating mystery"] is alien to all our present-day thought. William James set the style in his patronizing remark, "God is a very useful ally of my social conscience." True, we have lately seen a reaction. Neo-orthodoxy does now speak quite a lot of God as *Tremendum*, but not of His Fascination. Hence the scorn with which American theology generally speaks of all mysticism, and its contemptuous ignorance of Asiatic religion and all contemplation. But theology means the science of God, and if that phrase is not to be blasphemously impertinent, then theology must adopt the humbling, guiding rule of all the sciences that would ever really know (and not be content with the feeling that they are "knowing"): "Beware when you find what you are looking for."

The pure in heart alone see God for they see pure, [free] of all "knowingness." They seek God not because they know, but because they know they must know and know that they don't. They realize that all their present type of knowledge is really but part of an ignorance that covers the whole life of the senses. This perception of their ignorance is, as Socrates saw, the first essential step to real knowledge. The second is the intuitional discovery that another quality of knowledge is obtainable—what Professor Sarvepalli Radhakrishnan has called *integral knowledge*. A person cannot remember the saving knowledge they once had, but they can remember that they once knew what they have now forgotten. They are therefore driven to seek for what they cannot say. To their rational mind this need is inexplicable, but for their entire nature it is peremptory.

How better, then, may a person express the object of their desire than by this strange word "shy"—an object both alluring and elusive, fascinating and awesome: as powerfully, intensely attractive as are those dark ultra-massive stars, and, as are they, as imperceptible, as unknowable, save by their supreme power of attraction.

The Inner Voice

Originally published in *Vedanta and the West*,
Volume 12, No. 4, July–August 1949

A MAN WENT out to a shrine to pray. Three demons saw him approaching and decided to waylay him. They were of different ages and of course, as all devils are liars, the youngest looked the oldest and the oldest the youngest. Thus, the oldest one had then the right of precedence. And certainly, because of his disguise, he looked the most presentable.

"Where are you going?" he remarked to the man as he met him on the path.

"Oh," said the man, just a little discomposed by meeting a stranger and being asked a personal question, "I thought I'd just stroll out and have a look at a little shrine that's out in this direction. It's a pretty little place, I believe, and I felt I needed a quiet walk in the country. Good for one's peace of mind, you know!"

The demon said, "You look all right. I shouldn't have thought with your looks you needed rest, retirement. If you're feeling gloomy, it isn't solitude that will set you up. It's company you need. Why, I can see at a glance you're the type of man who pines when left alone and is the life and soul of good company. Someone has been putting inferiority feelings into your mind—telling you you're a failure, that people don't like you and all that. Just jealousy. Don't let it sway you, a fine, handsome, obviously popular person like you. Forgive the personalness, but to tell the truth I not only took to you the moment I saw you but I got the feeling that you'd been [upset] over something. Solitude's all right for mopes but not for he-men. Look, I'm just going along to a party—it's going to be fun. There's only one thing that isn't quite right. There are a lot of first-rate women coming but we're short on men. Won't you help us out?"

The man wavered. Perhaps, after all, a party would prove more helpful than prayer if he were really the sort of man who was a party [person]. But he couldn't help doubting that, despite the kind words and generous offer of this nice, well-set-up stranger.

"You see," he said, "though no doubt I look all right, maybe quite passable, the truth is I'm far from strong. My doctor has told me that late nights are quite wrong for me. Indeed, it was he who told me that I ought to take this quiet walk every now and then. Thank you so much, but I must be getting on."

"Oh, I'm so sorry." The handsome devil's face registered the most courteous consideration. "Of course I should have noticed. Forgive my selfishness. I was so keen on getting a few good-lookers together for our little dance. Of course, good looks like yours so often deceive—the typical T.B. appearance. Of course you are right to take care. But are you sure a long walk is the right thing for you in a damp wood? Exertion is the consumptive's most insidious enemy. Rest is your ally. Come along with me. I know of a wonderful physician who's had amazing successes with cases such as yours. He's told me he's saved innumerable lives with just one simple motto regularly applied: 'Avoid Any Effort.' Come along."

The demon took his arm. "You lean on me. I'm a close personal friend of this great specialist. I know if I turn up with you, though he's so busy, he'll make time to see you."

But the man somehow didn't like the touch of his new friend. "Excuse me, perhaps later, but just now I'll think over your kind offer," he said, and disengaged himself.

"All right," said the demon but his voice certainly didn't sound so, "all right, you croaking old hypochondriac, no wonder you're taking to God—the Universal [Waste Can]. Who else would want your company!"

The man turned his back and the demon vanished into the bushes. As he was the senior, the others kept silent and in silence the second obeyed when the [failed one] remarked to him, "You next."

The man therefore found himself again confronted. "I didn't know this lonely road was so popular," he remarked to himself. And the second passerby also came up to him. This second man wasn't, surely, as handsome as the first, but he was if anything even more reassuring. He looked so sound—a sensible, shrewd person whose advice would always be valuable. And he seemed inclined to offer it. At least he was inclined to be of service.

"Have you heard the news?" the second devil asked straightaway. "I thought not," he added as the man looked blank, "or, of course, you wouldn't be sauntering out into the country on a day like this."

"A day like this?" the man queried.

"Why of course. After all this depression and slump, the market's at last got up like a person after a long and refreshing sleep. It's kicking off its bed covers, and [wow!], who'd be anywhere today but down in the business quarter. There's nothing underhanded or get-in-first-and-leave-you-out today. Why, it's all [comradeship], all of us together. This is the common person's day. Business wants them with their patient savings. Capital is zooming. Put your money in now and by next year, why you'll be able to be a social benefactor, build a church or what have you, and never feel the pinch of giving. That's what prosperity used to be, and that's what it's going to be again if people, people like you and me, aren't escapists but come right in and all pull together."

"But," said the man, trying to avoid saying where he was going, "I don't think I want to make more money. I haven't much but it's enough. You see, I like a quiet life and my—my interests—really aren't economic, they're rather psychological."

The other didn't seem put off. On the contrary, his interest seemed to grow. He actually looked concerned. "You've only got a little?"

The man became a little more defensive. "Well, as I've said, I have enough but I'm not of course a rich man with money to throw away."

149

The other said nothing for a moment but sighed, then added, with a gentle smile, "Yes, I can see your interests are psychological. But did you never think that you are able to have your psychological interests because of your economic security? Would you, could you care—if I may be forgiven a very crude and inaccurate term—could you care for the state of your soul if the cupboard were bare?"

He paused and then went on, so quietly, consultively, patiently. "And we, whom no doubt you dismiss as crude dollar-diggers, ignorant of the rich deposits of the human spirit, I wonder if it ever crosses your mind how often we spend long, wakeful nights thinking not merely of the public welfare as a whole and how trade may be stimulated and enterprise rewarded, but just of the thing you've mentioned, psychology? Do you ever think how mysterious money is, how, if again I may use a strong phrase, how sacramental, how mystical money really is? Why, credit is just the faith that moves mountains. And credit like faith is dead if it hasn't works to back it. You must show that you believe [and] prove it.

"It's just because you little people, playing for security and thinking you have it, turn your backs on your responsibilities that you wake up one fine morning to find that you've let the day of opportunity pass and the very basis of your life has gone. Then you may whistle for your peace of mind, and it will be cold comfort to know that your silliness and indifference have allowed scamps to beat the market and get away with your pennies. No, my dear sir, do your duty today, and tomorrow—once again secure by your act of faith in your fellow humans and your cooperation with their effort, an effort needing constant repetition—tomorrow be free to take your quiet walk in the country and enjoy your psychological enquiries."

"Well," said the man, "thank you so much for the tip. I'll get along tomorrow and see my broker. Just today I have an engagement I really oughtn't break."

"All right," the demon echoed his leader's tone. "All right, and only have yourself, and no one else, to blame when you wake up some fine day broke!"

He strode off, and the man once again set his face toward the shrine, only, at the next turn of the path, to find a third wayfarer.

This third devil seemed in more of a hurry than the other two and almost passed the man before suddenly wheeling in his tracks.

He asked him, "Excuse me, have you just come from the city?" To the man's "Yes," the stranger then added another question, "I wonder whether you mightn't help me. There's a municipal election [going] on; most people don't pay attention. It's one of the hardest tasks of a good citizen to get people interested in their home politics. Naturally it is a difficult game, and then people think they can wash their hands of it when they've said that it's dusty, and of course, when things get damp, of course a bit muddy. But you've had to have first the dirt track before you had the cement pavement, haven't you? And what's that got to do with you? Why it's simple as pecking at pie. People are so bored with our hard work they just won't attend to real points. They vote, believe me, I know, just by faces. Now you've got just the face we want. You remind people a bit of Washington and then in another light of Lincoln with just a dash every now and then of Teddy Roosevelt or a gleam of Jefferson. Come along, we can put you up. We'll do all the work for you. All you have to do is to be photographed enough times and televised. We'll write the scripts for you, and you'll have nothing to say but the round good stuff."

"But I don't want to touch politics. I don't think people are altered that way ..."

"And so you're just going to stand back, sweep your robe aside, and all the dirt of politics will vanish? Because you refuse to approve—refuse to cooperate—the horrid thing will lose face, flush and hide itself, and we'll all carry on in philosophic anarchy without anything so crude as a machine or any [method] of getting consent from the people and keeping them content at least below revolution bursting point!"

"Well," the man tried to put in but was swept aside.

"And because you are too pure and high to go in, therefore of course politics being under the ban of your disapproval, no one else will dare take the place you have put under your interdict. The lowest type will shun what your moral anathema has declared impermissible. A vacuum of complete purity will descend on all [leadership], on all administration! No, you're not such a hypocrite to tell yourself such a story, such a [lie]! You know that, because you

151

won't take the offered place, won't let yourself be used (and use the opportunity to do the little good that so comes your way), then scamps will come in. You are not preventing evil by refusing to use mixed means—on the contrary, you are leaving the door open to those who will certainly spend all their time making a mess of things to their own advantage, and, my fine pharisaic friend, will make it hot for superfine secessionists like you as soon as they catch sight of you, mark my words! You're nothing but a conscienceless, dishonest escapist!"

The man was shaken by the storm of moral denunciation. "But I don't feel fit to rule."

"Well then you show yourself fit to be kicked around. It isn't democratic to desert your social duties. This is just moral treason, and you'll deserve the capital punishment that it demands."

Again the man was shaken by the moral fervor of his challenger. "I'm awfully sorry," he said. "I do see your point. It hurts me a great deal. I don't honestly see my way. I haven't a clear answer to what you say, and yet I can't see it's really right to do evil that good may come or even to act without knowing what the real consequences will be. You see, when you met me, I was going to ask advice on these points."

"Of whom? Haven't I answered your question?"

"Well, I was going to ask someone else. I was as it happens, if you must know, going to pray!"

The face of the moral reformer went purple with passion. "Hell!" he exclaimed with really intense conviction and darted off down the path.

The man felt quite giddy and a little sick. These three people—how very odd, how very apt, how very challenging—none of them had said anything that the man himself did not in part agree with, and to what they had said, he found he had no clear, clinching, convincing answers. They had been so sensible, so cogent; he [had been] so weak and always protesting, excusing, ill-thought-out. He had started out to pray just because he was a bit uncertain, and now he was twice as uncertain. He had thought he knew what he wanted to ask, and now he didn't know even that, he didn't even feel sure that he ought to be asking anything, whether he oughtn't to be getting back and doing something, either having his psychophysical health looked into, or his financial situation, or the state of the city politics. Wasn't he escaping out here, repressing the real problems? Oh what a mess he was in! He couldn't even pray now; he couldn't do anything. He stopped, exhausted, feeling at the end of his tether—the path, too, had become overgrown—he was lost.

Then a voice said out of the thicket, "My child, though you didn't know the answer, you knew [that] those who came to you to prevent your coming to Me [also] did not know it. Though when you started out you thought you knew what to ask, now you know your ignorance. Now you may stay still, and I will speak to you, for at last you are really silent, really listening."

Vedanta and
Western History, Pt. I

Originally published in *Vedanta and the West*,
Volume 12, No. 6, November–December 1949

A NEW [RELIGIOUS MOVEMENT] has come into history—that is Western Vedanta. For centuries, and perhaps millennia, Vedanta influenced and molded the East, passing from the richness of original Brahmanism to the austerity of Theravadin Buddhism, through the counterrichness of Mahayana and so again to the counterreformation of Shankara and the Vedanta we know. But, save for some tentative influences—such as the missionary effort of Asoka and the small though steady trickle of Indian ideas through Alexandria—Vedanta did not really strike the West. Christianity, had it not been torn from its original rooting spots by Islam and made to specialize in the Western legalistic form of Catholicism, would no doubt have exchanged many ideas with India. As it was, the Christian Church on the Coromandel Coast—claiming descent from St. Thomas—did not remain a live link, and the Buddhist missionaries who entered the Mediterranean world made no distinctive mark. True, there is a church in Sicily dedicated to St. Barlaam—a garbled form of Buddha's name made famous and saintworthy because of a garbled but very popular story of his life and renunciation. The width and subtlety of Indian thought, the range of its cosmology, the depth of its psychology never, however, succeeded in enlarging that narrow [Judeo-Christian] scheme of things, [with its] Apocalypse [narrative] and eschatology, which has ever since cramped and hobbled the religion of the West.

There can be little doubt that the Eastern churches of the Levant would have made some use of this treasury of knowledge when we see how many Indian ideas are present in Origen—how clearly he holds reincarnation, and with what liberality he wished to draw upon the East for insights, for those illuminations from "the Christians that were before Christ." The mistake of the Council of Chalcedon of the fourth century—in condemning reincarnation—removed from Christianity a view of things that till then had been liberally entertained, and with which the cruel finality of everlasting punishment for the mistakes of this one life would not have disgraced the "religion of love." [Ed. Note: Heard's assertion regarding the Council of Chalcedon condemning reincarnation is incorrect.]

Indeed, we may say that the appearance of Vedanta in the West as a living religion, and not as an academic study, is inevitable just because the religious heredity of the West has now outgrown the tight [Judeo-Christian] pot of cosmology in which it had been growing for two millennia. A faith that taught hell for those who did not get themselves saved in this life was suited enough to put "the fear of God" into barbarians or into people too busy to do much more than make a dash with their last breath for a deathbed repentance. But for people really interested in the spiritual world, really desirous of growing in spirituality and filled with a real longing to know and love God, such doctrines were, far from being any help, a terrible obstacle. Catholicism has become increasingly dogmatic, Protestantism increasingly secular and humanist. Where were people to find a religion that was intense but not cruelly narrow, wide but not vague, loose but not tepid? Vedanta in the broad range that it is given by the Vedanta [Society] of Southern California is the answer. [Ed. Note: The affiliated Vedanta centers located throughout America promote the same message.]

And the very breadth of Vedanta, combined with its force, is bound to embrace and develop much that is now lying latent in our Western thought and spirit. When Christianity went to India, it became in form and in much of its spirit Indian. When the Indian-reformed Brahmanism that we call Buddhism went into China, it took on many of the forms and manners of China—so much so that today when people imagine that warrior spirit Gautama, they think of a rather obese Mongolian dozing. So today when Vedanta comes to the West it will, now that it has been acclimated here—to which acclimating it owes so much to [the Vedanta Society of Southern California's Minister] Swami Prabhavananda—take on and make a distinctive Western Vedanta. What that will be we cannot say. Few historical studies are more interesting than to see what it is that the spirit of an area and province will pick as its peculiar accent and expression of a universal truth. For example, when Tantric Buddhism—an [odd] enough synthesis in all conscience—entered China by way of Tibet, and the Shakta–Shakti symbol of union was shown to the Chinese, they made no protest as far as can be discovered to this rather startling picture of spirit and expression. They simply dropped that symbol, gradually making their own iconography. So no doubt gradually the West will pick those Asiatic forms and from them make ones of its own that best express for it by symbol that which all agree is in its Essence inexpressible.

It is easier to speak of the Perennial Philosophy, the Eternal Gospel, the Universal Religion than actually to define them—or it. We can see that certain general principles run through the great religions that have affected humanity for many centuries. But when we come to consider what are the actual essentials and what are merely matters of time and place, topical and local, then the issue is far more difficult. Probably there is not a religion extant that does not in some way and degree meet the deep demands of its worshipers for relief from the false self, for some vision of a vast meaning in which all may find both loss of their separation and fulfillment of their deepest nature. But certainly religions, just as much as individual persons, grow old and in their decrepitude they may, like ourselves, produce ugly features and show evidence of disease.

The Congress of World Religions when being summoned in London in the 1930s [held] many sessions of its main committee to decide on how this act of union could be best expressed. The secretary very rightfully wished all religions to be invited. There was, however, a long and inconclusive discussion when a member asked whether all religions would include such tribes as might still wish to practice human sacrifice or even temple prostitution.

A great deal of thinking has to be done on Ramakrishna's ecumenical statement: *all* roads lead to God. It is possible to think of all religions as tending to enlightenment and liberation, but only if some of the more decadent and [disagreeable] are considered as those strange and tortuous paths whereby, as Blake put it in his gnomic utterance, "Were the fool to continue in his folly he would become wise." You may get to Catalina [Island] by sailing straight southwest from Los Angeles. You can also go there via New York, Lisbon, Cairo, Ceylon, and Wake Island, and hence come upon it from the seaward side. As the Sanskrit tradition holds that the gods themselves are mortal—only the imageless Brahman is unchanging—so it would seem it is with all religions; they may need to die and transmigrate, and their essential nature take form again in another guise in another epoch.

There is, however, another consideration that today arises when we think of the Perennial Philosophy and especially of Vedanta as its most ancient expression. There may not be progress in history in the way that the nineteenth century thought of historical progress—a process whereby people became better just by going on "and," as Tennyson says, "the thoughts of men are widened with the circling of the suns." But undoubtedly there is an element of irreversibility in history—a process is working itself out. History does not repeat itself—only, as in music, a theme given earlier may be repeated and developed further on in the composition.

There can be no doubt that no age resembling ours has existed before, and that in one respect we have an opportunity denied to earlier ages. Today the world is in touch with every part of itself as never before. We know that, despite the exclusiveness of certain theologians, religions themselves are strongly inclined, as [noted] above, to borrow from one another. Today there is no doubt we must look forward to and should anticipate a new syncretism of the religions of the world. In the succeeding article, some of the possible results of this intercourse and exchange will be considered, and the part that Vedanta will play in that process will be suggested.

Vedanta and
Western History, Pt. II

Originally published in *Vedanta and the West*,
Volume 13, No. 1, January–February 1950

DR. HEINRICH ZIMMER concludes his study *Myths and Symbols in Indian Art and Civilization* with a charming fable. He tells of a rabbi who dreamed a number of times that he must leave his own small house in the ghetto of Kraków and travel to Prague, for there on the bridge leading to the castle he would find a treasure. Finally the rabbi agreed to obey his dream. Arriving at Prague and going to the bridge he found it guarded. So he waited for a long while. At last the captain of the bridge, noticing the old man hanging about, spoke to him kindly, asking what he was waiting for. The rabbi, being good to the point of ingenuousness, told him. The captain, however, remained as friendly, indeed breaking into laughter and becoming confidential. "Why," he told the poor old pilgrim, "I myself had a dream of just the same nonsensical sort, but, as you might say, it was even more upside down! My dream told me to go to the house of an old rabbi in Kraków in the ghetto there, and behind his stove I would find a treasure! You see what nonsense dreams are! There's no treasure on this bridge I can assure you. And you and I know that the last place in the world to find a treasure—this bridge would be better—would be in the dwelling of a starving rabbi in the Kraków ghetto." The rabbi bowed and said nothing more—for he had forgotten to tell his friend where he had come from. He returned back straightway to his home. He dug behind the stove and found a buried bag of gold coins.

Dr. Zimmer used this illustration to point out how much India can help the West and that one of its main services is to send us back to our own branch of the great stream of the knowledge of God that has flowed down all the ages and through every land. True enough, our own stream has for the last three hundred years been mainly underground, but even then we may (as one may in New Mexico) trace where the water still runs by the green tree that here and there breaks up and stands fresh among the dry stones of the old surface riverbed.

Many people are still inclined to think that spirituality has never been native or natural to the West. That, however, is not true and could only be advanced by one who was not interested in history. Indeed we might say that till three or four centuries ago, the West was as deeply interested in spirituality as the East. Sir William Flinders Petrie, the great Egyptologist, once remarked that the East seems asleep to the West because when the East is awake, the West is asleep. Perhaps we may try and make the definition more exact and say that when the West is looking outward at the apparent world, the East is looking inward.

Certainly, as Dr. Raymond Bernard Blakney, the latest editor of Eckhart, has pointed out, today the Far East—[specifically] China, which he has lately been visiting—has become keenly contemptuous of the inner life, despises the Taoist mysticism, and seeks in improving the environment by mechanical means, the only "happiness" of humanity. Certainly today we of the West are wearying of our effort to create happiness outside ourselves, and our basic science, physics, is now tending to see the visible world as a projection of our minds or a selection made by them. Increasingly, the philosophy of science is returning to epistemology—the study of how our minds [perceive] what they take to be objective.

Nor need we think that we are being untrue to our past or taking to a metaphysic for which we have no gift or calling. Until four

160

centuries ago, the West was not only as religious as the East but also as keenly interested not merely in the path of devotion but in that of spiritual knowledge. The history of the West concerning pure spirituality is not only interesting but instructive. The great issue of worship of God with form or without form was worked out and disputed in the West, and what is more, the spiritual have, on the whole, tended to be those who have worshiped God without form.

The two sources of Western religion are the Hebrew and the Greek. Both of these religious traditions, when they rose to the point that they could become of use to a wide circle of their neighbors, had found it necessary to dispense with forms. To Plato and to Plotinus, to Hillel and to Philo, anthropomorphism was equally unhelpful. It was from this blend of Greek and Hebrew mysticism that there sprang up in Syria the teaching of the Dionysian school, that *via negativa* which, by a series of denials, flakes off all incrustation of image and leaves the mind with an essential [awareness].

It is important to remember that though the Western world in the fifth and sixth centuries A.D. was sinking in cultural and mechanic skill, it was this very advanced spiritual teaching that took people's minds. The works of this strange "pseudepigraphist" first passed to Constantinople where they were approved by a Church Council and thence into France. There they came into the hands of the great Irish scholar, John Scotus Erigena, one of the few individuals of the West who then could translate Greek in which the works were written. Erigena was such a passionate *advaitist* that he is said to have been murdered by being stabbed to death with the pencils of his students—a martyr to monism! The violent iconoclastic controversy of the Eastern Church time and again gave the victory to those who would have no images of God and who felt that only in the worship of the imageless could Western people be satisfied. The pure contemplatives of Ireland seem to have followed the same path. Only in India can an intensity of contemplation equal to that of Ireland's be found, for this fire of solitary contemplation burnt longer in the extreme Western island than it did in the Egyptian desert. And throughout that tradition there is a passion for the formless, a drive toward the *jnana* contemplation that today we consider as specifically Eastern.

So, too, with the great Rhineland mystics, though they were probably revived in their interest in pure intellectual love of God by infiltrations from the East. In the monastic system also, when the solitaries of Ireland (the Culdees or lonely anchorites) began to be gathered into small groups, here, too, the worship of the formless, the jnana approach, is native and cultural to the far West. The first monasteries of western Europe owe nearly everything to these Irish "religious," and the evangelization of central Europe is due largely to their efforts. Columbanus, the great Celtic monk, lies buried in Bobbio in South Italy. It is against this pure and advanced form of religious life and thought that Benedict, the Italian, offers his more formal, organized, liturgical way. Pure mental prayer, contemplation, is to be secondary—and inessential—beside the reciting of the offices, the repetition of the psalter, [and] the performance of the Mass. Naturally this is the easier way, and may be the safer, and so it naturally [prevailed].

But when the reaction came and these forms were challenged because they were worshiped formally and not with real devotion, and also because the reality that was claimed for them appeared to be superstitious—then the [Western] Church had nothing to oppose to the bleak critical puritanism. The mystic insight and practice, whereby the consciousness may be changed, had been neglected under the excuse of what was called liturgical piety, and the form, perfunctorily performed—an excuse for and not an aid to attention—appeared to be empty of content.

It is certain that all forms do wear out. We can watch in the well-documented and dated history of the West how first in the thirteenth century, motherhood is worshiped. As Henry Adams pointed out, throughout the whole of Chartres Cathedral there is in window and in stone only praise of the divine motherhood; the divine man dying on the Tree is lacking. Then a century after, churches of "St. Savior" are founded everywhere; the sacred body becomes worshiped (Corpus Christi), [then] the Five Wounds, and then the Sacred Heart. Then once more the Virgin begins to absorb devotion, is named as the sole channel of grace, and the cult of the Sacred Heart, once confined to her divine son, is now extended to her. And we must always remember that, as such shifts of the form of devotion take place, there is always danger—and this of course actually took place during the Protestant revolution—that with the form, the spirit will be banished.

The West is still little interested in true religion and pure spirituality today because the worship of God with form was challenged and had exhausted the attention of devotees. The old forms became empty; no new forms took their place, and the worship of God without form had not been inculcated or the method of such worship taught. True enough, for a while Quakerism seemed as though it might be the jnana of the West or at least a devotion to the formless. But the lack of method and of expert knowledge of the mystical approach and an increasing concern with social service drew off the minds of this small communion, and the early promise was not fulfilled.

Today, however, we are returning to our original interest in pure spirituality, and it must be repeated that [this] interest (as shown by our pure research in science) tends to be toward jnana more than to devotion of the emotions. Those who wish for worship with forms and images can find it in the West in Roman Catholicism. But those who cannot obtain from the multiformity of Catholicism and its strong tendency to anthropomorphism, the sense of the Presence of the spaceless and timeless Being, are in need of a free but deep worship such as Vedanta can promise. Some further suggestions of this possible development will be made in a final article [in this series].

Vedanta and
Western History, Pt. III

Originally published in *Vedanta and the West*,
Volume 13, No. 2, March–April 1950

WE HAVE SEEN in the two previous articles [the following]: (1) Western people have been in the past as interested in religion as the East; (2) that this interest, when keenest, was in the worship of God without form; (3) as the intensity of their devotional interest waned, this formless worship was gradually pushed aside by worship with form; and, (4) this worship with form tended toward polytheism.

Further, (5) when historical critical methods arose and history took on scientific methods of assessing evidence, these forms, being rigidly identified with personages asserted in every detail to be specifically historical, were regarded as untrue and dismissed. Finally, (6) came the vast revolution in Western thought caused by the revolution in the basic science of physics. By 1915 (as Sir Edmund Whittaker points out), classical mechanistic physics, which had been the foundation of materialism, was overturned. Western thought, seeking for a system whereby it might grasp more realistically the nature of the universe, found that it had to abandon mechanomorphism, the assumption that the cosmos is a vast machine. The universe was a nonmaterial power that functioned free of causality as David Hilbert had shown. Hence it was something much more resembling an alive organism. It will be obvious that such a notion certainly ends mechanomorphism. But it does not return us to anthropomorphism. The consequence of the thinking that has led to modern physics is to make a person find as the object of their worship (for worship means "worth-ship," and worth-ship is our total estimate or esteem of anyone) the timeless and spaceless, immanent and transcendent Being.

The first thing then that religion today must provide is a cultus that permits people who have been thus convinced of the fact of deity, to "worship Him in spirit and in truth." The future of world faith belongs to whatever religion will give hospitality and welcome to such believers. The religion that will welcome these, teaching them the ways of living (the moral rules) and the mental exercises—the religious methods whereby what is intellectually believed can affect conduct, character, and consciousness—such a religion must [succeed]. The future of religion throughout the world could belong to Vedanta if it will guarantee this "holy liberty." We must remember that, whereas a generation ago in the West, religion (being still based on anthropomorphism, still supposed to be denied by physics) found its main support among the uninformed [and] its main challenge among the educated—today this is reversed. The revolution in science (from physics to psychology) has turned the most open-minded thinkers toward theism, while the uninformed and reactionary still cling to a discredited fundamentalist Marxist materialism. So the new movement toward religion can be adequately met only if a highly spiritual method and worship is offered.

We must, however, make a distinction here. There are three worship possibilities to be offered to three types of worshipers. Sometimes people speak as though the choice were either anthropomorphism—the worship of God with physical form—or the pure monistic contemplation of Him who is one without a second. There is, however, a middle term—God without form but with attributes—in fact the *Sat-Chit-Ananda* of Vedanta. This is the outlook of most today who have come by natural theology back to religion. Their need, the terms in which they can conceive of ultimate reality, must then be respected, their mode of worship guaranteed and sanctioned.

166

On the other hand, it is as necessary to make clear to them and to all other enquirers or critics that those who come to religion through natural theology must learn and extend an equal tolerance to the other forms of worship. Many of those who come to religion today are scientists—that is to say, people interested in immediate observation of nature. They are not historians. It is only quite lately that scientists have begun to study even the history of science. Most scientists have to learn the historical, the anthropological approach. So they have to learn to respect the method–processes of those who worship God with form. An abacus seems a childish computer to one who reckons in their head. It can be employed with great speed and accuracy by one accustomed to it. To the mathematician, their symbols seem incomparably superior to words, yet great poetry can convey things that the neatest formula or equation will miss.

Granted then that the new movement, through natural theology to religion, needs an imageless (though not an attributeless) worship, and that this new movement must learn to sympathize with those whose minds (artistic rather than scientific) worship God with form, we come then to our final question. For those in the West who worship with form, what forms are significantly helpful to them?

There are, we know, two basic forms—those of motherhood and of fatherhood. They have, we also know, alternated in the history of humanity. The primitive matriarchate culture held naturally to the worship of motherhood. When patriarchate culture succeeded, Godhead was conceived as male. With the rise of those cultures in which male and female are seen as complementary, those two aspects have been worshiped as (1) the gynanthropic forms of Helladic archaic Greek cultures; (2) the mother and son pattern, e.g., Isis–Horus; and (3) the twin consorts, e.g., Cybele–Attis.

A further extension was given by totemism. Recognition of kinship with all life and of deity as being within all creatures appeared in the zoanthropomorphic figures (as the Egyptian jackal-headed Anubis, etc.). These latter have not lasted in the West and maybe are passing away for good. They do not help in the approach to religion through natural theology. Further, there are the "wrathful" or "power" forms of deity. These are shown by (1) the destructive, and (2) the procreative iconography. The destructive was shown in Egypt by Sekhmet, the female "wrathful" power symbolized by the lioness-headed woman. The procreative, the "Min" figures, were largely destroyed in Western religion by the puritan revolution of Akhenaten in Egypt, and later in the eighth century another such revolution among the Semites.

As the European religion developed through the Middle Ages, in thinking of the male concept of deity, Western people abandoned all attempts to render the fatherhood in form—save for such efforts as shown on the Sistine [Chapel] ceiling. Iconography concentrated instead on that of the divine young redeemer and his mother. She is a virgin and he an emaciated sacrifice. Hence sex symbolism and erotic devotion are replaced by pathos. This is probably due to two things: (1) chastity was found to be the safe and sane way to illumination, whereas orgiastic erethism was discovered to be extremely dangerous; and (2) pathos—compassion—was a more safe and more enduring emotion (e.g., [as found in] Buddhism) than passionate romantic love. Hence the West, learning the value—and indeed vital importance—of strict continence if complete consciousness ([i.e., including] ecstasy) is to be [attained] and held, abandoned not only the Shakta–Shakti iconography and symbolism, but also that which is its complement, the "wrathful" and destructive aspects of form-rendered deity. It is also worth noting that the completer and finisher of the universe in the Western Trinity is God the Holy Spirit—a hypostasis without form and whose attributes are peace, purity, and inspiration.

To summarize then, two features seem to emerge from the contact of Vedanta with the twentieth-century West: (1) most Westerners are looking for a religion that shall express and render to them an experience of the transcendent–immanent Eternal Life that physics has now deduced to be the nature of the universe. Vedanta can give that—All is Brahman; thyself art He. (2) Those Westerners who, on their way to that experience, need help of forms, are helped by such as are (a) purely compassionate, and (b) are specifically psychologically satisfying and that are not involved (as are those of dogmatic Christianity) with statements as to the historicity of the form–features which are found to be psychologically helpful.

Finally, those who are helped by form should not impose their forms on those not so helped, while, conversely, those to whom form is an obstacle should not deny or feel contempt for such [aids] when used by those who are so assisted to grasp or contact the Ultimate Reality. The proof of the efficacy of a form or a formless method must in the end be found in the life it produces, [and] in the freedom from greed, emulation, fear, and anxiety that is achieved.

Is Old Age Worthwhile?

Originally published in *Vedanta and the West*,
Volume 13, No. 3, May–June 1950

OLD AGE IS A FAVORITE [TOPIC] for Occidental moralists and literary persons. The Romans, when they wished to be cultured, turned to it as a convenient theme to practice on as essayists. It had the double advantage that it proposed to the elderly that senescence after all might not be so bad, and [it] dictated to the young a proper respect for those who, though [they have] become infirm, yet continued to cumber the scene. But Cicero and Seneca are not very convincing, while when we reach Marcus Aurelius, we find suicide proposed as a solution for the awkwardly advanced physiological conditions.

In short, the "consolations" of old age are not those we find really efficacious when employed on ourselves, but rather [consist of] those euphemisms, uttering which, "we find it always possible to endure the sorrows of others" and to extract from their miseries seemly moralizings. Nor, as "progress" has swept our Western culture onward, do we seem to be getting any wiser about old age or resigned to its processes. The Romantics of course made no bones about it. Youth would not endure, but it was the only time worth having; old age is the very mischief. The attitude is neatly epigrammatized in Leigh Hunt's touching effort ["Jenny Kiss'd Me"] to draw bravely his "post-mature" balance:

> Say I'm weary, say I'm sad,
> Say that health and wealth have miss'd me,
> Say I'm growing old, but add,
> Jenny kiss'd me.

Jenny being the vivacious Jane Welch, herself so rapidly to ripen into the formidably acidulated Mrs. Carlyle. John Milton had written—when a young man—that it was possible to live,

> Till old experience do attain
> To something like prophetic strain.

But when he was old himself, the strain that was felt by his daughters was one of exasperation, not of inspiration.

It is hard then to see that the West has shown, as Albert Schweitzer has maintained, an attitude of life-acceptance. As a matter of fact, the further we advance in power over our environment, the more we seem to be determined to take only the hors d'oeuvres from life's menu, and to turn with disgust from the rest of the table d'hôte. We have monkeyed about with monkey glands and other Tithonus tricks. They have proved—as the Greek mythmakers knew—far from happy, and lifting faces hasn't lifted hearts.

Of course such an attitude is not even good naturalism. We are refusing to face up to the physiological facts. For, as Dr. Julian Huxley has pointed out in his *The Uniqueness of Man*, we are the animal that is marked specifically by the strange characteristic, the unique feature, that only when our reproductive acme is over do we enter into our particular, outstanding way of life. "Man *qua* man" is the not-young, yes, and further this person is the "post-mature." Ever since becoming human, [man and woman] had to decide what to do with this extension of living when impulse was over and reflection had to begin. To define middle age, then, as merely "the feeling that tomorrow you'll feel better" is of course to refer to the standards of sensation, an experience that should be judged by the standards of evaluation. Middle age is when humans become specifically human and they are human then because they have learned to disregard euphoria and focus their attention on understanding.

We see anyone must achieve so much who will not show himself or herself to be too old at fifty and unfit for maturity. But lately we have added another story to the castle of life. As human beings, we achieve a middle age hardly ever known to any animal in the wild state, and the advance of our society depends on the fact that we can and do enter onto this plateau of reflection. But further, this power of research and reflection has made possible an even newer thing—healthy old age, at least physiologically healthy, provided the "reducing rules," the diet of "involution" is observed. Alas, however, little as most people like leaving body-identified youth for mentally interested middle age, fewer—far fewer—relish the prospect of leaving the moderate and chiefly rational pursuits and activities of midlife for the quiet acceptances, deeper insights, and death-spanning vision of a non-adhesive old age. We have, in short, been granted by our status as human beings a new upper-level apartment of middle age and have done little to fill it with adequate psychological furnishing. Then, by our status as physiological researchers, we have placed on the top of this second story still a third—and this, which we should have filled with the observatory equipment for studying the heavens we have shrunk from, trying to skulk in the basement of life's building—though the inevitable elevator of time has our skirts caught in its gate and is dragging us remorselessly toward the roof.

We may then say that the chief problem that confronts us, not merely individually but socially, is the problem of life's new offer—a third term. And we may add that, as youth is not youth without hope, and middle age is not middle age without reflection, so old age cannot be old age, but simply an inability to die, unless it has achieved vision.

That, however, people today nearly all agree in this hemisphere, is easier said than done. Indeed, instead of finding space for middle age's capacity to review experience, we hustle the oldsters off their feet and out of their minds. Nor have we done any better [for] the ... youth. We have certainly not given them much reason to indulge in the exercise of hope. That being so both for the first and second stories and terms, no wonder old age lacks vision.

Yet all of us who have had the opportunity of learning from the Eastern hemisphere's tradition know that in that system there is contained precisely that triple psychology which we need to furnish [in order to] make purposive sense of our present physiological [aging sequence]. Youth, which should be inspired by hope, can generate that hope because under the *brahmachari* vow, the young live for a future that now they are earning. There can be no hope without denial—a fact the West has objected to recognizing. Then follows the life of the householder who, by self-control, has learned to enjoy that balanced situation of authority and responsibility which is the sober joy of those who understand this middle, transitional world. When this second state has fulfilled the first, it in turn becomes the way to the third.

The Sanskrit view of life turns around and points rightly forward the sequence of life, which we have gotten the wrong way round, and so must live, not in hope, but in continual repining. For old age is seen, in the traditional way of life, not as a decline and frustration but as an explication. We unfold from us and put aside those gloves and swathes with which we have had to handle this world, and with a freer touch and wider reach we stretch out already through our thinning integument, able to handle the unseen and immortal.

It will certainly require a revolution—in the literal sense of the word—a revolution in our whole outlook, if we are to get this matter of old age straight. But if we don't, not only shall we have an increasing number of elderlies on our hands, creatures alive but, like Saul on Gilboa, repenting that their life is still whole in them, a pest and bore to themselves and to all around them, but we shall have a society gravely handicapped by this sagging load at its upper end. We shall have a generation of senescents costly to keep, useless for production and, final frustration, utterly unlovely and unlovable. The outlook is grave enough to startle us—it is grave enough already to have startled all those who view human population and its age groups as a problem in worthy living.

Further, when we examine it, we see that the problem of old age is only that extreme point, like gangrene in the foot, where the sick state of the whole age groups of individuals—the three generations of youth, middle age, and old age—becomes first evident. Middle age and youth are just as wrong today, and [so] we have the problem of old age because youth was not taught how to wait and middle age how to act without possessiveness toward action. Peace of mind, acceptance, and their consequent vision cannot be extemporized.

174

Those who should [comprise] the third state of humans when they are ready to be free of incarnation, are the result of the first two parts of life being lived well and with understanding.

There is, however, no need to despair. Because the collapse of the body does not end the causal "field" but only leaves it free once more to involve itself with such an envelope–instrument [i.e., a new body via reincarnation], everyone, however old, may set themselves at once to re-educate themselves. They may not in the time that remains be able to root [out] the basic wish to repeat pleasure rather than go on to fresh understanding, but the mixture of desire and knowledge that is the nature of all people who are in this middle world may, before the next shift of costume and scene, be altered a little, perhaps quite a great deal, in favor of knowledge and against craving.

As for the younger groups, of course their outlook is more hopeful, but at the same time the drag of desire is more strong. Sometimes it would seem as though, for most people, there lies a stretch of comparatively open water and good breezes between the storms of passionate youth and the ice pack of old age's exhaustion. It may be, as hygiene and the discipline of diet gain on us, we may recover the extensive period of healthy old age that seems to belong to people who have lived according to the [health-minded] tradition. If that is so, we may yet see, if we will only make our spiritual knowledge equal to our physiological, a recovered old age when many may go far toward freedom for themselves and to become real inspirations to the age groups below them.

Christ Jesus

Originally published in *Vedanta and the West*,
Volume 13, No. 6, November–December 1950

THE WORDS ARE NOT DIFFICULT to define. [The first, *Christ*, means] the anointed deliverer, the appointed saver. The interpretation of the second word—Jesus or Jeshuah—said in the Gospels to have been supplied by the angel of the annunciation to the virgin mother, is "he shall save them from their sins." The first word, which we translate from the Greek, was taken by the Greeks as their rendering of the Hebrew word "messiah." There seems no doubt it means a providential rescuer, saving us from some acute crisis and sent for that purpose.

But what of this power of salvation? What is this acute crisis, and from where has the rescuer been sent? Montefiore, one of the greatest Jewish authorities on Jewish thought during the couple of centuries we name 100 B.C.–100 A.D., says that we have some documentary idea of what Jewish thought [understood] the Messiah to be before 100 B.C., and what Jewish thought held on that opinion after 100 A.D. But we have for those critical in-between years no certainty as to what precisely were the characteristics and qualifications of the rescuer. Was he political in his aim or spiritual? Was he a divine being that had "pre-existed in heaven"? ([Jewish] thought never seems

177

to have clearly envisaged the possibility of reincarnation.) Or was this being a heroic soul, a blend of prophet and lawgiver, seer and social strategist, in whom the founding spirit of Moses and the counter-compensatory character of Elijah were fused?

We can, however, say that very soon in the second part of our first century, the Jewish–Gentile sect that was beginning to be called Christian, had mainly made up its mind as to what Christ Jesus was. In the first place, he was a spiritual being who incarnated; he was an *avatar*. But more, he was the only avatar. He was unique.

He was also not only the temporal aspect, the human manifestation of the preservative, restorative aspect of the Trinity. That is, he represented on earth not only the aspect that the Hindu calls Vishnu, but he was the Logos also, the creative word. In short, he represented Brahma too. Finally, as the final judge that destroys the world with fire, it is clear that this avatar also represents Shiva, the completer.

Indeed, it is an interesting fact that when the doctrine of the Third Person emerges—a doctrine forced largely on the rest of the [early] Church by the extreme and finally ejected sect of the Montanists—still this Third Person, this Holy Spirit is seen as the beginning of all things but is not allowed to be the completer and the end. It is the Second Person, the Son, the Redeemer, who preempts for himself the role of judge too—the part of the final disposer, the ender of all things.

Naturally, such a being is (1) born of a virgin. (This "bearer of God" soon herself rises to such a height of human estimation that the place which was being granted to the Third Person in the trinitarian pattern now increasingly falls to her as the channel of grace.) [Such a being is also] (2) able, though he is slain, to rise again from the grave; (3) able himself to raise the dead; and (4) able through his death to secure salvation for every human soul that calls on him for his grace.

The Mediterranean peoples of the first centuries A.D. took the phraseology from current Hebrew and Greek metaphysics to describe this figure. And it was this figure that for the next twelve hundred years was to be, in Jung's phrase, the mythos, the man–god through which Western people were to interpret all history, see all cosmology, and judge all ethics.

The emotional force that surrounded the Christ figure was therefore intense, and as we shall see, unique. But after that date, [and] later with the rise of the Renaissance, European society had grown so strong that the critical spirit—the belief that asking questions regardless of consequences was better than submitting to authority for fear of consequences—began to challenge the tradition. Expansion began to get the upper hand over cohesion. Dogma now was required to show reason.

The [Christian] Church was not unprepared. Islam had done Christendom a service by presenting the West with the problem of Aristotle. The question of science, of factfinding and fact-facing, had been put before Europe by the [nonnative] Arab before it was raised in the very camp of the Christian faithful. Thus the Church had already an answer, really a power to delay action, in the *Summa Theologica* of Aquinas. To the appeal of history and the assertion of authority, the Church was now able to add the persuasion of argument.

This largely accounts for the fact that it was not until the middle of the nineteenth century that the real crisis broke and the Western tradition and metaphysic found itself openly and generally challenged. For it was not until the close of the first third of the last century that a new tool appeared, a new line of research opened. The revolution in historical studies was as great as that in the sciences of nature.

The success of the latter had masked from most people the great, maybe greater, effect on their lives of the historical revolution. The Church had claimed its right to supersede the older mysteries because it was referring not to mere "inspired wish and God-given hope of mankind." The Church based its claim on the fact that actual events, factual happenings in the world we know, had started its history and secured to it its overwhelming rights. And it was this very basis of its argument that had once made it victorious against the mystery religions, which now threatened to overthrow its supremacy.

For when the Church said, "Look at history for my claims," the Modern Age with the new lenses of historical research, looked. And it found not a simplex but a complex. The documentation was undoubtedly early and unquestionably referred to original evidence that brought the researcher down to the first century. But, and this of course was the heart of the issue: Were these documents on which the Church built its claims—that its avatar was a historical figure and had given it all the powers it claimed—in agreement with each other in building up the picture?

It was clear that the documentary evidence fell into two divisions. One included the Epistles, which worked up to the Church's full conclusions, together with the Fourth Gospel. The other included the other three Gospels, the two most decorative of which, Matthew and Luke, were clearly dependent for their historical narrative on the much shorter, less dramatic, less theological Mark.

The result of this conclusion we all know. There arose what is generally called liberal Christianity. This large loose school held that we must abide by Mark; all else is accretion, indeed superstition—a religion about Jesus, not the religion of Jesus. For it seemed clear to the liberal that Jesus was a teacher of righteousness—one of the prophets of social conscience and social reform. On him and his simple doctrine had been imposed the imposing but unhistorical trappings of the mystery god, the mysterious unhistoric being that is constructed of the fertility priest–king who is worshipped as the epitome of the fruit and harvest spirit and then sacrificed that a new crop may spring from his dead body. As for the actual history of Jesus himself—that was clear to the liberal Christian. He, gallant reformer, was inevitably killed when he attempted to bring to a sudden arrest—and without an army behind him—the clumsy gears of use and wont.

The issue seemed curiously clear to everyone: the choice was simple, the battle was joined. Either dogmas or documents! The conservatives held that the documents must be shown to agree with the dogmas. The progressives claimed that the dogmas must be shown to agree with the documents.

The issue, however, did not prove as final as had been supposed. Soon there arose a middle party with a new solution. These were the Modernists. They would accept the documents as seen in the light of historical criticism, but they would also cling to the tradition, to the dogmas. This was done largely by making a distinction. There was the historical Jesus and (largely [mistaken]) teacher who thought the world was coming to an end at which time he would become the messiah king of a new age, a fresh eon. But there was also the eternal Christ, the Second Person of the Trinity, [similar in concept to the Hindy deity] Vishnu the preserver. The Modernists offered this as their compromise to the Roman Church. Of course [the Church] refused it. The Pope of the day, Pius X, not being a capable statesperson but rather a simple fundamentalist, called the new offer of help a compendium of heresies.

But more than an accident of church politics accounts for the failure of Modernism to live up to its own chosen name assured its defeat. The whole thinking of the movement was preanthropological. It had [hardly] studied the psychology of peoples outside the assumptions and frame of mind of the Renaissance. For Modernism, therefore, there was only one alternative: either the story is true and shows a man without magic powers, or it tells about a miracle and is hence untrue.

That this simple Modernist dilemma was far too crude we can all now see. Carl Jung has pointed out that there are great mythoi, great patterns of social heredity—inherited notions that shape the cultures of peoples—making what we inaccurately call races. Further, we see that the ideals of these patterns have immensely influential shaping power on the lives of those who carry on in the tradition. We, generation after generation, tell the story; conversely the story also tells us, inspires us, categorically imperatives our lives and makes us quite different than we should be without it. Under the influence of the pattern, we do more than play a part. We become possessed by it. Our little private personality fuses and is cast in the vast feature of the race's ideal.

It has been said that it takes three generations to make an avatar incarnate. There is the preliminary generation of seekers [and] expecters—indicators of how the promise will be fulfilled and that the messenger of the covenant is at hand. Then there is the second generation, in which—the expectation having become intense and immediate—someone says, "I am he of whom it is written that he shall come!" And finally there comes the third generation during which the local, topical, and individual features are stylized away from the actual historical man, leaving a timeless figure to stand for millennia as the archetype of the race's pattern of prestige.

But though there is much truth in this analysis, we must guard against its blinding us to the fact that the actual historic figure need in no wise be such a simple structure. Today we realize that we cannot safely assume what will happen to that particular person who finds themselves in the path of the mythos at the time that this spirit is ready to incarnate. There seems to be no reason to suppose that there is any accident in history. The conjunction of the person who is prepared to be possessed, and the spirit that is ready to possess, is not due to chance. When therefore we have a "genius" of such quality ready and able to open themselves to inspiration of such force, why then should we suppose that the resulting "possessed person" should resemble the pattern of behavior of the times? Because we like looking at paintings or listening to a little good music, should then the artistic powers of Michelangelo or Beethoven or Bach be compared to those of our lesser selves?

An incarnation, therefore, should be a fact that as a matter of historical evidences we should not reject. Further, we can and should allow that an avatar is of necessity unique. It appears quite certain—it seems a fact of history—that there will never be another incarnation like that of Jesus of Nazareth. Why should there be? History does not repeat.

The redemptive spirit, the restorer, must throughout the time process take specific forms. In the Heroic Age, we see it as Rama and Hercules—the heroic deliverer. In the individualized periods of social conscience, private responsibility, and personal salvation, we see it as the Buddha figure of self-sacrifice. This culminates in the concept of the suffering servant incarnated finally as the crucified savior who, because personally they oppose the system into which they are born, is personally killed. And thus their death, because they are racially the incarnation of the mythos, becomes the symbol of redemptive love in its most dramatic form. What in Gautama the Buddha was mainly a teaching illustrated by a life is, in the Christ, a drama that has a teaching as its libretto. Now it has found its ultimate expression, and from then on it is that form that is seen in completely crystalized representation.

We see that each of the three great social heredities of humanity— the Mongolian, the Indian, and that of the Fertile Crescent which stretches from Palestine around the Syrian Desert to the Persian Gulf—each solved to a great extent one of the three problems that haunts humankind. The problem of [the individual] and society was more nearly solved by China than by the other two. The problem of people and their deeper layers of consciousness, [and] the problem of psychology—in that India has proved supreme. The problem of people and nature, and so of humans and death—that was the concern of the Fertile Crescent.

So from Egyptian religion, which gave rise to the mystery religions taken over by Greece and finally stylized by St. Paul as *the* mystery religion for Western peoples, [and] down to the Mass today—that is the concern of real Christianity, the essential catholicism.

Roughly speaking, we can say that China succeeded best with karma yoga, because its solution to the conflict of individuals and society has proved most successful. Second, we can say that India has been outstanding with its *jnana* techniques because of its profound and supreme analysis of consciousness. Third, the Fertile Crescent with the intense poignancy of its crucified savior has created the symbol with the strongest *bhakti* appeal.

Today each of these could recognize the value of the other two and so a true perennial praxis and universal religion could result. In such a world religion we could reverence and practice a full cult that would meet each of the three levels of our entire spiritual requirement. As there are four types of humans, and only in the highest are the other three consummated, so it may be that in one of these three actual praxes, peoples of different levels could find their fullest natural religious expression.

Yet as they did develop each its own vision to the utmost, and in charity with the others, it would find that its vision ended in a common all-embracing light beyond all form. The danger of past religions that arose from past avatars was their exclusiveness. The need of people today is an avatar who will teach that all roads lead to God. Back we come once more to the great universalist statement: all routes if earnestly followed point toward the highest.

What Vedanta Means to Me

Originally published in *Vedanta and the West*,
Vol. 14, No. 1, January–February 1951

"DEFINE YOUR TERMS," the reader will say, as they have a right to. For the phrase used above as a caption is, if not ambiguous, certainly double. It calls for both what I *mean* by Vedanta and also what Vedanta *does* for me. That is, what do I take Vedanta to be; and how for me does it seem to work?

Clearly then, I must take the first question first. The definition given in Vedantic literature seems to me satisfactory: the threefold statement that a person's nature is divine, that it is the aim of our life here on earth to unfold the divine nature within us, and that this basic truth is universal—that is, that every religion which has inspired humankind has been trying to state these facts. In short, Vedanta offers that system of thought and way of life for which people have been increasingly looking:—a universal religion in which could be combined all people of goodwill.

I think, too, I would and may add something to the above answer to the question of what does Vedanta mean. What makes it seem to me the best theory of and reaction to the whole is, in a phrase, that its span is commensurate with its grasp. That is to say, it is vastly tolerant, or to be more precise, charitable. And it is also precisionally free from sentiment. In it, kindness and truth are not in conflict. It secures these supreme values, these necessities of a universal religion, by its teaching that God is at once immanent and transcendent. To use a condensed technical term, it sees the problem of evil as arising from the problem of time, and the riddle of an objective world—which appears largely irrelevant—it perceives as an issue of epistemology. As a consequence, it is neither careless nor despairing about pain and sin. It neither says they are just accidents soon to be swept away by more accurate science, nor does it say that each individual makes their own world. Either alternative is seen as too simple.

Vedanta would allow that we have made this world as it seems to us, but it would also add that the "we" who make it are no more the various egos who think themselves the final units of consciousness than that "we" are the creator gods who in [regressive] myths are said to be the makers of the world. Vedanta, as far as I know, teaches that within time there is evil as ruthlessly real as time itself. But rise above time and there is no evil. All the great religions have of course taught that God is eternal—not everlasting, for that is to be extended in time. Therefore, He does not dispute with evil. But only the mystics have consistently taught that rising to union with Him is the one way in which that problem can be transcended; for only the transcendent and those who are united in the unity of the One are beyond evil. To say that evil does not exist and still to desire the appetites, love possessions, and claim recognition is to demonstrate ignorance, not transcendence.

Vedanta is then cosmologically satisfactory. It shows that what we call evil is a [misconception], but it is a [misconception] more real because [it is] more persistent than that of the hypnotized patient whose skin swells into a painful blister when they are told that the cold penny let drop on their flesh was "really" red-hot.

Of course one great religion, Buddhism, which sprang from Vedanta, criticized its parent for having *any* cosmology. Buddhism treated systems of metaphysics as fetters. But that Vedanta's minimum was and is necessary has been proved by four things.

First, Buddhism split on this issue and the Mahayana built up a metaphysic as vast if not vaster than Vedanta's.

Second, the Pali, "Southern" school, rejecting all metaphysic, tried to operate with nothing but a psychology. As a consequence, it has always been in danger of forging an instrument that could be used for bad quite as much as for good purposes. The most striking illustration of this is given by the development of Mahayana in Japan where the Zen teachers, anxious to rid themselves of the vast ritual and speculation of the late Mahayana [period], again tried to reduce Buddhism to an empiric psychology, and made from many Zen initiates perfect instruments for the fanatic nationalism that brought Japan to defeat. In the meantime, in the Ceylonic schools we can say the doctrine of holy selfishness—a phrase coined by St. Jerome—was preached with a grim logical frankness. For where there is no doctrine of grace and no clear teaching as to what the enlightened state is and its relation is to the needs of others, then it is impossible to regard compassion as other than, in Dr. William Ernest Hocking's phrase, the "noble inconsistency" in the Noble path.

Third, Buddhism had for some time no message for the layperson and could not have. When it did, it was committed to what it accepted as, and what in the West has been called, the doctrine of the two lives, lay and monastic. Inevitably also, as was the West, it became committed to a doctrine of *four* lives: that of the simple active, who can keep no more than the code of justice and avoid wanton cruelty; that of the just merchant; that of the chivalrous knight; and that of the specifically "religious," who was to aim at the law of charity.

Fourth and finally, Vedanta not only originally taught that there were four lives—that is, four kinds of humans incarnate—but Vedanta was as rich laterally as it was longitudinally. It had not only four stations for various types of people on the ladder of being; it had parallel places for those who might be similarly advanced—of equal spirituality—but needing different methods to help them to the final liberation and enlightenment. All religions lead to God and all converge on that final God—quite true—but till late on the path, people of great goodness may need to use different methods. This fact has often led to bitter intolerance, with ritualists persecuting those who were unhelped by its dramatic forms, [and] non-ritualists treating as abominable idolators those who used images. Vedanta has avoided this danger also.

It would seem then that in Vedanta—once its universalism is understood—must lie the religion of humankind. As it moves over the world, it will tend to express its eternal and universal truth in the vernacular of the era in which it is conveying its message.

These, then, very briefly seem to be some of the main reasons why one may believe that Vedanta, with its interpretive charity toward the other great faiths, may become the spiritual spokesperson for humankind.

And now as to the further question: What does Vedanta do for a particular experiment and experimenter? There one may say that its particular blend of empiricism with metaphysic, the width of its cosmology, the vastness of the picture that it gives of human destiny, and the immediate practicalness of its advices and practices—this amalgam seems most suitable to anyone who wants a method which is psychological and a worldview that can match modern knowledge of the cosmos.

The knife-edge in this respect runs between a faith that is rightly urgent and a knowledge that is vastly patient. In Vedanta there is what may be called "the choice of [fates]": a nonhuman birth; a repeated human birth that is bad, fair, or good; gradual postmortem enlightenment through passing through the *brahmaloka*; enlightenment at the moment of death; and enlightenment while still in the body. This richness of choice makes for neither panic nor for slackness. Many religions have sought to produce urgency by teaching the irrevocable finality of the choice made here, and even the choice at the moment of death. As a matter of actual experience, this attitude too often leads to either despair or carelessness, the very things the teaching attempts to oppose and cure.

Vedanta does not neglect the importance of the death moment, but it teaches that you will not be able to avail yourself of that moment's full power of choice unless all your life you have been preparing for it, and also, that though the moment of death decides the course of the soul—maybe for an immense period—yet nothing is irrevocable but the final end of the story, to which all must come sooner or later—union with the One.

This doctrine then is neither slack nor does it make an offense against the moral law and the concept of compassion as to the nature of the universe. An eternal hell, whether it frightens a few people into panic behavior or not, is one which is metaphysically [and] theologically impermissible. For its existence means that God has been defeated for good and all by some part of His creation. ... No thinking person can entertain a proposition that is so absurd.

The other knife-edge that Vedanta seems to travel is between the opposed dangers of a doctrine of grace that removes all need for self-effort and one that teaches that there is no worker but yourself; you save yourself or no one can. This, again, of course, dates from an inadequate psychology that thought of the individual as the one irreducible and unexpandable unit of consciousness. [Ramakrishna's] teaching that the wind of grace is always blowing, but you must raise—and keep raised—your sail, is the only doctrine that in East or West has ever made complete saints, people who achieved entire wholeness. It does more; it also gives the first insight into the doctrine of karma, a doctrine that we must now remember is being forced on Western peoples, not by religion but by genetics—that we are born with a fate that we can modify but never disregard and indeed can modify only insofar as we accept it.

If we are really all much more members and parts of each other than the Renaissance conception of individualism thought, then Vedanta is not only more scientific than the Renaissance outlook, [but] it also offers a way of life more truthful and at the same time more practical. Human nature can be changed, once we realize what human nature is. And the person who changes themselves *is* actually changing others. Private salvation is a contradiction in terms. For we are saved from isolation, privacy, [and] egotism into the One who embraces all.

Human nature—that phrase leads to two further points which appear as important definitions of Vedanta, showing how it balances between "life rejection" and "life acceptance," between despairing pessimism and unsubstantiated optimism. Western asceticism has tended to take that aspect of mortification which regards the body as a foul prison—this "vile body," as the English translators rendered St. Paul's phrase—and this life as a vale of never-ceasing tears. The *Theologia Germanica*, following this tradition, says that Christ never had a moment's joy in his whole life, a remark that the Gospels would certainly seem to deny. Luther refers to the body as nothing but a sack of worms. Later Protestantism, reacting from this, whirled around and has tended to say that the body should, with rational hygiene and giving it its [primacy] as far as the appetites are concerned, become a lasting delight. Likewise the world, properly tidied, should prove a paradise.

Vedanta teaches that the body is invaluable and must most carefully be kept in health, because—and only because—it alone can be the egg in which the soul may hatch. Likewise the world, [as] it, too, is the shell of that egg in which we hatch. And the further we advance in growth the more we shall be able to see that this world appears as a heaven to the person, but only to them, whose body and mind have become truly translucent. To them this experience of time and grace is as God sees it—nirvana: the state beyond all conflict and separateness.

Vedanta, then, in regard to the physical body and the temporal world, finds the true attitude and balance. This is a middle world in which we are embryos, tadpoles of eternity. Heraclitus' phrase, "Here we are as in an egg," may be taken as a good definition of our physical condition and what we should do about it. We may define our environment in that saying of Jesus preserved for us, not by the Western canon, but by the Indian emperor Akbar when he had carved over the capital he deserted as soon as it had been built: "Said Jesus, may his name be blessed, 'This world is a bridge; pass over it, but build no house upon it.'"

Such then seem to be very briefly the reasons, general and personal, philosophic and empiric, for our [both] availing ourselves of all that Vedanta can teach us, and striving to practice it. For so only may we really learn to understand ourselves and become at length mobilized for the rightful service of others. The actual terminology in which such a system of thought and action is conveyed must always be modulated to the place and time in which it is being conveyed. Vedanta is so ancient that we can see it doing this throughout the ages. And because of this, we can perceive the essential and unchanging under the topical and can now at present see that here and now, by its present teachers and practicers, it is growing for itself the instruments of expression and practice whereby it may speak in the vernacular of our contemporary lives to Western people.

Effort or Non-Effort?

Originally published in *Vedanta and the West*,
Vol. 14, No. 4, July–August 1951

BESIDES A PERENNIAL PHILOSOPHY, religion has perennial controversies. Of these, none is more provocative of misunderstanding, and therefore of schisms, than the two schools of Effort and Non-Effort. This universal dispute ranges all over the world and as far back as we can find people wishing to argue and wanting to question. The cry of Isaiah that everyone who thirsteth should come drink "without money and without price" [Isaiah 55:1], may well be a protest against salvation being sold for cash, but it does not mean that enlightenment and liberation are to be gotten without cost.

That, then, is the first distinction we have to make. It is true that your pecuniary resources cannot buy you freedom. But it is not true to say that sacrifice on your part has nothing to do with liberation. As Gandhi kept saying to Vincent Sheean (as reported in the latter's *Lead, Kindly Light*), "Renunciation first! Without that there is no enlightenment!"

The next turn which the controversy seems to have taken is one that we usually associate with Pali Buddhism, although it is probably worldwide. The favorite quotation of the Southern school from the words of the Blessed One was generally rendered [as follows]: "Be ye lights to yourselves." So it was construed to mean the doctrine of self-salvation. It is now, however, allowed that the real meaning of the phrase is [this]: "Let the [higher] Self (the Atman) be the guide of the [lower] self (the *jiva*)"—a doctrine close to that of the Inner Light as taught by the Society of Friends. The former rendering of "Be ye lights to yourselves" has, however, been the accepted one for millennia in the Theravadin schools, and as it was often called the doctrine of self-effort, it did excite countercriticism. For very soon, people discovered that principle which in this century the French psychologist Charles Baudouin aptly named the law of reversed effort. The more you strove the more stubborn became the inner resistance. Gradually it was discovered that practically everything that you commanded with your surface will, your deep directive powers refused to do. Indeed, they often did the reverse. If you ordered yourself to sleep, you lay painfully awake. The doctor said, "Keep your eye open." You tried to obey, but your eye shut. "Put down your tongue." It rose and closed your throat. "Swallow." You choked. "Relax." Your muscles tensed.

The obvious answer to this dilemma has also been given its slogan in this century: "Leave your mind alone." You can upset your digestion, your breathing, [and] your heartbeat by thinking about them. So just distract yourself and all will go well. Lounge about and life will lunge you on. Ruysbroeck—perhaps the greatest of the Northern European mystics—met this sophistry in his early life. The Brethren of the Free Spirit and their successors, the Beghards, opposed all effort and all restraint and made a lot of scandalous noise wandering about, indulging their appetites, squabbling incessantly in the name of effortless peace, and refusing to work. For, as a matter of interesting fact, few Quietists are quiet. Indeed, the most literarily famous, Madame Guyon, who aptly called her spates of automatic writing "torrents," reminds one of Lord Morley's comment on Carlyle's incessantly self-advertised taciturnity: "Mr. Carlyle has succeeded in eighteen stout volumes in compressing his doctrine of silence." Even Molinos, the master Quietist, left behind him after a few years of teaching many thousands of letters, as well as a book or two.

This volubility about the unspeakable certainly suggests that here is a problem far more complex than Quietists allowed. And certainly a way has been found between the horns of the dilemma of "swim and you get cramps; don't swim and you drown." Today we have begun to be able to map the matter in modern terms. The technique, however, has been known at least since primitive Buddhism. Gautama himself is said to have ruled, "Even with knowledge of the law, without *dhyana* there can be no enlightenment." What is dhyana? In modern terms it is the method of getting in touch with the thalamus, the midbrain: the seat of the will and the emotions.

When, in the middle of the eighteenth century, what had called itself the Age of Reason began to turn into the Romantic Age, it was because such different authorities as Rousseau and Wesley agreed that reason might manage the outer world but not the inner. Rousseau said, "Go back to your primitive nature." Wesley taught how to shatter, at least temporarily, [a person's] addictions by an emotional explosion from [their] subconscious. Methodical techniques that worked well enough with nature, the Romantics urged, couldn't work with human nature. This defeat, however, has not endured. Method does work. Skilled effort can and must be made. Training is possible and essential. What Grantly Dick-Read has shown in childbirth and J. A. D. McCurdy in training air pilots (these detailed and particular methods are specific illustrations of thalamus training)—the way, the only way, to speak to the deep will, [and] the way to avoid the frustration of "the more I strive, the less I achieve." The "I" that has to be mobilized is more than the ego.

There may be considerable differences in the procedures. They have, however, all of them, this common element: the deep mind is not saved, not even stirred, by the smart syllogism, nor is it open to any sort of rational argument. It is by constant repetition that it learns, as we say, by heart. Ritual is then the way for some. The rite is a para-rational demonstration to the total attention of the superconscious state. Discrimination helps others through the *via negativa*.

The commonest way, however, has been by *japam*—by the *mantra*, the "song word." This is the way so tellingly demonstrated by the anonymous intellectual, the author of *The Cloud of Unknowing*. From the Greek Church we have lately learned of the popularity of the same method. In *The Way of the Pilgrim* and *The Pilgrim Continues His Way*, now available in a combined volume worth our attention, we have a nineteenth-century account of the technique of constant rep-etition kept going at the reverie level until the rhythm becomes autonomous.

How and when does this happen? And what are the results? [The achievement of this state] certainly requires constant skilled effort. The "word" is fed into the stream of the reverie "at the back of the mind" whenever the surface mind becomes aware that the beat has stopped. (The best times for doing this are, of course, when waking or going to sleep, and in the small hours of the night. Anyone who so practices will cease to complain of insomnia.) The more time given to this exercise—which is really not so difficult but is, what we really fear far more, dull—the sooner the time comes when the reverie level accepts and makes the word its own. The mind becomes con-tent to keep to the one idea.

Such complete automatizing generally takes, for the person in the world, some years of skilled feeding, and unless the sleep times are used, it would probably take much longer. The result is prayer without ceasing and without effort.

There is nothing odd or strained about such practice. At base it is of course the method that all artists have always used in their training. The confusion that we have fallen into when we would apply such effort to the whole art of living, to the wholly religious life, seems to be due partly to a semantic confusion. By effort we too often mean strain, and conversely, we use the word "relax" (that is to say, let down) when we should use the word "release" (i.e., going forward, letting free). For we are not, if we have any idea of the life process and the meaning of having a human body, aiming at returning our-selves or anyone else to a "norm." This life to anyone who thinks searchingly cannot be considered as other than a growth, a prenatal condition.

Effort must be strenuous; it is not debilitating. Everyone who even takes walking exercise knows that there is an optimum stretch that builds up muscle more than the exertion breaks it down. With effort there is always atrophy. Further, when there is a goal worth the striving, fatigue, we know, can be indefinitely postponed. Bore-dom and exhaustion come because the goal does not seem worth the price. Attention is humankind's supreme power, and attention means tension towards. [But] there is a right tension. Between the relaxed state—which in musical and feeling–tone terms is flat—and the tense state—which in musical and feeling–tone terms is sharp—there is the tonic condition, the ideal tone of attention. The great art critic, Roger Fry, coined the useful phrase "alert passivity" for the state of mind with which we should confront a work of art that challenges our former complacency. In the religious life, this alert passivity is the state wherein the soul waits. The song word, the mantra, is the incessant knocking, the sounding with which the soul echo-sounds [pings] the deep ocean floors of the spirit.

Continue, and after some years we hear the counter-knocking, the reply wave. We are being answered. Seek and we do find that door. Knock and that door does open. Ask and what we most need is given.

But we must treat the ultimate judge of our sincerity as though it were a corrupt judge only to be stirred to action by our intolerable importunity. For such is our basic dishonest laziness, until we can rouse in ourselves such attention [that] we really do not want that for which we pretend to ask. Only when our persistence is so great that we have ceased to care how long we have to go on asking, only then can the gift be given. "*Only* as many lives as there are leaves on this vast tree, and then I *shall* see Him!" Only then, when we can say that, will the time be over and we hear, "No, child; in this life you shall see Me."

It is worthwhile. All the cost is as nothing. But to say that it does not cost every ounce of effort of which the soul is able, can only be said by one who has no real notion either of the process or of the prize.

Kindness

Originally published in *Vedanta and the West*,
Vol. 14, No. 6, November–December 1951

WHY SHOULD WE THINK about kindness? Surely it is obvious, basic, and easy. Talking and thinking about such great, sane common-places as kindness simply spoils them. Just go ahead and be kind! Everything then will work out. Why make what is clear all muddled by discussion? We make things difficult by definitions and devices.

That is what the practical person often says. That is what they have against religion. It makes things complex, elaborate, technical. As for them, they are content to be straightforward and direct. *Just be kind.*

But the trouble with the word "kind" is that it is no longer sim-ple. Even when it seemed simple, it was paradoxically double. It is only when it is vague that it seems to be easy. When it is definite it is difficult. The word by gross overuse in careless hands has become a dangerously blunted term. Blunt words are more dangerous than sharp knives because they lead to deadly misunderstandings. The word "kind" is difficult because it is precise. It means "*kin*—of the same sort."

When we tried to make a science of life, the first thing we had to do was to distinguish the different sorts of life. The first division is into species. "Species" is the Latin word for *kin* and *kind*. Species means those groups that can breed with each other because they are kin, and won't breed with any of the other species because they are not kin.

Turn from science and biology to humans and history. We see the same thing. Kindness does exist very definitely—in the exact sense of the word "definitely." Small, intense centers of devoted kindness are always breaking out and building up. Most people are passionately kind and loyal to their family, town, clan, and tribe. They are less kind to nations, less again to empires. Small communities have lasted for millennia, nations for centuries, empires for generations. Sometimes the biggest empires last only for decades. The bigger the area the weaker the kindness. Naturally, inevitably, the range of the senses is the limit of the emotions. As humans grow in power but not in self-knowledge, they deny this fact. Instead of cities squabbling, nations campaigning, and empires grappling, we have ideologies mutually annihilating. Crusades pour [forth], which are the most widespread and cruel of wars. For now, to my natural dislike of and non-kinship with strangers, I [am determined] to make them similar to me, to convert them. Once we said frankly: "Go away. I don't like you." Now we say: "I'm coming after you to alter you until you're similar to me." Naturally, we meet with a warm reception!

This determination to like humanity lets hell loose. There's the devil to pay, and he alone gets paid. To say you love humanity in this way is tantamount to saying you are prepared to massacre humanity. For hell has one fury more hellish "than a woman scorned," and that is a missionary rebuffed. After each ideological crusade, after each determination to be so kind to all that I will have a right to alter them until they are so like me [that] they like me, there is a reaction.

The last patcher-up of peace after the last crusade of crusading kindness was Talleyrand. After the ideological explosion of the French Revolution, this lame old realist, in whose long and devious life Napoleon himself was only an episode, was given the task of making people live together. They had shown they could not like each other in a state of equality nor even endure being under one efficient master. As he built up the diplomatic corps (that more or less kept European anarchy from becoming wholly homicidal for a hundred years), the old teacher's first advice was: *pas de zele*—above all, no enthusiasm. Learn that people are not lovable and not kindly, any more than you are. Be moderate in your hopes. Give people what they want. Understand what they need.

First ... [a private romance that includes sex] is a person's first need. Without a private romance, a person may start a public conflagration just because they are bored. Next, for sex itself cannot be relied on wholly to satisfy people, give them food. "Eating," said [a] great anthropologist, "is the only pleasure that can be practiced three times a day, and with care can be made to last each time an hour." So the master diplomat won Europe a reprieve of three generations. Then once again the deluge of crusading kindness flushed out the quiet and stagnant pools of culture.

And now, what of the morrow? Well, of course humans are far tougher than we thought. I am using the word "tough" in its precise sense. We can endure frightfully rough handling that would make a tiger lose its nerve and a python schizophrenic. The periodic cloudburst of emotional crusading is nearly over. The dictators have had their day. We can hear at the door the limping tread, the tap of the ebony cane of the old diplomatist. Is that then the invariable third act of our ever-recurring tragicomedy and Grand Guignol farce? It will be, if we won't understand kindness, for verily "the children of this world are in their generation wiser than the children of light" [Luke 16:8]. What is wrong with our kindness, and is kindness, like patriotism, not enough?

Kindness is enough; love is the fulfillment of the law. But it must be real kindness. And ours has not been. Our kindness has a little realism in it as far as it goes, as far as it is natural—but that is not very far either in area or in time. We are kind to those with whom we are really kin.

To start at the foot of the ladder, many mothers love their children. This is right and good as far as it goes. But it doesn't go very far. It is animal love, and animal love is wonderful as long as the young want it. Then it ceases. But we humans will have nothing of the sort. Why? Because our love is an alloy. It is one-third real devotion and loss of self in a cause larger than self. But it is two-thirds prestige-building and self-seeking. Motherhood is a prestige part. Crusades command crammed cradles. Women want to have children, because [it is falsely assumed that] to be childless is to lack a certain tassel of social dignity. But, further, even that is not enough for us. The mother, having demanded of the community that she shall be praised for following the animal pattern of her nature, requires also that the child shall pension her for the honor she has done it.

Now, this [kind of thinking] is dangerous nonsense, as dangerous as any crusade of kindness. As Dr. Ian Suttie has pointed out in his important book, *The Origins of Love and Hate*, the relationship between child and mother is one of symbiosis—they are a joint organism and each gets intense pleasure from being in play with the other. That can't last, but when it is over you cannot send in a bill to nature or to society because of your self-sacrifice in performing an instinctive pattern. As well, might one who had dined well ask their host to pay them for having undergone the biological task of taking nourishment. A person who falls in love is not deserving of payment for their self-sacrifice.

Our kindness then starts as, and for a little time is, real kindness, kin, liking. Then it gives out and we cheat. Our kindness then is sham. It is cupidity because it wants to be treated as an exceptional benefactor instead of as one who has already been well paid as an equal and a partner. "Verily I say unto you, they have their reward." To ask to be paid twice for one small service is to be not kind, but a ruiner of common kindness—a cheat. So from the parents that are always talking of the ingratitude of their children, to the politicians who are always talking of the ingratitude of democracy, we view the hypocritic front of humanity. Our kindness is doubly false. It is pride, and therefore it has no sense of kinship for people that it says it loves and serves. But it is not too proud to be also fraudulent. It wants to be thought dignified, but it stoops to scrounge a fee for the exercise of its own indulgencies. Can it be wondered that such a synthetic thing, such a corrupt alloy, crumbles and breaks? It is thoroughly adulterated.

What then are we to do about it? Honesty is the first step. We must see ourselves as we are. That will lead to humility, and humility will bring us down to the threshold of kindness. We shall no longer feel superior to others and so wish to patronize them or desire to be praised for our selflessness and paid for our self-sacrifice. Kindness, of course, is its own reward; and if it isn't, it isn't kindness. Nature has provided throughout that we shall be paid for our natural kindness. [Nature] has a grim way with those who send in a fraudulent account for payment already received.

But are we then to remain at simple animal level, basic brute justice? The tormented Medea, finding herself trapped and all her animal passions set against one another by her betrayal, cries: "I have learnt one thing, to be a true friend to those who befriend me and to be terrible to those who betray." That, of course, is the old law: "Thou shalt love thy friend and hate thine enemy" [Matt. 5:43].

But we cannot go on like that. What are we to do? The outlook is not too bleak. We are learning. We are taking the first step in anthropology. We have found that the first step is to be interested in those who are different. We want to learn from them before we attempt to teach. Now, that is real kindness. Because we start on their level, as kin. We can only teach those from whom we can learn, for only thus can they learn from us.

The second great step in anthropology is to turn that same uncensoring interest on ourselves. Being arrogant and *un*kin (unkind), we assumed all the others were superstitious, ignorant, contemptible. We alone were reasonable, sensible, informed, and right. We turned a corner when the Lynds made their classic study of Middletown.[71] That was the first time that unkind, arrogant, modern people turned the camera on themselves. When we are truly kin with our own selves, we can then begin to be kind to others.

"But" say the impatient hot-gospellers and the communists, who, instead of being in common with all, are always excluding somebody, purging somebody, liquidating somebody. "But you wish to keep us at the animal level. Even if your method worked, it would take centuries before this slow osmosis of kindness could percolate through humanity. It takes too long to understand people. We must be cruel to be kind." And then, because we seem so low and animal in our modest aims, many of them will suddenly quote: "Be ye therefore perfect, even as your Father which is in heaven is perfect" for He is kind. Precisely. And when we quote scriptures, we must not play the devil's trick by leaving out the latter half of the quotation.

Why is He unlimited? Because He is kind to the just and the unjust, the evil and the good.

Now this won't do at all for the hot-gospeller. God must take sides. He must be with *our* crusade. Hence, the pathetic nonsense of saying that if God doesn't suffer, then He is no God for me. This phrase always has as its corollary: if He doesn't win this war, then I'm done with Him. But if He is kind to the just and the unjust, that is because, being so unlimited, He does not belong to one chosen people or one particular species. He is kind to the tapeworm as He is to the baby that to the tapeworm is its lovely warm home. Naturally, people want to force their kindness, their sense of right, their idea of happiness, their belief as to what the end of the universe is— naturally, such people resent and are horrified by such kindness. They don't want to be kin even with their fellow humans who happen to think not quite as they think. To be kin with a parasite they consider treason to life!

But if the end of the universe is really to set all life free, if the only way to do that is [with] an infinite patience and an infinite interest, then God's way after all may not be so abominably indifferent, inhuman, [or] alien. On the contrary, it may be because He is so much closer to the evil, the failure, and the perverse, that He sees [these] with a deeper compassion and a greater hope for its possibilities than we can perceive.

Kindness, then, we see is a gigantic mystery. It is part of the mystery of suffering and of sin, of evil and depravity. And we ourselves, little, odd, self-tortured, unkind atoms, are slowly migrating from animal kindness that serves the purpose of life and takes its wages of animal happiness, and are migrating slowly to God and to the God's-eye view, for which the Latin word is *contemplation* and the Greek word is *theory*: the power to see all things from the standpoint of eternity.

We may judge then our kindness as to how far our interest grows in others—not merely tolerance, but a real wonder as to why this is so and why [they] should so behave. That is the wonder of which Plato speaks when he says, "By wonder are we saved"—from our narrow unkindness, saved from our narrow glib assumption that we know and have a right to manage.

That, too, is the compassion, the high compassion of which Buddhism speaks, the high compassion that has gone beyond heartbreak and far beyond righteous anger. That compassion never takes sides any more than God takes sides. That compassion is the mark of one who has understood, who is enlightened and sees that all is very good, who is liberated and so works incessantly for the liberation of everything that still can suffer from this ignorance.

When we attain that, then and then only shall we be able, through the temporary freedom that we will grant them, through our humility and patience, to bring all humanity and all life to that eternal freedom to which we have attained. At last, we shall be kind to the just and the unjust, to the evil and the good, because at last we are perfect; we are unlimited as our Father in heaven is perfect—infinitely kind, unlimited.

Fun

Originally published in *Vedanta and the West*,
Vol. 15, No. 5, September–October 1952

Fun—surely that is an extravagant, outré subject for a dignified journal! But, as a matter of fact, whenever religion really works—when suddenly the unseen manifests in the seen; when what we call a miracle takes place; when a saint as a byproduct produces "psychic phenomena"; or an alcoholic suddenly is inspired to stop drinking—we generally say "funny" and we *don't* smile.

This common, [ordinary] word has then two senses: an exoteric laughing sense, and another, a hidden, esoteric dark sense, the sense of the uncanny. Such a word is therefore worth examining, for how can two such opposites as the uncanny and healthy share the same short noun?

But tight, monosyllabic Saxon words are hard to break up. We had better first look at its cousins, its possible synonyms. "Play" is surely the likeliest. We say something is "in fun" or "only in play." This word "play" has been worked hard, giving rise to at least three highly illustrative meanings. Let us start with the most exact and see where play comes in with the simplest, most familiar of our associates—the machine.

We say if a machine has no play it will seize, its bearings will not endure such total lack of freedom. If a machine is to work, it must have play. Second, turn to animals. Life is a serious hand-to-mouth business for all of them. Yet here, too, play is absolutely necessary. The importance of play for young beasts has been exhaustively proved. An overplus proof has resulted also. The play of the animal is not merely exercise to attain the perfectly automatic, utilitarian action. It is also explanatory, the expression of a reaching-out beyond the closed circle of use. Third, human society has to employ play. Despite all laws, something has to be left to the far freer, less definable rules of the game. Society, when most civilized, is a game rather than a business. Hence, we speak of fair play and foul play, freedom used for cooperation or for assault. Indeed, all richly creative activity is play, so we speak rightly of the playing of an orchestra and of the play of minds in conversation.

If play therefore is found as the growing edge of all development, may not the word "fun" prove as rich? Fun is the atmosphere and feeling–tone of play. Certainly this tight little bud-word, this three-lettered monosyllable, when let expand, shows a number of petals. For "fun" is first of all *Fahne*, the "banner" waved, the gallant eccentricity. And the word expands still further from *Fahne* to "vane," which is the sheen wing of the butterfly or the weathercock that gives first warning of a shift in the wind. This lightness is not frivolity or irresponsibility, but that sensitiveness to delicate forces, that penetration to profound tides, that awareness of [what]

> The world's coarse thumb
> And finger failed to plumb.[72]

Fun avoids the narrow dogma of reason and use. It is different, too, from wit. Wit is intelligence. Wit will so condense, so streamline, and so point its penetration that down its clean, lean shaft we may all pierce to the heart of the matter. Well enough. But that is only half the truth and may be not the better. For knowledge depends on width as well as depth. The superficial is not necessarily the unsatisfactory, provided it is sufficiently wide. Wit is something that strives to gain insight by being detached, objective, above the battle, with the God's-eye view. But consequently, there is about it

206

something of the pretentious. For can we ever take that station of eternity? Are we not indeed nearer to it when we own what von Hügel calls our creatureliness? Can we ever step out of our skins, cease to be provincial, become sophisticate citizen–cosmopolites of the universe? Of course we cannot, and we are least ridiculous when we most realize our absurdity.

Next, humor, the gentle idiosyncrasy of "fun," is the recognition that we can really never be great universal wits seeing all people with monumental, colorless detachment. Our objectivity consists in recognizing our own private and personal subjectivity. Seeing our own peculiarity, we see ourselves with detachment. Your point of view is your uniqueness and sincerity. Thus and so, at that hour and place, through this lens and prism it was revealed and [understood]. So seen, the vision of the least is in that degree everlastingly authentic. You with your honest humor, in your particular eccentricity, you are one of the myriad million lenses of consciousness through which "He who sees all yet has no eyes" directly [perceives] and delights in His mirroring universe.

And that thought, that reflection on why humorous fun so often has darted higher and deeper on its iridescent vanes than has the arrow of wit, brings us to fun's vocalization—laughter. Wit sometimes smiles, but the smile is generally frozen because of the great height of superiority at which it spreads: an ice cloud where the air is so rare that it is supersonic, and not even a chuckle can be heard. But humorous fun laughs shamelessly, not abashed at being obvious but delighted that so many common things, rather than appearing banal, seem funny. Things do not have to be tragic or majestic to interest the humorous. Their humility provides that they are not easily bored and very easily amused. The silliest joke makes them chuckle.

But this is undignified, unworthy, we say. It is here we touch upon what is perhaps the West's profoundest weakness. The fear of ridicule may not seem a very serious fault. Some Jesuit casuists ruled that a slight on a man's name was as grave as severe physical injury. The importance we attach to our personal selves and its dignity is morbid. We know it [matures] when people wish to be independent, solemn, respected figures. And, when they fail, they cannot laugh at themselves. They comfort themselves by believing they are tragic.

Now we know that tragedy in art, mechanism in science, and puritanism in morality all emerge at the same time. They are, in fact, three aspects of the same constriction—the sudden sense of being a private, lonely person in an alien universe. This constriction takes place when comedy dies. The sense of sin, especially [in] the sense of sex, becomes dominant, with the universe conceived as a system of inflexible law. Now God becomes so inflexible that at length He is turned into a machine.

This, however, never happened in the East. There, the gallant hero–*avatar* performs, as with Rama, great labors, but he does not become a tragic failure. With Krishna, it is the same. As shepherd boy or as charioteer in battle, he is never tragic. Prometheus and the "suffering servant" seem both to stem from the concept of the prophet who is so convinced that he is right that he can believe what is certainly hardly ever true: "They hated me without a cause" [John 15:25].

Somehow, the West became dominated by the nomad–seer. This person, coming from the desert, always simplifies their [own] problem. They have the solemnity of mind that never doubts they are wholly right. So they persecute those who differ from themselves. The persecuting religions, tolerating no sect but their own, all seem to come from the desert or steppe. As long as this humorless prophet can persecute, they are sure they are right. When they are checked, they believe that the universe is a place of tragedy: truth cannot prevail; the whole world is the kingdom of Satan; the righteous always perish. This is untrue. The truth is kindlier, but it laughs at the fanatic. It says: "If you persecute others, they will persecute you. If you cannot learn from others, why should they learn from you? If you cannot laugh at yourself, you will find it [such] an intolerable insult and a mysterious tragedy that others will find you comic."

We can see then that comedy and its fun are very important. Without fun we are always falling into that stiffness which soon can become the rigor of insanity. The masklike face is the surest symptom of oncoming mental trouble. Today, then, we should welcome the return of fun. Tragedy is ended, and we are waiting for the return of the new comedy, metacomedy. Mechanism has gone out of science, and the puritan has failed to impose their narrow, repressed, persecuting morality. Tragedy may give a partial catharsis of tears but, providentially, tears are really never dignified. For a real cathartic "cry"—not the glycerin dewdrops of cine–fairyland—ends, everyone knows, only in hiccups and a swollen face. It is a form of intoxication.

Comedy does far better. Laughter can produce tears, but it also produces the general massage that makes the sides ache. It is then, when we laugh, that we have sudden insight into a central knowledge. That is why Hobbes calls laughter a "sudden glory." Of course there are two laughters: the dissipating and the culminating. The dissipating restores our assurance. The child suddenly perceives that the glaring, fiery monster is only a pumpkin with a candle in it. That is something, but culminating laughter is real revelation. Suddenly we see that the whole picture of things—the banal, the squalid, the futile, and the tragic: this is not incoherence. But neither is it rational coherence. We are past the horns of the puritan's dilemma: this must be useful or useless, meaningful or nonsense. It is neither and both. "What does it mean?" The answer is the sudden glory of laughter. If you laugh you see; if you do not, no reasonable argument will give you the vision, the delight, and the liberation. You remain like that British pillar of salt, Queen Victoria, unmoved, "unamused."

But when the huge frame of things, the vast *maya*, begins to appear as the Divine Comedy, then we see the answer cannot be sound sense and, when we cannot extract that from it, tragic. The maya is not unreal, nor outrageous, nor "sensible." It is *lila*, the dance of God. In that whirl of creation, at that tremendous tempo, the opera, which if played at our petty pace becomes a funeral dirge, now becomes cosmic comedy. In the terrific figure of [the Hindu god] Shiva, we have a dynamic, united concept against the static arrest of unyielding, anguished Prometheus on his rock and inflexible, angry Zeus on his throne. Our age, which has broken out of mechanism, realizes that the universe is best conceived of as a dance, the play of life best conceived as comedy, and morality as that abandonment of the pathetic pride that clings to its arthritic dignity. If the harlot and the huckster go into the kingdom before the dignified scribe and Pharisee, surely we may say that heaven is not far from the clown and the buffoon who have found liberation by the loss of dignity and the way to enlightenment by the mystery of fun.

Pain

Originally published in *Vedanta and the West*,
Vol. 16, No. 1, January–February 1953

To MOST PEOPLE it seems defeatist to talk about pain. For pain is not modern. It is a hangover from an unhygienic age when humankind's helplessness compelled it to make a virtue of necessity. Pain is a most un-American activity. The American Way and United States "know-how" should soon get rid of its last traces!

This hope is not confined to this continent. Europe has entertained such hopes. In 1929, one of the British King's physicians told [this] writer that in another thirty years, cancer—public enemy number-one—would have ceased to be a killer. That same year Professor J. B. S. Haldane, a great physiologist, said that such was the growth of neurological knowledge that, in this generation, pain would come completely under medical control. We do not need to ask: Have such well-informed prophets seen their vision fulfilled? We do need to ask: Why, with all their knowledge and skill, has the promise not been kept? The answer seems to be in that law which Emerson made famous, a law of life that appears to be even less easy to avoid than the principle of entropy, namely the law of compensation.

Life is a balance. Consciousness itself seems to spring from contrast. In the fairy story of the crumpled rose petal, the princess sought comfort, the comfort not of strength but of ease through insulation. But of necessity, her nervous system adjusted to the condition. Her sensitiveness proportionately increased as the number of feather mattresses was added. At last she had achieved such exquisite sensibility that she could be kept awake all night because below the lowest mattress a careless bedmaker had neglected to notice there lay a crumpled rose petal. Must we then resign ourselves to sitting on one horn or another of the painful dilemma: resign yourself to becoming a tough; anesthetize your hand and heart by plucking nettles; be a pachydermatous pugilist; or else keep up the drug dose until not only can you feel no more, [but] you are conscious no more?

Certainly if we don't think about this problem, these seem the only alternatives, and life will force us to take one or the other. But if you don't shun pain or assume that it must be wrong and must be bundled out of the way as a thing that is as useless as it is unpleasant, then we may find out not merely how to face it but how to make it profitable. People have never really wanted to think out pain. But that seems the only way of getting out of the dilemma with which it confronts us.

The moment we look at the word, it does begin to throw a little light on what the thing actually may be. For pain is derived from the word "penalty." Pain is a punishment, a consequence and resultant of having done something. Pain is incurred. We know that is partly true. We know that if we want to do anything that requires great exertion, one of the prices that will be incurred is that the work will exact from us painstakingness. The eighteenth century was a century that prided itself on its rationality. Nevertheless, a supremely efficient craftsman was called a very "painful" person. Once we consider that aspect of pain, we see that the problem opens up a little more. For when we say "painstaking," we show that we mean that the person willingly accepts the exertion. They *take* pains. They do not have them forced upon them. They adopt them in order that their work should have perfect finish and show freedom from all limitations of crudity. They use the pains. But the pains do not exploit the person.

There are, we know, two forms of pain: *patheia*—the anguish of being broken down, corrupted, and decayed; and *agonia*—the skilled effort of the wrestling match when the athlete opposes their skilled strength against the force of their sparring partner. We cannot then fly from pain, and our pursuit of comfort is bound to fail if we aim at insulating ourselves from efforts, from taking pains, from agonia.

And yet it would be a false diagnosis of our present state if we said other than that the main aim of the United States is to avoid discomfort. Our great-grandparents' chief concern was sin; our grandparents' principal dread was senselessness—you must have a utopia to gain, you must hitch your wagon to a star; our parents' fright was social shame, slipping down on the social scale; and ours is sensory discomfort.

Nor when we analyze Homo Americanus can we say that they are wrong in this diagnosis of themselves. As they would say in their telling argot, they do know one thing about themselves, and that is that they *feel* "a hell of a lot." Hence their unprecedented consumption of that master depressant, alcohol. The modern person is, of course, more of a time-binder than any other of humankind. By that is meant they are more self-conscious, and their self-consciousness involves that sense of the past and of the future—they look before and after, and sigh for what is not. The animal—and even less reflective, less restless people—cannot suffer as modern people suffer because [animals] have a greater power of living in the moment. The power of pain, we know, consists not merely in memory of the past and apprehension of the future, but in the power we have to extend the "specious present" and so make the pain impulses, as it were, continuous. It would seem that all the standard anesthetic, nitrous oxide, does is to change the time sense so that the impulses cannot be brought together into one anguished spell of recollection.

The evolution of consciousness then seems to be an inevitable part of humanity's development, and with that goes the realization that we must accept pain. If you will have pleasure, you must have pain; but more, as you intensify pleasure it turns into pain. That seems a dreary enough outlook, and when it is faced, most people hunt about till they turn up what seems at first sight a [rather] good defense. Granted that pleasure leads to pain, and the more evolved you are the more what was pleasurable to the coarser palate becomes revolting to you; what was stimulating to the tough becomes torture to you, [but] that still is not the whole story. Trace the physiological facts and what do you see? As humans goes on, as they emerge as the supreme animal, it is true that their nerves become capable of pain the animal does not experience.

But that leads to a further development. We know now that senses become specialized out, as for instance the eye and sight evolve out from a general photosensitivity of the whole skin, as the ear and specific power of hearing grow from a general sensitiveness to airwave vibrations. And in such cases, the nerves that originally signaled as pain nerves—as evolution goes on, they become specific. Many of the nerves running to the eye, for example, signal to it not by pain but by flashes of light, and those running to the ear signal by sounds that warn it of something wrong. In short, it would seem that as we become more [functional], our nerves do not need to goad us so much. They send us a message and leave our reason to understand it and take the right steps to keep the body intact and free from damage.

Does not such a development show that one day we shall have no pain at all? Won't we have done with such crude goads and spurs? Won't all the early blind impulses of anguish have been transmuted into signals which tell the intelligent mind that a repair job should be undertaken?

That should be the answer if we were what the humanist and the naturalist have thought we are: a creature that could be fully explained as an animal, a supreme animal evolved out from a simpler form, and at last—by the use of [our] huge central nervous system—[we have] come to be the most efficient of all living things, a creature that can hope to become completely adjusted to its environment. But there are certain facts that seem to [advise] against that [as] the right and full explanation of the strange being that has called itself Homo sapiens.

It is true that some of our crude sensitive energy has been used up and specialized out. The brain itself is largely incapable of pain, and as Harvey Williams Cushing pointed out, [it] can be cut and carved without the patient being aware of any inconvenience. But certain areas of the body do remain terrifically sensitive, showing no sign of becoming less so, but indeed [providing] evidence of gaining in their pain-giving power. For example, such are the nerve endings just under the skin, and it is the damage given these by fire that makes death from burning so frightful. Considering this, one would think we were like trees, where the real life goes on just under the bark, and the heartwood is not the area of growth and development, but simply a stolid core of support. It is considerations such as these that would seem to bear out the hope that humans might become creatures of complete vitality and so [neurologically] specialized as to be incapable of pain. Such a hope, such a picture of the future, is too simple, too crude.

Can we bring out any other [future] in its place? Yes. In the Indian tradition there seems to be a concept far more subtle and richer. It is, to put it in our simple Western phrases, the concept that evolution and progress are facts. But this evolutionary progress is of an entire being, not of an animal. Humans are not made for adaptation to this environment; otherwise, they would only come to be a super cockroach. For the roach is the most successfully adapted creature of which we know, having succeeded way back in the Permian Period, and being content to carry on repeating its accomplishment in the longest success run ever known. No, humans are made to *transmute themselves*. If that prophecy is the true one, then we need not be surprised that we have not, in spite of our high and specialized evolution, gotten rid of pain. If we were animals we should have. But because we have yet so much evolution to achieve, we still have a vast store of raw energy left in us for our further evolution. It cannot be used up by our present system even at its highest efficiency. No wonder that in our search for physical comfort the force within us outwits us.

We are trying to live in permanent healthy content. It cannot be done by humans. If humans will not choose ecstasy, the power to transcend themselves, then they must have agony. They must rise above themselves or be drawn above themselves; they must break out and hatch—or be extracted. With a streamlined right effort, or by breech delivery, humans have to go through their second birth and be born into a life that at last can and does transcend the play of pleasure and pain, comfort and distress, ease and disease. Then at last they will welcome the challenge of that tonic stimulation which is an outrage to those who are ignorant and joy to those who know.

The Supernatural (abridged)

Originally published in *Vedanta and the West*,
Vol. 16, No. 5, September–October 1953

FOR A RELIGIOUS JOURNAL, it is hardly possible to find a title more corny, more suspect, than this. It reminds us of the occult, the cult, the phony. An appeal for realism is made to us by politicians, by practical people—yes, and by most of the academic world. As they send us to that Caesar, to that Caesar we must go. There is today no place for dreams, no place for wonder; in compensation there is no place for terror or dismay. The universe is commonplace.

But this appraisal does not stand even the most superficial examination. When you really look at nature, you understand that it is terrifying and inexplicable. Julian Huxley said to me repeatedly that he could understand people, confronted with what is now known by research as the nature of nature, recoiling with a sense of terror capable of pushing them over the brink of madness. But what he could not understand is that anybody could ever be bored, or that anybody could face the challenge of our own vast "beyond that is within" and simply dismiss it as being uninteresting. We teeter-totter, of course, upon that knife-edge between two abysses, into the depths of which no one at present has been able to look and see any bottom or ground—the vast unknown extent of our own nature, and the vast unknown extent of that other Nature.

Where, therefore, shall we put the boundary of what we call either the natural or the supernatural? When that vast system which for centuries managed to have a reply to the problems of varying civilizations and intermittent barbarisms—the Roman Catholic Church—has chosen to use the term "the supernatural," we cannot lightly dismiss it. We can say, "I cannot see how you can reduce this term to forms that will be useful to me in trying to think what nature is, but at least I shall pay you the compliment of saying that you are discussing something that is real, something that is of significance." What is it, therefore, that the Scholastic system, now being so largely revived and offered the respect of lectureships in large universities, means when it uses that phrase?

There is the idea that certain experience is natural and certain experience is [unnatural]. The former is right, but the latter tears up the systems of coordinated response and makes nonsense of the universe. Such can't be true, for no one could have made a universe like that! This, I think, is the real challenge that lies behind the words which balance each other in a system of morality that is now in ruins but is still awe-inspiring in its decay—the concept of discipline, the concept of braving events, however terrible, and denying oneself any of the ordinary escapes. See therefore the confrontation of those two terms, the supernatural and the unnatural. One may explain the terror of actual experience by saying, "This is impermissible; this is the unnatural; this is the horrible. This is the intrusion of the accuser, the frustrater, the enemy—enemy of reason, enemy of sense, enemy of beauty."

And on the other side is the concept that not only is there the denier, but there is also the affirmer, affirming beyond any position which can be covered by logic the proposition that there is some wider frame of reference in which all the conflicts are reconciled. My own opinion is that had Scholasticism had the courage to stick to that double system, it would have seen that it need not be trapped in its curiously limited idea of what the natural is. It would have come to the conclusion [that] it is upon the elasticity, the tolerance, the tensile strength of my own mind, upon the charity of my own power of entertainment, that the whole concept of meaning in the universe depends. ...

The whole process of life is translating the constant challenge and fear of *patheia*, of suffering that makes no sense, into *agonia*, the suffering that does make a transcendent super-sense. You see, one of the terrific struggles that is going on as we consider concepts like the natural, the supernatural, and the unnatural, is the [forcing] open of the human mind, which it dreads above all things. Natural selection is now taking place in the mind; we take the pressure of its selective power there, in the choices we make. Can I accept an experience in which there is no answer? It does not mean I must face futility. It simply says: any answer that could satisfy you now would be inadequate. It would give you a false sense of where your true security lies. It would say that, in a locked and closed universe, now you have something firm. The whole doctrine of the dynamic view of life has always said: it is in the power of knowing who you are, that "Thou art That," that a person can have a person's sense of the worth of being. They are struggling, and there is no answer in time that is "full of repose, full of replies."[73]

The choice of natural selection is just this: How many questions can you sustain? If we took away all the answers but left you only with the divine gift that childhood so gladly welcomes, of being able to ask questions, which would you choose? All the answers given, the book closed, the canon sealed, the systems and so-called natural laws all working, no place for escape, no place for the fear of being turned out once more to wander in that waste of the Godhead where no person is at home. Which would you choose?

We see what is happening. You can leaf over the greater part of our immense academic achievement in this particularly favored country and see quite clearly that most of the makers have chosen the closed area. They have taken the wrong turn in the maze, and they are not at all distressed when they find the blind alley. For at the end of the blind alley there is a little seat, and you can sit down there and doze. You haven't got out, but when other people come down that alley, you tell them, "I found there is no way out. You had better sit down and doze with me."

219

You say, "Yes, you can obviously make a case that there is a great mass of evidence which points to the fact that there is a lot in this universe that doesn't get into textbooks. There is a lot in this universe that people don't like facing. But can we not dismiss such as little anomalies, and instead of disturbing the magnificent system we have, can we not disregard them?" But the history of science gives absolutely no sanction for that kind of escapism. It is because the anomaly was entertained, because people were willing to see the old answers burst open, that new, immense questions came peeping in through the gap. Because people kept the divine curiosity of the child, they were able to push on beyond the safeties of the syllogism, beyond Scholastic finalities, beyond the society that was continually watching as to whether anybody was irregular, unnatural, or dangerous, on into this terribly risky climate of freedom. It is because of that that we are here at all with our present power over the environment, such as it is, and of which we are so unconscionably vain. It is undoubtedly impossible for any kind of advance, any kind of growth to exist unless we entertain the anomalies.

There is a hypocrisy infinitely more tragic than that to which Edmund Burke gave his famous label of "the tribute paid by vice to virtue." There is the tribute paid by despair to faith, a tragic tribute, and paid with something worse than criminality—the collapse of nerve in those very people, the salt of the earth, on whom the survival of society depends. It really hardly matters how many criminals there are: "If only there be ten righteous men, I will not destroy Sodom" [adapted from Genesis 18:32]. We utterly underrate the enormous power of those whose vision has shown them [who are] passionately searching for truth that there is meaning, that it has significance, and that it is possible here and there to catch a glimpse of this thing working—and to look at it until you stand moved. Already inside you the divine *imago Dei* ["image of God"] is working within its chrysalis, and at that moment it cracks a bit, and at that moment you know that you will never really return again totally to defeat. You may be driven back, but this will simply show that you are not spending enough time with those people who are authentic, who cannot be reduced. The fact is that you realize that as you look at them, you see that they are transformers in which the immense current that could not come close to us is stepped down.

We wait and we know. You've only got to wait; it will flash out again. And gradually you piece together this fact: So this is Reality, and why did I not see it? The Lord was in this place and I knew it not. It is the most vigorous, the most active discipline continually to blame oneself when one does not see a thing. Look what has happened in modern art. We know perfectly well that we are completely dependent upon those pioneers who dare to look on the forms that are too complicated, too advanced for us to take in. And we take it on rightful authority from them. They say, "Do not accept this unless, after a certain time, you have seen it too. But I promise you, if you look in that direction you will see it."

At present we are so largely, in spiritual things, sheep without a shepherd. And we are looking in all directions. We are looking in many directions where the sun is not actually shining. When people are totally blind, they may just as well look in the west for the sun to rise as in the east. You need, therefore, people to tell you, "This is the direction [where] we have seen it. We promise you it is there. Look, and gradually that radiation will clear the cataract from your eye and you will see. We have done it often enough to know that it is true."

One of the most successful books of today, *Annapurna*, is about a peak, one of those amazing, inscrutable peaks of the Himalayas. ... To climb Annapurna is an athlete's ordeal. If you read no other part of the book, read at least the tiny preface written by the [author Maurice Herzog], mutilated for life when he was at the height of his strength—handless, wounded, having gone through what seems to be a futile accident. A futile accident, because it looked as though it was bad luck that, at the moment of his victory, he was destroyed forever in the world in which he was to be supreme as one of the successful ordealists of our age.

Was it accident? Is the Greek story true? Is the Hebrew story true? Are all the stories true that if you see God you must pay for it? Even in our own blood-and-bones tradition, Wotan gives his eye for knowledge. Herzog gave his hands, the hands by which he climbed, which were to him both feet and hands, the power of leadership, the power of withstanding the heroic agonia, the immense tonic of achieving. And at the very height of achievement, when he had broken all records, he was struck down. Let live, but let live under

221

conditions which—offered to him when he was young, offered to him at the beginning of the expedition—hardly could he have accepted. Never to be a free man again, never to hold a penny or a hat again, to have a hideous mutilation after months of agony and pain. And yet, what does he say? "In overstepping our limitations, in touching the extreme boundaries of man's world, we have come to know something of its true splendor." We [perceive] another frame of reference. And he says, "I had won my freedom. This freedom, which I shall never lose, has given me the assurance and serenity of a man who has fulfilled himself."

And as he, with these simple words, stumbles to repeat again the real challenge and slogan of the Perennial Philosophy, what does he say? "It has given me the rare joy of loving that which I used to despise. A new and splendid life has opened out before me." He closes his book with this, [which I'll paraphrase]: It is not necessary that everybody should go the particular path I went. I went through the wars. They did not teach me this. I found it in those inhuman desolations—doing a thing that seemed to be a gratuitous act, a sort of defiance of the hero against the gods. And then the gods did show themselves, and they were not envious of the mortal.

There is the dance of God, burning you up and yet making it possible for you to say at that moment: I became free in a freedom I shall never lose. You can't dismiss those sentences. Too good to be true? Look at the man's hands and feet—a ... sign of somebody who has been through patheia to agonia. And he knows it. It is the power of this eye of the soul agonizingly to open to its full aperture under the appalling blaze of utter reality. And it does come back because, of course, He is there also. He has never forsaken His universe, is never embarrassed. He is in the appalling desolation of those great peaks, but He is equally present wherever we are. Here we have thicker masks; there He lifts it from the face and says, "If you will take my mark, you may come unto my station."

Herzog says, "There are other Annapurnas in the lives of men." Everyone has this power, the power to take the ordeal and transform it into the initiation, new birth. "Unless [a kernel of wheat] falls to the ground and dies, it remaineth alone" [John 12:24]. This husk has to be broken open. [This is] our job, our task, our concern. For one thing we can do for humanity, for civilization, for our own country, for our own associates, for our own soul, is one total thing. It is to be able to make the ordeal—day by day to know that there is no chance or accident, to know that with the infinitely loving cunning of the divine Master, He will bring the pressure exactly to bear where He wishes to force open the suffocating cocoon that is around us, and to release us into the larger life. One act and one act only is required of us—the act of faith. We will not call Him a fool or embarrassed, but we will give Him the benefit of the doubt and we will continually be able to say, "Though He slay me, yet will I trust in Him" [Job 13:15].

That is the problem which we face with the supernatural. The average sensual person, looking at it, first of all denies it and then says, "Well, it's supernatural." But the supernatural is simply the gasp of the average person facing this and saying, "It cannot be human." All right, don't call it human. Call it divine. Realize that in the blaze of that moment, He who made it recognizes what He made and the deeps call to one another. Then there is no wish to have answers; then there is no need to be afraid of questions. Then you can ask for more and more and "Ask and it shall be given unto you." "Given unto you" not in order to defeat you, not in order even to give you power or success in any terms we understand, but that you may enter into this fabulous condition called in Sanskrit "*ananda*," which in our own simpler tradition is called the joy of the Lord.

Vision (abridged)

Originally published in *Vedanta and the West*,
No. 117, January–February 1956

VISION IS UNDOUBTEDLY A TERM that we rather enjoy when we are not involved in action. People speak of taking long views, being able to see things in perspective. Vision is not, of course, the characteristic of the person of action; but, on the whole, as increasingly we want to be cultured, we have a feeling that, though we may be active go-getters most of the time, there should be certain periods when—after having driven sufficiently fast and far—one is prepared to sit down and enjoy the view. And yet Western people have always been in a quandary, in confusion, with a certain uneasy attitude toward that very basic word, vision.

The term, "a person of vision," carries with it a certain kind of all-over, commendatory flavor. We like to think that we have among us a few people who have been too longsighted to succeed actually at the moment. It is an extremely useful phrase when one is dealing with the peroration in obituary notices about people who ought to have succeeded, and didn't. You are able then to say that they saw too far for there to have been any immediate return.

"The person of vision" is an acceptable term. But not "visionary." That is different. The visionary is the person of vision *before* they died, a rather awkward liability, when their effects have not as yet been edited and shown to be poetry and not fact. The word "visionary" certainly has a bad flavor.

When we get to such words as "seer," they are practically subversive. A seer is a person who may be investigating *anything*. They are not merely looking at long horizons; they may actually be looking under the table. The Latins had a grim motto when they were dominated by secret police and a totalitarian state: "Who guards the guardian?" Who investigates the investigators? And the danger of the seer to the community is that they may be investigating things which are best left under that table, best not looked at.

And now we touch another very deadly word. What if our person has another focal length of consciousness? What if they are an individual of "second sight"? Well, we usually try to dismiss this and say it is part of their dangerous pretentiousness. But there is enough evidence—if we can bear to investigate evidence that does not fit very well with our prejudices—that second sight can exist. It is a very awkward fact that the best authenticated cases of this power of real long sight, of seeing down time and not wearing the blinkers of immediacy, have to do with the phantasms of the dying, with the unpleasant fact being dinned in upon the human being: "Thou too art mortal."

For these reasons people feel, I think, that it is best to keep "vision" simply a poetic phrase—let it be placed in a suspense account against the need for obituary eulogies on the dead, about whom, as Horace said, "Nothing but good must be said." But when it comes to a practical point, of recognizing vision here and now, then it is a much more serious thing. Heinrich Heine, in that extremely touching poem, says that the life of vision, for the ordinary person, is very much like a rainbow—a rainbow in the tragic sense that when you look back, it is touching the earth, and when you look forward it is touching the earth; but it is never touching the earth where you are.

If this is so, we have to be very suspicious of that word "vision." There is nothing more serious than when poetry and prose come apart, and when words get the bit between their teeth and go off by themselves. Because they do not remain mere words. They become dope. They become ways of not being able to face up to facts. They are immensely powerful defenses, torpedo nets, fields that prevent the mind [from] ever being fertilized by the great, pregnant thoughts that are moving in the world. We contain them. We say that they are poetry, that they give us uplift, and we have them safely caged.

Yet, let us consider the very discipline in which we believe most and that has given us most power, called by that rather dangerous and inaccurate word, "science." Science [is] the method of using measurement and persistent experiment. What is the technique that science has trusted to the exclusion of all other channels of [understanding] of the outer world? Precisely this: vision.

Not until science arose did anybody think of trusting sight—vision, the power of seeing things—to such an exclusive extent as that to which science actually does trust it. We know that when we move as tolerably successful animals, we use common sense; we gather together in the heart of the brain all the messages that come to all the different senses and make sense of them. But that is not the approach of science. We know now, by careful tests, how elaborate are our powers of discrimination given by the other senses. The trained ear can hear with extraordinary precision. Even the trained taste buds of the tea-taster, the coffee-taster, the wine-taster can be brought to points at which one or two molecules can be registered.

Touch can be, again, the same almost uncanny sense. For example, in France after the First World War, when there were so many blinded young people, experiments, when carried out on a really sensitive subject, showed that the hand, not even touching Braille at all, but the hand merely held over print, became so sensitive that the person was getting the [perception] of what was printed there through the fingertips. Either some sense other than touch was working—yet only when the hand was over the object, close to it but not touching it; or there might be such supersensitiveness that the difference of the heat radiated from the page by the black of the letters and the white of the surrounding page could be detected. I only give such an outstanding example, in what we consider a rather clumsy sense—the sense of touch—to show what [tremendous] powers remain undeveloped in the human being. When St. John of the Cross wants to talk about the absolute [perception], he, an extreme ascetic, no longer speaks of vision or insight. He actually says that it is these *touches* upon the soul that give it its deepest insight.

And yet, to return to that point of science, science has put all this aside. It has advanced until those things that cannot be measured, that cannot be tested by the eye upon the reading charts, upon the levels, the dials, are considered not to exist. Seeing is believing for science, although the French, who have a great deal of experience of living, say that "feeling is knowing."

The scientists have taken the secondary characteristics, such as color, and said that they cannot deal with them unless they can be created as a radiation which can be calibrated and measured. The fact that the color is the color has nothing to do with it. The tone of a musical instrument gives out a vibration, and you can see the vibration. The magic of music—the fact that something takes place in you that moves the soul, producing emotions and aspirations—that again has nothing to do with science. It can give you the number, it can give you the quantity, it can give you the rate. But all these things can be tested by sight. Seeing is believing.

The very process itself has advanced. In studying what is going on, the basic instrument of science is vision. It is vision in the sense in which the poet, the seer, and the inspired use it. [This is] because it is never a simple calibration or measurement; it is never simply weighing masses. It is seeing the thing in its richness. It is forming a judgment. That is the only possible aim. And the more we study what goes on in the eye, the more we realize that we are only at the beginning of the mystery that is present. To take the most rudimentary experiment: scent can increase sight. During the last war, the Russian pilots discovered that if you gave a shock to the olfactory nerves with citronella, the sense of sight was dilated. One could see for a moment clearly. The charge going down one nerve—which is the simplest but possibly not the whole explanation—charged up the other nerve, and one saw better.

An enormous number of creatures have not been content with what one would call ordinary seeing. Even when you take a degenerate form, like the small snake, the adder—for a long time it puzzled both anatomists who dissected it and those who were watching its behavior, to observe that this creature saw in the dark. They thought they would discover in it some extension of the nerves of the eye, but it was not so. Under the eye, [and] a considerable distance away from

228

it, there is a small pit. To that pit there was found running a nerve. It was this that permitted a creature possessing practically no sense of smell to strike at its prey and catch it in total darkness. It could see by infrared. It has a focus that takes red rays and transforms them, without a lens, into an impulse to the brain. The creature sees by heat, and it has, therefore, two visions.

So, already we are outside the world of common sense, the world to which our senses respond. We watch these other immensely efficient creatures, and they operate partly in our world, or by what we call visible light, but also partly outside, and by using not merely their eyes but the tactile sense too, so that in that little hollow pit, in that degenerate animal's face, there is a second eye.

With ourselves, too, know perfectly well that if we did not have so much artificial light, we should have a great deal more experience with our second sight. For our second sight is, of course, night sight. It takes twenty minutes to come into action. You cannot hurry it; you must wait. Then it can [activate], using only a very few photons of light, with which it is so sensitive that it can guide a person. An extraordinary and perhaps interesting point is that when you are using night sight, you must never look at the object. This idea runs through all the great myths, all the pictures of what people are: that there is a vision that does not attempt to break down the thing, to focus it, to fix it, but rather looks at it obliquely and [perceives] it as a whole. Night sight is this ancient form of sight, evidently, in the eye, and it operates with great efficiency in what seems to us total dark.

We have, then, two forms of sight. But already we have begun to push both aside. We have removed sense after sense, as being just an amusing thing without having anything to tell us about the world. We have actually focused ourselves down, narrowed ourselves, until we are only using by probably a tithe of the [perceptions] that are used by people when they are really [under trying circumstances]. The Australian Aboriginals are supposed to smell water; they certainly can find it fifty miles away. Some [perception] exists there, brought to a fine point by the absolute teachings of necessity. With us, that is not so. We could not even smell whiskey fifty miles away. Therefore, when we are viewing the process that is going on, we must remember that science itself today is moving toward a [perception] for which we have to use our total sensoria, our huge range, and we must bring it to athletic keenness if we are actually going to see what is happening.

Otherwise, you are running blind. You are in the dangerous situation of unconsciously having put aside a number of the cards. You are in peril of doing that very thing which was considered one of the most dangerous things in the scientific discipline—finding what you are looking for, and suffering from wishful thinking. You must take the whole thing in, and you can only do that if you are functioning yourself at your full pitch of [awareness]. No human being has ever done that up to the present. Before we get on to thinking that the world is divided into seers who are magnificent believers in the impossible, and practical individuals who only believe in what pays, we must realize that this division is unsound.

Because, in between, there are endless stages. There are people who have practiced the discipline of critical study, and yet have not lost the power of enormous generalization. There are people who claimed to be visionaries who have been narrower than any fanatic who believed in materialism. In between there is the emergence of people like ourselves, who are aware that this either/or attitude is not quite true, and that somehow we must discover how to work as a whole. We are always repeating this today. We are driven to the conclusion that unless you realize yourself as a whole, you will split yourself, and the result will be conflict on both sides. You will be reduced to the stage to which so many nineteenth-century thinkers were reduced: the true is the unpleasant, and the pleasant is untrue.

This is not so. There are these steps; we are not asking people to make the leap of death. We are asking them first of all to make a diagnosis of themselves. What are you, in your totality? Are you using yourself at anything approaching the capacity that is in you? Don't you wish you did? We remember that when J. M. W. Turner was attempting to paint right into the sunset, he showed some of his work to one of the polite ladies of the day, who said, "Mr. Turner, you know, I never see a sunset like that." Now he was not a polite man, but his response was necessary: "Don't you wish you did, ma'am?"

That is the first thing. Without humility, there is no advance of vision. And the visionary who is not humble is not really a visionary. For we have discovered, in the last ten years, that the chase after objectivity was a vain dream. We have discovered that there are plenty of animals that see things other than we do; that our own sight can shift; that people have various faculties which permit them to [perceive] things differently from us; that many people live in separate worlds as far as their values are concerned. And there has been undoubtedly a danger—and it will be over us for the rest of this generation—that this will lead to reaction. Progress has been vain. The idea of going on is an illusion. [When] only the past [is] understood, [then] retreat! There you will find comfort. Of course, you will have to give up a number of "useless" acts; you will surrender your will and your wish to understand. But you will have found comfort.

But one is not really willing to settle so easily. You have got to be continually exploring, and that sets up the creative tension. Now, when we regard the situation of Homo sapiens today, we see that people are being stretched almost to the limit of what they can endure. They have to live in a very complicated society in which, on the whole, it is much simpler to live if they assume that what they are told is what they ought to do. And at the same time, they are perfectly aware that this can only be provisional. It is still possible to say, as is often said, that society is half right. The mischief of it is to discover—which half? And always, anybody who is a living citizen, an individual who wants to be integrated and to understand their relationship to the nature from which they have emerged and to which they go, must be straddled across this to the limit of their span.

Therefore, when we talk about vision, we say that we are not talking about something which means that the visionary must either take refuge in their private world or surrender to a blind authority which says: "I have all beauty, all comfort, and all supernatural vision at my disposal. For that, leave the world alone and, when you touch it, come to me for the explanation and the behavior pattern that you are to employ." No, it would be comparatively easy if that were so. What we are presented with is a third choice. There is another solution in which you accept the fact that vision is possible. There is a continual process of stretching.

We never cease, through all our lives, to be born. We wage a wrestling match with life that will lead to an emergence into another frame of reference, provided [we are] ready always to go forward. And this is the one question we have to ask ourselves, "What is my intention? Do I wish to understand? Are curiosity, wonder, interest, [and] sympathy still in me? Why do I entertain these new, unsettling facts? Do I entertain them in order to be able to say that I have not an alibi, that in a world [which] is so incoherent [that] I have a right to retreat? I see more than you silly fools who only see the carrot in front of your nose. I see the long, desolate track, and I'm not going forward."

Or do you go forward, because you see that at the very limit of this track there is a light, there is a promise, and this sheer power of exploration is the proof, the guarantee, that you yourself belong somehow to a process [that] is yet unfinished, and [which] can only be finished by you?

All the attempts to make sense have been partially true. Remember, we are the first generation, as far as we know, of any human beings that have ever really tried, not merely to stand in other people's shoes, but to look through their eyes. And that is the first thing, I think, that vision has done—a perfectly practical thing.

Anybody who reads with any detail, and absorbs to any degree, the attitude of the eighteenth-century rationalists, is astounded at the provincial narrowness of those individuals who considered that they understood the world. They wore a mass of frizzled horsehair on their heads, and imagined that they were people of reason. They alone saw the world as it actually was, and when they went to any culture other than their own, they simply explained it away as being completely barbarian.

When that extremely open-minded man, the Earl of Chesterfield, wrote those fascinating letters to his natural son whom he hoped to educate (and failed to), he said: "You will go and see the Greek works of art, because ... they pointed to the Renaissance." [He also] pointed [to] the eighteenth century, which had refined away the crudities of Phidias and had given us the extraordinary things of Canova. An elegant world! But he added, "Waste no time upon Egypt, for there you will see an exhibition of misguided barbarism."

Egypt, an exhibition of misguided barbarism! A culture that succeeded in lasting far, far longer than anything the eighteenth century set up. Ozymandias might be in the dust in the end, but only after an enormous time. And no one imagines that the eighteenth century will be remembered four thousand years afterwards. We know that it is present in us, that tradition, that it still flows in our hearts and minds. That was our first great step. We stepped back into the past, to be better able to see ourselves. Because, you cannot step into the future to see what people will think of you. And then we took the next step. Past civilizations began to look rather stately. They left, as far as they left anything, the best. For the best generally lasts well, especially if it is carved in granite.

But what about the people of our own time? Then came the discovery that the Bantu tribes, the Australian Aboriginals, even the [disliked] Chinese, were not so inefficient. They understood. They had [produced] a reaction, and many of them lasted and did not suffer from psychosis and neurosis. We began to say, "They too have vision." We cannot use it; we do not accept it. But it does give us an idea of the width of the [comprehension] of, and, what is so important, the enormous charity of nature—how many forms it will permit, provided there is present in them this one thing: the will to live, to understand, and to make sense; the will to take your total [awareness] of your particular environment and heredity, blend them together, and say, "Out of this I can make a creative response." ...

We shall not reject the past; we shall use it; we shall see that we have to add to it. Do you see what is coming? Long ago poor old Hegel saw it: first of all the thesis that I am right; then the antithesis, we are all wrong; and then the synthesis, that we cannot take the past. You cannot go back to any religion. The religions themselves have been changing all the time. Even the most ancient of the Western religions is not the one that never changes; it is the one that changes last. That is an actual fact. In 1810, the Church of Rome, without any fanfare, decided that the time had come to move [forward]. And it put the Newtonian hypothesis as a possible answer to what takes place, and accepted Kepler and Copernicus. You see, it did move. But it took much longer than it need have taken.

And that is the point. What is the optimum velocity at which we have to move if our vision is to open up? There must always be two things going on. You must have that divine curiosity, which is noticing this wonderful anomaly with the fascination of a child. But you are an adult too. When you become like a child, you do not actually go back to infancy. You take all that the child has got, in its avid and wonderful power of acceptance and joy in the strange which is not the repulsive, and at the same time you are continually building it into a frame of reference because you are an adult, because you must direct your life.

You see what this means. We, privately, as individuals, inherit a very interesting culture which has learned by anthropology that other people see other worlds, and yet basically we are one. [We] made wonderful past discoveries, but they must be in contemporary terms, and revivals are a mistake. We must know the past. We must be able to assimilate it, and yet keep it in absolutely contemporary terms. That is what we must each do in our own lives if we are to be people of vision.

But vision is never a private thing. If you begin to see things nobody else sees, then you have to take great care. You may be a person [with foresight]. But it is much more likely that you are a person who has fallen in some way behind. If the mind is afraid of sharing its vision, then we may be certain that there is fear at the back of it, and not curiosity. Every single person of vision, whether painter, musician, or scientist, is under the urge to share. Truth, to be good enough, must be anonymous. There is no private salvation. There is no private revelation. And they who seem to be successful in imposing their private vision upon others, are simply the paranoid. They succeed for a short time, pouring their suggestions into other minds and infantilizing them. They must not do it! That has been the tragedy of most cultures. They could not go on learning. The canon closed. The powerful person dominated, and the whole thing had to be cracked open again.

I do not think that we need look upon the future with discouragement, with a feeling of, "Well, that's what human beings have always been." Our [grand] view of history shows us that you can never say of human beings that they have always been the same. They radically and profoundly change, and never so much as lately. The speed is on us; the pace is here. And we can live up to it because we are not forced prematurely into action. Our knowledge is pouring in, and if we will only be open to it and ready really to learn, we shall very soon find that the reactions are there which will permit us to make a creative response. For we are beginning to see, through the mercy of Almighty God, that we are not succeeding in stamping out all other cultures, or in putting our narrow and grotesque idea of what nature is into the categories of what has not even suited us very well.

We cannot go on saying that our frame of reference is the only one; we must say that it is a thing that must be grown. We must continually grow, and we cannot do this unless we crossbreed [our cultures], unless we are prepared to take from other people everything they can give, and to give back.

The visionary is the person who can excite vision in others. And they do not make others see what they see, but they make them see to the full compass of their own sight. They give others sight. They do not impose upon them what they will do. The Buddha sedulously refused ever to say what the enlightened person saw. When you have given a person sight, they do not need to be lectured as to what vision is. The whole process of any kind of sharing today is specifically that. It is the encouragement to people that they go and see for themselves.

Our society today demands people of practical vision, people who see, and go on seeing, and who know that there is going to be no limit to what they see. And all the time they are trying so to live that they will give a creative response to life. What is this creative response? Fundamentally, it just means that I always accept *this* as being, basically, wonderful and good. When I cannot see the meaning myself, when the eternal music seems ugly and the latest picture irritating, I do not charge the person (if they have shown the authenticity in their life of discipline) as being a fraud, or as a person who for some reason has become suddenly incompetent. ...

I must be prepared to act. I must use force, but never violence. I must be able continually to say, ... "I shall not try to kill this thing; I shall attempt to understand it." Long ago [that] fine historian and convinced liberal Lord John Morley said about the revolutionaries whom he was studying: "We will not denounce you. We will explain you."

But to explain is not to explain away. You will see that this is the test, given at the very beginning of our tradition—that you may only judge a tree by its fruits. And you may try, under a narrow botany, to say, "It can't bear any fruit, because that is not a tree I've recognized before." Do not be so certain. Test it, and see what it is giving.

Vision, therefore, is not confined to my own attempt to see everything. It is combined with my attempt to see from your point of view, even when that seems very anomalous to me. Finally, of course, as it says in Sanskrit, I shall see the point of view of total [awareness], because there is integration given by total vision. There must be association with others, for I cannot have a total vision unless all your visions are coming in and I am making them mine, and handing you mine that you may use them.

But also, of course, there is the tremendous power of realizing, and it is not merely a sublime piece of Sanskrit rhetoric. That light which has made the eye, has made eyes all over the place. The eye of the octopus is utterly different [from] ours, and so is the eye of the bee, of the ant. But they are all eyes. They have responded to light. They have powers of vision, given in order to make creation.

This is not subjectivity. Let us not think that this is retreat. It is an immense advance. It says: you are a creator, because light made you to reflect light, to see light, and to be a light-bringer. But you can only be a creator if you are a co-creator. If you arrogate to yourself the power of creation and say, "Whatever I see is right; God meant me to be happy; I intend to work miracles for my own use because I have this power within me," you will be a deluded person. And if, at the same time, you say, "This is a hostile universe; it has its iron laws and I can do nothing about it," again, you are a deluded person. It is the razor's edge. In between lies this creation. You can actually co-operate with that light. He that is within the sun is He that is within your heart.

That is why objectivity is over, and the end of it is not disaster and need not lead to chaos, reaction, or revolution. Because the end of it leads to the vision whereby humankind is able to say, "So You, utterly beyond my comprehension, are also myself. And if I can trust You sufficiently, by that act of devotion to You, I shall understand others and I shall understand myself. And, in that triple chord—of association, integration, and orientation—You will have achieved that process that You intended in me, and in Your creation."

[This] is good. It is going to be better. And, in the end, when I realize what You are, in that [tremendous] saying, "Tat twam asi," then I shall be able to say: "In the name of that One, everything is made new."

Evolution

Originally published in *Vedanta and the West*,
No. 123, January–February 1957

IT SEEMS A DULL ACADEMIC SUBJECT; but as it happens it is one of the most gravely neglected hypotheses of living. We use the word with the same carelessness that we use another ill-defined term—instinct. Because some animals seem to have developed eon by eon, we assume that the stars are evolving.

An age that desires comfort more than anything else dislikes the notion of cataclysm. It is interesting to note that when the sciences of life began, people could still remember and heartily fear the convulsions caused by religion; hence life theories at first tended to be cataclysmic. Then as the eighteenth century thought that it had arrived, through reason, at permanent placidity, the theories became uniformitarian. As the Romantic movement began to disturb the nineteenth century, uniformity and permanency were changed for progress. And finally, as the twentieth century began its violent wars, mutationism took the place of gradualism. The process was considered blind because it was capable of producing anything. But through a lucky chance it had produced, among innumerable and mainly unviable [mutations], humans—who thereupon christened themselves Homo sapiens. It was therefore easy to carry on the core of Victorian optimism, at least in America, and to hold that "one increasing purpose runs, and the thoughts of men are widened with the circling of the suns."

It was all chance of course! But out of slime had emerged a superhuman, [and] out of jelly, genius. Chance, however, is a difficult thing to settle. To the layperson, the laws of chance sound almost a contradiction in terms. Surely there can't be any such thing! Nevertheless, as we all know, not only does a science of probabilities exist, but statistical probability appears to be the only real guide that science has. And statistical probability has made some competent statistical biometricians question whether, if random mutations are all that can have worked the change from mud to man, there has been time, since the cooling of the earth, for these randomly directed build-ups to have taken place.

Whether that be so or not, evolution—which means simply the unfolding of something that is present there in a compressed form—is not the word for the process as the evidence seems to show. Once the first microscope failed to show a microscopic man, or homunculus, at the center of the human seed, it was clear that the process should be described by some more accurate term, namely epigenesis—[meaning] that the germ or embryo is created entirely new, not merely expanded and unfolded by the procreative power.

There are also a number of other odd questions that the evidence—on which the evolutionary hypothesis was founded—now raises. To give but a few, embryology shows that every child, before it is born, has proportionately a much greater brain than that with which it emerges into life. Can it be that our evolution is not finished? That is a deduction that the evidence certainly suggests. And when we consider the very stuff we are made of—protoplasm—what an odd thing it is. When biochemistry began, the founders of that science said openly that, with a generation of research, they would have got rid of the "bio" and left only the chemicals. It hasn't happened. Proteins remain curiously distinctive. The protoplasm of one animal is not exactly like that of another and, what is more, that of one body may change as the body grows. This is not chemistry as any chemist understands it.

And the process has generally been described by a false analogy. We think of life as a flame. We talk of it therefore as consuming things. The reverse seems to be true. A great number of researchers believe now that life is not subject to entropy. If we are to have a simile to describe it, it looks as if it is nearer to being an electric field in which there can be built up forces that release energy beyond that found in the world of inorganic materials.

There is no reason, then, against the hypothesis that, instead of life being something that [depends] on a fantastic accident in a minute area of the physical world, it may be a new synthesizer that is kindling the universe to a new quality of energy. Yet most people feel that even if this thesis is true, it really doesn't matter. The whole process is so vast that we can't do anything about it. But even that may not be true. Even if we take the time spans during which past life developed and compare them with the speed of the development of our own stock, the rate is so highly accelerated that it can only be shown by a logarithmic curve. And when we take the advance of humans since they have had writing and cities, the speed of what is usually called their social heredity has accelerated even faster.

It is not true, therefore, to say that in one generation we can make no difference to the process of human development. Indeed, the more we study what has been referred to above—embryology— the more we see that there is a biological basis for what child psychologists now maintain: that if we chose to give each child the best spiritual environment which even we are able to conceive, its progress and that of its society might be truly mutational. It is good for us to reflect on these things, because we tend to believe that the more we educate a person, the more informed they are, the more they are capable of debunking anything that might be described as a "hopeful" outlook!

Still this is no casual optimism. If there is evolution today it not only could be at an unprecedented speed, but it also need not take place at all—unless we choose to cooperate with it. [This] is because the present outlook, on the evidence, seems neither pessimistic nor optimistic that it suggests a moral challenge. For faith (and the resultant life of faith) is not a belief in something that is contrary to the evidence. It is the continual athletic choice of the most meaningful

picture—the noblest hypothesis; and once that picture has been accepted, the resolution to live in the light of this sufficient truth.

Communication (abridged)

Originally published in *Vedanta and the West*,
No. 129, January–February 1958

WE HAVE DISCUSSED VISION [see article above]. Considering thought in its broader sense, it might seem a big, ambiguous word in the English language. And because in the end it seemed that there can never be true vision unless it is an aspect of communication—between that and this, between you and me, between the past and the future, between what we call the objective and the subjective—therefore, it seemed necessary we should link it with this even more difficult, because more familiar, subject of communication.

We saw when we were considering vision that it must result in communication; and we shall see, as we consider communication, that it is a form of vision. And yet that seems a paradox. As we know, whereas vision has around it a not-altogether pleasant aura of the visionary, of the phony, of those overstatements of poetic phrases that are then put into circulation as rather doubtful and inflated paper money of the spiritual world, communication has a harsher sound, really. One often thinks of it as "talking down to people," being a popularization that always leaves out the true richness of the discovery.

Of course, there is also always the great fear that a communication is issued by an authority, and that it is slanted, colored, meant to produce a reaction in us. The great word "advertisement," which has become so important to government, means "turning others." It means that you aim this at them so as to manage to deflect them from their present position and fit them into the position that you wish. The analogy too often used—and yet with a great deal of truth in it—is that a random society is like a piece of unmagnetized metal. There are the atoms, and there are the structures of the metal in a random condition. Then apply a strong magnetic field, and they all with their separate charges become one-pointed—not in any transcendental sense, but in the practical and immediate sense. That they think one thing and say one thing—that makes government easy. [This] makes it possible for the attention of humankind to be directed in those channels that will lead to the maximum output of organized effort.

We cannot too often repeat in our present sociological crisis that all governments are half right; all governments rule by default. All governments are trying to manage us, because we must know that, as a community, we do fail to manage ourselves. No human being resorts, as far as we can see, to violence, until in bewildered fear of anarchy they have perceived that such apt forces as reason, persuasion, and example in their own case don't [work]. And the result is, as St. Dominic said himself: "I've used reason; I've used example. I've used these forces." He sold his few precious books—when books were worth their weight in gold and for him almost essential—to give to the poor when he was traveling through Spain. This hard ascetic was so moved by the fact that these people needed bread. The founder of the Inquisition was not at that moment energized by the thought that they must think rightly. He felt that they must be fed. And yet that is the very man who in the end was driven to make the most terrible instrument that has ever been devised by the human mind: the coercing and damaging of the will, which inevitably—because it is contrary to the process of life—led to the wrecking of the very institution for which he gave his life. [Ed. Note: St. Dominic was not "the founder of the Inquisition," as Heard claimed, though he personally founded the infamous Order of Preachers, which carried out unthinkable acts of gruesome torture, barbarism, and religious exterminations after his passing, as heartily sanctioned by Rome.]

So we realize that communication has rightly got a bad name. And we are suspicious of it in that level where our suspicions are most effective, most defensive, most impossible really to coerce—in the levels of our actual reaction. Without our knowing, when we are most loyal, when we most assert things, we have our saving clauses, our quiet reservations. One need only give a number of examples. Psychology has rubbed that lesson in, that whenever a person over-affirms a faith—wait, wait, in a little time they may take it up. No one is really a greater risk to those people who fear subversion than the very person who seizes on every possible means to impose what they call "the right way of living." That is not a statement made without ample historical evidence.

It was that strange genius, with probably the drive of an epileptic visionary, Paul or Saul of Tarsus, who was determined to save Judaism as he understood it. When his own church was hesitant, when wise individuals like his own teacher Gamaliel were inclined to wait and see and throw their weight in favor of tolerance, it was he who drove his hard, pointed spear of bitter opposition against the new development. And yet, when Saul himself was sent out upon the very process of completing what he thought was the extermination of a dangerous, but, thank God, easily liquifiable minority, he was seized with a seizure, and woke up to fight with equal fanaticism for the very side that he had attempted to destroy.

And therefore, when we feel a fear of communication, we must watch ourselves. When we feel, as many of us do, that any kind of move perhaps at the present time is unwise and we should wait, and that we should as far as possible not ask questions but obey slogans, we should remember that our assent to that proposition is not whole-hearted. It is the mark nearly always of a premature convert if they tend to be terribly anxious that everybody should come to the light as they see it. And the reason is their own uncertainty of whether their vision is true. The only possibility of being able to make that vision true is that other people, absent from the coercion which can be directed by a fanatic in those moments of their utter conviction, see that vision, and see it from their own point of view. No person who clings rightly to their sanity is satisfied when anybody takes an opinion that they utter simply because they uttered it. We are in communion with others when by other paths they have arrived at the same result that we have, when by other methods they have achieved those things that we feel we agree with them to be the things which we should achieve and yet have not achieved.

Now, how did this particular process of subconscious dislike and fear of all kinds of communication grow up? When you understand a thing, you not merely can explain it, you understand that it served a purpose; it was expedient that this thing took place. Pain, frustration, disappointment, contrary opinions, oppositions, suspicion—all those things are very good thoughts because, not merely do they [cause] us to examine whether the methods we have used to persuade are accurate, [but] they are also, of course, questions. They may be asked with an absurdity that naturally causes a considerable cauterizing effect upon the tender growing edges of one's own egotism. But, when one has got over the sting and tautness of the cautery, they are also information.

There is, we can always remind ourselves, more information in a question than in an answer. But it takes great vitality to see this. It is much easier to imagine that we have got an answer than to want an answer. And the whole suspicion of communication did grow up when people had begun to discover that the answers that were given were not necessarily untrue when they were given, but that they were no longer adequate as a comprehensive answering of the contemporary question of the world as it seemed at that moment. We know now that no bolt falls from the blue, that no revolution takes place without warning, that no disease attacks the organism until it has been in the precancerous or the pre-tubercular or the prediabetic condition for a very long while. It isn't even true (in Plotinus' telling phrase) that nature speaks twice and then she strikes. She speaks again and again. There is no cataclysmic element present unless you have stretched the elasticity of the organism, of the environment, of its fellow people beyond all possible tolerance, and it smashes back. ...

The trouble, as Plato says, is that our eyes look backward and our feet go forward. We always retreat ... to the position that is actually going to be the new one, and do not know that it is. It is a very encouraging thing—if we have the nerve to recognize it—that this is what we are doing; that our very recoil from things makes us collide with truth. Our tremendous effort to resist a certain point of view means that we are driven to realize that our own point of view is really inadequate. In the desperate effort to get a case, to be able to defend ourselves, we shall snatch hold of things that will compel us to move on from the too narrow position which we have occupied.

So we can see that we are in a third phase, [noted below]. First, that of authority; secondly, of the right to private judgment—the passionate belief that what I have seen is true. And those two points seem to be in eternal competition. At present we should use the rather cheap and vulgar phrase that this is the dispute between science and religion. It is the dispute between those people who believe in reason and in all empirical data—or say they do—and those people who say: yes, but this won't help you to live.

And where shall I find a system that gives me a series of coordinated reactions? As Chateaubriand said, I return to the Church, for in the Church alone can I find the sanctity of the home; the destiny of my own life to face its utter loneliness and its final dissolution; and a conception that behind this vast incoherence there is a plan, a purpose, a designer, and a path. Yes, that is perfectly true, but there cannot be any returns in life. We may go back and reconsider, but in the end, we have to realize that we are considering things as individuals, that our vision is partial.

The solution to that very serious problem between anarchy and conservatism, between anarchy and tyranny, lies, I believe, entirely in the third phase, in which we begin to understand communication. It is going to be painful, whether we do it or not. But it means precisely this: others have rights to their vision, and we must live together. And at the same time, one is quite certain that what I have seen is, within limits, my authentic vision. As long as we use that word, "within limits," we are going to grow. It is natural selection working on the soul. For it says, "I have seen something and there is some element of vision in me. But this will never be complete until I have the power of seeing as others see in their infinite multitude."

The *samsara* is nirvana. The multiplicity is the One—but only when the multiplicity is total. As long as there is one person seeing something and unsatisfied—not made to submit by coercion, whether that be lobotomy or propaganda, not made to surrender their vision but be able to contribute it—then and only then shall we have not only sanity but creation. In the end of that moving book *Wisdom, Madness and Folly*, written by a man [John Custance] who has been [manic depressive], the summarization is [this]: We must never persuade the insane to surrender their vision. We should point out to them that we, too, have a vision. We do not maintain that our vision is absolute objectivity. In our vision, too, there is construction, there is hypothesis, there is magnificent fantasy. But we ask them to contribute. We do not drive them out. We ask them to do the agonizing exercise of seeing their vision and trusting ours.

The real act of faith is not in the idea of what we in our limited way call God. Beyond all terms of relatedness, beyond all limitations, it is whether I have the courage to perceive that you, too, reflect God. But you reflect Him from a tiny and peculiar point—intensely valuable, but valuable as is every single note that the human ear can hear, not by itself, but because it can be combined.

We are part of a fabulous composition. And that idea is very, very new in the modern world. It is the first time we have been able to say: it is not this or that; it is not a choice between the sane, the conventional—the people who are practical, and the people who are visionary and a bit over the edge and must be coerced. It is that we all have partial vision. And yet the very partiality of that is our authenticity. It is the most torturing thing to realize that what I see is true and it can contribute to what you see; that it is not true in the fact that I could ever impose it. It will take part in this whole frontage of this immense facade of understanding. It will take part in the gigantic composition that is in the outworn phrase "the music of the spheres." But it does not have any authenticity by itself, and yet it has authenticity with others.

We see at once that we are involved in the fascinating issue of communication. We know that we have to acknowledge perfectly that from the beginning of a person's attempt to understand "where he was, what he was, and who he was," there is absolute truth, though a hard truth, in the tremendous saying of the Tao Te Ching: "Those who know don't say, and those who say don't know."

You must not at this moment think that your proposition can be more than a stimulant. It suggests there is something more to see.

We have made the only real progress we have ever made with the problem of insanity when we have begun to respect the insane, when we have been able to say: it is possible we should entertain the hypothesis, the disturbing idea, that you did see something, and it was so intense that after that [and] up to the present you have not been able to ... behave yourself in a profitable way to the rest of us. But then, if we saw ultimate reality, would we be able to do something about it? ...

We are on the threshold of a new power. It will be discovered piecemeal. [Scientists] did not think for one moment that they were near atomic power when they were, as we know, within four years of it. Power is closing in on us in a new vision. And each of us is capable of their authentic response to it. Communication is not merely words—words are on the very lowest level. Communication is sound; communication is vision and color and light. The whole body is open in an enormous gamut of [understanding]—[understanding] that gives us [understanding] because it refuses to be comprehension. It always says, "Little person, don't think you have ever caught me. Humbly know that for the moment I have taken hold of you!" And the result is [that understanding] is a deadly state only leading to an overwhelming anxiety unless it has in it the humility which at moments even that genius we have mentioned, Paul, had when he said: "I judge not, brethren, that I could have attained to comprehension, but I believe I have attained to [understanding]. And I stretch out further that I may attain more." [Ed. Note: This is Heard's liberal rendition of Phil. 3:12–13.]

There is the real humility of the person who has had an authentic experience. If they could have turned away from ambition, then the history of Western people might have been very different. As it was, they had to give us more answers than questions, and the result is that we had to be imprisoned within their system, as in that of Aristotle, and as in that of Aquinas, until we had to split ourselves out of it and be born again. They did not realize that the very phrase they used would be used against the very shell that they were shaping.

When, therefore, we come to this point of what communication is, we realize that every single human being has an authentic vision. They have seen a minute part of the reality. But they cannot themselves begin to see the whole thing until they have communication. It is not merely the statement: "How can I know what I'm going to say until I've said it?" Even people who are perhaps a little too fluent on the pulpit do actually prepare what they are going to say. You can prepare, but like old Balaam with his [donkey], you do not necessarily say what you meant to say, because something better is given you by those who listen. For there is the real problem that we are dealing with in communication: Why did communication go wrong? Simply, because it failed to be communion. The person wanted to tell something. Yes, they were very earnest about it. They were anxious to pour out this particular thing. And in the end, they were ready to give all the answers and to enroll people as charter-paying members. If the person could cling to the hypothesis—this I have seen, but I know it is partial; but knowing it is partial, I know it can be part of a contribution. And in communion we can come to see it, for then I could see what you are seeing.

It is not, of course, even standing in somebody else's shoes. It is seeing through their eyes. ... We are reciprocal creatures. And our magnificent achievement and promise lie completely in this, that it is the number of people with whom we can reciprocate that is the criterion of how far advanced we are. ...

But you could not have had the communication, you could not have understood *that* out there, unless the others helped you. There are people who say, "I don't hold with people coming together. I go out and communicate with the All." We in Britain used to call them "blue-domers," because they always said, "I go out under the blue dome of light, and I don't like coming together with other human beings that haven't such an immense vision as I have." And of course it isn't true. It is a silly remark of the self-made person. No one ever begot themselves. It isn't possible for us to be here unless endless care had been directed upon us. It is quite true—we have been damaged, but we have been much more given to than we have been damaged. And when we can get that into our minds, we are almost cured. ...

Bernard Shaw once said in my presence: "*Tout comprendre est tout pardonner.*" ["To understand everything is to excuse it."] "That," he said, "is rank sentimentalism." It may be if it simply means [this]: Now, don't think of it any more. Tear up everything. Let's go back.

Let's be jolly and have another beer. It doesn't mean that. I think it is a truer thing if we said, To understand everything is to interpret everything in one's own terms. To say not merely, "In those circumstances I would have done the same," but to say, "In those circumstances that thing was done. It remains as a question mark, and we ourselves will accept it and understand it."

We shall—as I have often quoted Lord Morley, talking of those old revolutionaries who finally murdered so many people in the name of humanity—we shall not merely denounce you; we shall explain you. Yes, but that is too superior. We shall not merely interpret you. We shall understand it, but understand it without any surrender of our own vision. Think what a conflict of opposites that means. Think what a gigantic tension. This is true; this is my vision, and yet your vision isn't quite the same, and yet [still]—the chance of the noblest hypothesis of the greatest possible act of faith is precisely that. Your vision is true for you, and my vision is true for me. And none of these visions by themselves is enough; and all of them only have in them—thank God—the promise of further questions. We shall go on; we shall pass this thing on. This is the apostolic succession of the unclosed questions. An open-ended universe is said to be the universe in which we live, which leads to an open-ended life process, which leads to the open-ended consciousness—always opening out, always refusing to close. No question is closed. ...

We are back again at this tremendous concept of the "hope deferred." Every question provokes an answer; every answer provokes a question. The thing can never stop until we are beyond the conflict of the opposites. That is the principle which undoubtedly has been revealed to us today. It is, I think, the most necessary provisional hypothesis we should deal with, that wherever you find the challenge, there you will find the possibility of the answer, and the answer is safe insofar as you definitely accept it as being the challenge to a fresh question. There is never going to be any settling down. No science is going to be complete; no vision, even of the highest mystic, is ever going to be final; no music will ever lead to the piece in which at last the journey of people toward satisfying harmony and understanding and rhythm is achieved. No painting is more than a hint, a little design put down to remind you: This person saw from this point. Now go on from this. ...

Don't let us therefore be afraid that what we say may be misunderstood. God is being continually misunderstood, why should not humans? We are continually of course saying things wrongly. But in any way we say may be this challenge. No statement can be made of any sort without producing some result upon another. For God has compelled us to be the universal communion. And we can do nothing in this universe without affecting others. What we may hope for is that our humility makes us realize that.

Communion goes on continually. He is always giving Himself to His universe, but because He wishes us to become givers and creators like Himself, He is always giving us questions. He is always rousing us. And it is when we are puzzled and distressed, it is then we may stretch out our hand to Him and say, "This is your question. This is your challenge to me. You are treating me as somebody who is growing up. You are treating me as somebody who, one day, You will want to be united with You."

That does not mean returning to safety. That does not mean authority. That does not mean that we are going to be able to get all the answers. It means that we shall go on to a process that we cannot conceive; that we are going out to an adventure which we cannot underrate. We all know that in the depths of our hearts, charity is the carrying wave of understanding. We all long to have it. When it is present in us, we know it is there. That is the profound communication. That is the communion of all saints and all souls. And in that spirit, we shall be together until in that tremendous moment, as Plotinus says, we shall see the One in the many; we shall see the vision in the communication; we shall continually radiate, unrestrained and unbaffled, each to each. And, as he says, "The glory will be endless, for we shall know even as we are known." [Ed. Note: This is Heard's liberal rendition of 1 Cor. 13:12.]

Death

Originally published in *Vedanta and the West*,
No. 162, July–August 1963

BIRTH, SICKNESS, DECREPITUDE, DEATH—it is said that the Buddha named these the Four Fetters. It would seem he held that these four give fourfold sanction for the view that human life is suffering—suffering so great that any person who will count the cost of it cannot but see what wisdom counsels; namely, that this present life should be spent in making it certain that another such life (subject to these same fetters) shall never be entered on by them again.

It may be said, however, that modern hygiene now presents to this generation a very different picture of the human predicament. Birth can now be achieved without anguish for the mother or damage to the child. Sickness, if far from being banished, has had its claws clipped, its fangs blunted. As to old age, it need not be a disgraceful limitation, a terminal stage in which, crippled by increasing incapacity, the victim can neither live adequately nor die cleanly. All this may well come to be true.

The fourth and final fetter, nevertheless, modern physicianship has done nothing to set loose. Indeed, our "doctoring" has made it worse. Everyone by adolescence should have learned the practical psychological truth that to run from fear is to turn it into a night-mare. Yet what else does modern medical care do with the elderly? By a series of operations ever more ingenious, drastic, and futile, that sad swelling contingent called—to avoid the truthful term "se-nile"—"senior citizens," are amputated from organ after organ. Increasingly, prosthetic artificial members awkwardly and painfully substitute for the body's natural instrumentation. Meanwhile, the physician–biochemist plays their companion part in this futile es-capism, first by increasingly drastic drugging and now by an even stranger pharmacy that hopes to retard malignancy or postpone the stilling of an outworn heart by altering the whole axis of personality and producing in the body another type of character alien to the for-mer person. Although lobotomy—the sundering of the brain and so of the mindbody in order to "relieve anxiety"—has been dropped af-ter a battlefield of casualties, these violent attempts to solve a spiritual problem by physical means go on.

And they will and must. For they are based on the medical pro-fession's conviction—the conviction of all the ruling sciences—that a person *is* their body and any other view of them is dangerous meta-physical superstition. How can this almost unanimous conviction of this, the most powerful intelligentsia, be altered? It is not enough to point to what is now all too obvious, that every bit of this painful (and costly) manipulation of the body has only increased the fear of death [and] has only swelled the huge, hugely expensive army of the de-manding useless, whose obsessional concern is to fight off a little longer the inevitable at any price. These unhappy creatures, the most successful advertisers of despair, and the highly trained pro-fessions that live off these who can no longer live but would rather be moribund than die, have at present no choice but "to continue in their perversity," to proceed to ever further extravagances of bodily outrage and spiritual denial.

The one cure for this deprivative disease of the soul is of course to return to the conviction of immortality. But how can that grow again in our social soil? This is now so sterile that, while it is materi-alistic right through, it unwittingly proves its sterility by maintaining that "America has never been so religious"; "America is *the* country that believes in God."

The approach can only be from the physical to the spiritual. Of course we all now know that the new physics (through which we chose to produce the atom bomb) disproved materialism and broke the deadlock of senseless mechanistic "natural law." But despite the fact that physics is still held to be the validating basis of all the other sciences, the applied sciences—especially the medical and the surgical—still consider the revolution as purely theoretical [lest] their enemy metaphysics return in a still more ingenious disguise.

That part of the new frame of reference that can command their respect—and so make our ordinary selves believe it is not dishonest for us to hold that hope may take the place of despair—is, it would seem, in biology. Such careful and authoritative biological studies (especially Sir Gavin de Beer's *Embryos and Ancestors*) that deal with the lifespan of the many species whose expectation of survival has been established, show this: provided a person is born of parents with the average expectation of the human species—barring accidents and excessive strain—they should live naturally into the first half of their eighth decade. (There are not, too, uncommon stocks whose lifespan lies in the sixth decade and others whose expectation extends to the ninth decade and a few over that.) Then the endowment of genetic energy is spent. To fend off this process of natural elimination is a cruelty to the individual and their society.

Such established findings allow us a first sane viewpoint toward death. For with this evidence in hand, we can recognize a vital homology. We know that the fetus—on whose growth in the womb will depend the whole structure and span of the postnatal creature—needs nine months of unremitting growth-work to be ready for a healthy birth. We see now that the postnatal human needs, for the completion of their life-journey in the body, nine hundred months. The fetus needs its full time, its "nine moons." But if it overstays, hanging on in that confinement though its work is done, there must be tragedy. So it is with our postnatal life. We do need full span. But if, out of fearful ignorance, we cling on to the husk when we have been prepared to be born again, then the tragedy of the embryo, which clung to the first life when that life was over, is inevitably repeated.

But is an established homology enough to wean us from our terrible materialistic mistake? It has often been observed that horses in a burning stable become so terrified that they cannot move and will refuse to be led out to safety. So it would seem with old humans in our materialistic society.

> Beyond this place of wrath and tears
> Looms but the Horror of the shade.[74]

Why shade should be, for those long out "in the sun's hot eye,"[75] so horrifying, is hard to see. The fact remains that in prematerialistic societies we still find examples of persons who, ripe for their second birth, only welcome it, but, knowing when it is due, can achieve it voluntarily.

The four ordeals of life are called, one presumes, "Fetters" because they impose an involuntary captivity. Put then that word "voluntary" or its synonyms "spontaneous," "liberating," as the epithet before each of these tests and turning points in the life process.

Voluntary birth we now know how to practice, and the practice is spreading widely. The potential mother, trained not to dread or shun the natural process, cooperates with her inbuilt nature and so, without drugs or violence, herself consciously delivers her child, with exultation—without fear for herself or damage to her child.

As to sickness, the second Fetter, that, too, is yielding to the full view of this life as an embryonic experience. If we live strenuously, shunning comfort, sedation, and all arrest of the life-process, in right exertion and exposure to the apt stresses of a purposive life, we do generate those antibodies that keep us for the time we need to be, actually healthy and happily aware of our ties with others.

If, having so lived, we undertake the elimination of completed and discharged activity patterns of our well-spent life, then we are prepared for and welcome this happy span of contemplation. Freed of ties, we look forward to the release into a life as above the restrictions of those imposed by the body as this one was above those necessarily imposed on the fetus in its womb. Then inevitably comes the crowning gift—the capacity to achieve delivery, the voluntarily liberating death which is the master-birth for those who have lived, purposively and earnestly, their bodily life as a preparation for that which alone can crown it.

Only such a view of a person's purpose can, we can see, give the individual true fullness of life and keep their society from despair, frustration, and self-destruction.

Karma: What Its Realization Entails

Originally published in *The Aryan Path*,
Vol. 9, No. 7, July 1938

THERE HAS, PERHAPS, BEEN NO TIME in human history when the Doctrine of the Deed was so needed. Yet it must also be recognized that there was seldom a time when such masses of humanity were behaving as though karma was only a story with which to frighten children. Leaders and led are acting with a complete irresponsibility quite impossible to those who realize that as a person sows so shall they reap, and that the deed once done, its consequences are inescapable. We must then first ask why such a common-sense doctrine is apparently neglected by the generation which asserts that it is practical. The answer to that question gives us insight into our age. It will also show us how we might emerge from our international and social anarchy, and discover a new order.

World religion is today undergoing its second aeonic revolution. The first religious revolution was the change over from a religion that was primarily social to one which was primarily individual. At the present time, religion is once again changing, changing back from being individualistic to becoming again social. The convulsive efforts of the totalitarian states [and] the bewilderment of the democracies are symptoms of the same thing: people have discovered that they cannot live as individuals and are seeking for a larger life in which to blend and fulfil themselves. This change affects radically our whole attitude toward the Doctrine of the Deed. In the early, "integral" societies, responsibility was general and could not be thought of otherwise—it was collective and complete. There was no life but the common life. In such a society, karma would be self-evident. There could be no debts or credits contracted outside the community; every act of its constituents entered into its balances, every loss and mistake had to be remedied by an equal gain and rightness. There was no escaping consequences, because the common life of which all were part, went on forever.

When, however, these primal integrated societies began to disintegrate, their constituents could only seek to arrive at personal and private settlements with the divine law. In the language of all the prophetic teachers of the seventh and eighth centuries B.C., teachers who extend from China to South Italy, each person must make his own settlement with Reality. This doctrine led to karma becoming a personal and private concern. "No man may make agreement for his brother"; "The doctrines of vicarious merit and grace are superstitions"; "Each man saves himself or loses himself": such sayings are the commonplaces of the great reforms that swept over the old collectivist religions.

This stress, partial though it be, was at the time necessary. The old religions had mostly ceased to teach a true conception of karma. Indeed these elderly foundations were already individualized without knowing it, for their doctrines of grace no longer taught collective responsibility, but that by depending on a wholly alien being the debtor's trespass would be cancelled. Such teaching is highly dangerous, not only to the individual but to society. It was, then, a social revolution that compelled a recasting of responsibility in individual terms. Personal survival after death had to be brought forward to take the place of the eternal life of the community. This new sanction for moral conduct was, however, a makeshift. First, it developed what Saint Jerome calls complacently "holy selfishness," and then, because this was essentially false, the belief itself began to crumble.

These are the reasons tending in our time to renew the search for a collective instead of a private responsibility. Aiding this wish are the findings of modern science—that we are only partially individuals. The question put to Jesus of Nazareth when a blind man was brought to him, "Did this man sin, or his parents?" is a question that increasingly concerns all the sciences of life. We realize as an empirical fact that no one can say, "I discharge my whole liability by paying out of merits I solely earned, all the debts I personally contracted." It was partly because the doctrine of karma has been said by some so to teach, that it has been discarded by many as being both unsocial and untrue. Those who are accustomed to reflect upon the Self, know that the above proposition is not necessarily inaccurate if the Self is understood in its immense ramifications. To the casual, hurried reader of the West, however, such a statement seemed to show karma to be a doctrine unfounded and unworthy.

The restatement of the doctrine therefore deserves some care, for without it there can be no true morality. Before, however, we can render it in our contemporary vernacular, we must examine a little more closely our actual position at the present moment. We are, by our thinking, driven to the conclusion that we are not wholly individuals. That our feelings confirm the findings of our thought is proved by the desperate efforts people are now making everywhere to find their full and satisfying [identity] in a nation or a race. Science also shows us that we are not separate persons who can set sure bounds to our responsibilities, but, rather, are nodes where the threads of innumerable heredities cross for a moment before again passing out to make fresh nexus. This position, however, is far from satisfactory, for although it indicates that we all belong to a larger life than that of our physical bodies—and even that we have a blind craving to live in and feel that life—it does not show us how to attain to such a condition. Neither mechanistic science nor the teachings of the dictators give a way of life that can be said to lead to a higher mortality among people. Indeed the contrary is so much the fact that today many faced with our social chaos are wishing to flee life and can hardly escape complete despair.

We need not, however, give up hope. If we persevere in our enquiry, we shall discover the missing links that are needed to make a dynamic morality of our present knowledge. What we require is a direct sense of our kinship with all life. For this sense would give driving force to the intellectual proposition of Western science that all life is one, and it would also give a real and sufficient basis of loyalty in place of the false and fatal (because narrow and exclusive) loyalties urged by the dictatorships. What is befalling us today (and although painful, it is hopeful) is that we are feeling our way back to organic society—to a living relationship with our fellow [human beings] (and through that to all life)—a relationship in which alone we can have an adequate moral life. Individualized morality has done its part and served its turn. We are, however, in a painful state of transition because, though most of us now know what we don't want, few as yet can see clearly enough to know what we do want.

What we need if we are to take the next step, is that direct experience of our unlimited social liability and this is only possible when we have found a way of living not based on the cash nexus, not based on mutual self-interest, but on an awareness of a common life, an awareness as vivid as the consciousness of self. This is not a vague aspiration. There is now ample evidence of how essentially therapeutic the simplest intentional social pattern can be. Practical sociology has proved that most criminals will recover if they can be placed in a community where they cannot fail to see the social consequences of their acts. With such experience, karma becomes a doctrine that simply states as a general law that of which everyone has their own personal knowledge. As such, a group life is continued; it grows in integration and aim. Each constituent becomes aware that they live because they are part of a general eternal life. They see that only by so living in that constant knowledge will they come at last to be an undivided part of that eternal, conflictless Being.

That desire for union with the One is the common experience of all seekers for fundamental order and peace in their spirits. Some Western authors, however, for example the great Dr. Albert Schweitzer in his interesting essay on Indian thought, have said they find here a serious ethical obstacle. Though they cannot avoid the conclusion that the mystical attitude and activity toward life is the only true outlook and approach, they feel that it must lead to asocial conduct. This difficulty is mistaken but all too common. We can try to rebut it by saying that the acceptance of being part of life demands of people the highest social behavior—behavior that alone is free of the unfortunate consequences of Western and all individualistic morality, [and] that individualistic altruism is really egotism: I do good to others to benefit my highest, irreducible self. This, however, is argument, not experience. People, and among them some of the best, will continue to think that the devoted search for union with the One, and even the doctrine of karma, are only "escapes" whereby thinker and saint leave the world in its ignorance and squalor, unless they can be given not merely argument but actual experience of the karmic, organic way of living.

The doctrine of karma therefore today prompts us, compels us to the most active social living, because it not only tells us to find our fulfilment in our [companions], [but] it goes, and today must go, much further. Today it tells us that if we are to live up to what we know, we must not merely keep the present society going, [but] we must start reconstructing it in such a clearly patterned form, in such a design for living that in it all, from the simplest to the most advanced and proficient, may have direct experience that they are living a life of unlimited liability, a life of union that expands naturally and fully, beyond the limits of the individual life and ego.

That, then, is what the doctrine of karma today compels us to do: to act more creatively than any other belief can compel us to act. And these are not vague words, for unless we so act, we shall undoubtedly perish; for if we do not make for people a collective way of life, they will make for themselves a collective way of death. One thing is certain: the old individualism is over and no one now can pursue their fate, treating the world as something indifferent. "We must all hang together or all hang separately." What happened during the epoch of individual salvation was that the engine (the saint) became uncoupled and went ahead, while the carriages, our ordinary selves, either stayed where we were or slipped backward. We have today to recouple the train to its true engines. Otherwise false tractors are ready to drag it over the precipice.

In practical words, that means simply building up once again a society that is organic, just as the physical body is organic. Yesterday the world lacked leaders. Today it is full of blind leaders of the blind, one of the most powerful and active of whom actually has spoken of himself as a sleepwalker. [Ed. Note: That one "blind leader" was Adolph Hitler, whose "sleepwalker" self-reference occurred during a March 1936 speech.] Against these leader–seers who see only illusion, we must put true leader–seers. Briefly, this means building up a hieratic society against a militaristic society. The individualized democracies are helpless against the organized societies even when these are organized on a false basis and pattern. The most mistaken inspiration, as a matter of brutal fact, is more effective than the most lucid rationalism. The only valid answer to the dictatorial state is the divine society. We have no time to use vague circumlocutions. Karma, both as a doctrine and as a fact, both as an intellectual proposition and also as the causative force working in our history, today compels us to set up once more a caste-patterned organic society.

Just as the physical body has a graded order of organs working cooperatively, so we must have a social body, graded from the eyes that see to the hands which shape. Caste only collapsed because the position of seer was too often held by those who were blind. If, believing in karma and the unlimited liability of each to all and all to each, we frame a truly organic society, we shall find that such a society will take on the shape of a dynamic caste order: seers, the eyes of the body at the head; administrators, the hands; fine craftsmen, the muscles of the body; contented servants, the feet. Such an arrangement is inevitable. Armies that have to organize not according to rights but according to realities have such an order: general, staff officer, noncommissioned officer, and private. The river of life is spanned by a bridge of never less than four piers. That is to say, types of consciousness that incarnate range between the seer and the routineer. They who denies this fact contradict life. It may be cruel but it is actual. How then are we to eliminate the cruelty while facing the truth? Liberal, individualized democracy would not face the truth: dictatorial, militaristic dictatorship mocks at the cruelty; only an organic caste system can face the truth and yet remove from it the sting of cruelty.

In the hieratic–dynamic caste society, based on a full realization of karma, there is both the facing of the facts of life and also a complete elimination of cruelty. Justice and Mercy kiss one another. For here we have a society where the wisest can see and inspire, and the three orders of the practical are all led to carry on according to their gifts. The vision of those at the head shows that the whole body politic is one, and those who now serve on the word of a just and inspired authority will in turn come to direct, open vision. Working faith ends in sight. Here are provided the patience and the selflessness without which there can be no social or physical fruition. Private virtue without public pattern is stultified. Public pattern without private virtue is helpless.

This, of course, is not to revive the old decadent form of caste. Each person must be given the position to which they are called by their manifest gift and by their devotion to its development. If they cannot sustain their rank, they must sink to their inherent level. Those at the head—the seers—must be free of possessions: the Eye sees all and possesses itself of nothing. Further, as Manu knew, the Eye does not even shape. It reports reality, and the hands then act according to the Eye's finding. Such, then, is the living social pattern, the highest world–social morality that humankind must find or perish. And this organic life, this extension of unlimited liability to all humankind, finds its inherent sanction in its constant experience of the Doctrine of the Deed—karma.

[Ed. Note: This article, discussing the desirability of "a caste-patterned organic society," but so as "not to revive the old decadent form of caste," was published in a journal based in India, where the ancient caste system had dominated social life for centuries. Heard endorsed the idea of a non-inheritable society-wide merit-based class system, based on the best intentions of the India model, in his 1935 opus, *The Source of Civilization*.]

Spiritual Direction

Originally published in *The Christian Century*,
Vol. 57, No. 10, March 6, 1940

SOME THIRTY YEARS AGO, just before people realized humans were about to fly, a new name was coined for the clergy. It was meant to be manly, breezy, humorously complimentary: "Sky Pilots" they were called. Today the title calls up airmail throughout America and Armageddon over Eurasia. But even if the realists hadn't snatched the title from the idealists, it is doubtful whether the latter could have held it. Those hearty curates, those physically fit ministers—lineal descendants of Charles Kingsley's muscular Christians—certainly shook off the "shame of the cross." Their fists could make them respected where their faith seemed milksop fairy tale. They swung into the slums. "The social gospel" became the progressive pulpit's slogan.

The First World War torpedoed them. It struck them below their waterline. They had never thought out what they believed about force. Charles Kingsley had said that Christ charged beside the gallant British boys at Balaklava or Inkerman or in one of those forgotten Crimean bayonetings. It was a natural reaction. "Blessed be the Lord my God, who teacheth my hands to war and my fingers to fight" [Psalm 144:1] was regularly sung as a divinely inspired psalm. If God gave you fitness, fists, and skill at "the fancy," He couldn't mean you to stand by and see a drunken ruffian beat his wife. Enquiring how it all started is out of the question. Quoting the brute texts wouldn't make him see the light, but you might win his respect for you and your cause after your left uppercut had made him see stars.

The Great War—and the Reaction

So when the papers said that a little girl of a nation was in the clutch of a sadistic beast of an empire, well, every decent fellow doesn't wait to ask the wrongs and rights or by what mysterious method of sacrifice God redeems the world. The healthily social Christian minister, just because they were so simple, direct, and brave, became the most implacable of foes. They had made a double oversight in reading one of their Master's key orders: they were about as harmless as a hawk and as wise as a pithed frog.

When the first round (1914–18) was over, the more talkative and unreflective ministers tried to forget the things they had said. The world, though, was far from inclined to let them. The public is generally glad to find an expert out. When they are a respected authority, it is nearly always delighted. The New Testament gave a number of awkward texts to the secularists anxious to discredit the churches. Ministers might still be good sorts but they shouldn't, after this, ride too high a horse. They had been taken in like the rest of us by propaganda, and they had let it fly to their heads rather worse than most of us. Whatever social uses might be found for them (and no doubt there would be plenty as assistant poor-relief agents and public health aides), they couldn't expect to be accepted again as spiritual guides.

Yet spiritual direction, always essential to people, is now their supreme need. "To whom shall we go?" Who has the words for sane living, let alone of eternal life? Hence the outburst of analysis. This is no old-age fumbling for future-life comfort. It is reported from some of the larger campuses that some forty percent of the students seek the modern "medicine man" to help them in their heyday living. Granted that a few are really psychotic cases, can anyone who knows anything of the universities of this land doubt that what the average boy or girl wants is just to know clearly what life is, what it expects of him or her, what it means, where it goes, and how they are to cooperate with it? To answer that—anyone knows who has searched their own soul—is far harder than making a psychotic cease giving trouble.

The Minister's Neglected Task

That is the task, the largely neglected task, of the minister of religion. They may have many other ancillary interests. They should of course understand physical hygiene, housing and athletics, and education and economics, [which] should all come within the field of their wide-angled lens. Their focus, however, must be the human soul. They may well know something of the speculations psychoanalysis has made about the [depths] of consciousness. But their special knowledge and mastery must be of people's spirit at its peak. At this point at least they need not shun being an Aristotelian; for them, "man's nature is his highest capacity."

They must, then, first know what to expect of men and women. People are mainly what we expect of them—if we can show them why such first expectations can be held and how the soul climbs to its rightful elevation. That "how" is the minister's second requirement. Acquiring these two knowledges and then practicing them is a fulltime job. Even the first part is as fascinating, though, as unearthing a forgotten civilization.

There has been a sort of dark age of knowledge, a conspiracy of silence, about the upper levels and ranges of human character. It would take too much room here to explore the possible reasons for this. Suffice to say, as Proust remarked, [and] we reflexly remark, "Too good to be true" about any exceptional account of goodness; we never say "Too bad to be true" about reports of evil. Debunking hagiolatry was a natural reaction from superstitious veneration. And it served a useful purpose. The acid of practical contempt ate through the meretricious gilding of propagandist pietism and neurotic emotionalism. And in a number of cases, at the heart of this synthetic spiritual pearl was found not a spark of the eternal life, but only the withered germ of an arrested soul.

On the Trail of the Saints

But some of the saints shone out all the brighter for the abrasion. The local and the temporal were eaten away, and underneath, the timeless was exposed. When the half-saints go, the true saints survive. We are beginning to wake to this fact, the fact that James Leuba, in his classic "writing down" of the watered stock of Western mysticism, leaves as his final irreducible mystery [that] there are, scattered through the centuries and the churches, men and women who are psychologically inexplicable. We may dismiss as psychologically contemptible the explanations they give for their condition; [but] the condition itself is indubitable, is irreproducible by us, and is awe-inspiring. In short, the saints tell us what humankind can rise to.

We find on rechecking the saints' recorded altitudes that we have estimated far, far too low a "ceiling." True, many—maybe most—who assayed the ascent collapsed. But some achieved. True, they had strange natural endowments. But we may quite as fairly put it the other way and say they had immense natural handicaps. An inquiry into the correlation of health and mental achievement in schools has just disclosed that the two are actually in inverse relationship. Health, like too great an endowment of natural technical facility in the arts, [works] against true creativeness.

Condemned to Sainthood

Few things are more informative than the rare rough sketches and untouched likenesses of the saints. They all show manifestly the stupendous reconciliation of opposites. These men and women by God's ... grace had no choice. They could never have been sober, sensible practitioners of the world, contented and approved. For them the only alternative was heaven now or hell at once. They had either to love all people or hate with hopeless self-pity the happiness of the most innocuous child. They could only joyfully embrace the Eternal or be utterly unhinged by the torture of each moment of the temporal. The faces show that, by God's power, there is another alternative way beyond Arnold's desperate dilemma, "Madman or slave, must man be one?" The thwarted energy which, left alone, would tear apart body and mind becoming "the temple of the Holy Spirit"—that energy imparts a new quality of living intensity. Carbon pressed beyond all measure becomes diamond—and not otherwise.

That is the first knowledge a true minister to the soul must have. They must know the soul's capacity and destiny—that under the pressure of the intangible, under the full radiation of the invisible, it can and does transmute the inert and even the base metal into becoming radioactivated. Second, they must work ceaselessly to decode in the vernacular of our contemporary lives the instructions of these great empiricists of transmutation. They tell us primarily two things that we can understand almost at once. The first thing is what they call God's grace. People differ; some are called to the highest effort to advance to the limit without delay; others are permitted to wait in reserve. This is a mystery but it is an empirical fact. All must be ready, for no one knows at what age (God is no respecter of ages any more than of persons) the call may come to the advance line.

The second thing is that a person's effort answers God's grace. There is a training that must be done by each. The rules of the spiritual life—what we may call, if we will, the principles of the further evolution of consciousness—are quite definite, and most of them apply to all of us. If we would enter in the full timeless life of God, we must be born a second time. This is not Oriental hyperbole. "Now," said the founder of Greek thought, "'we are as in an egg." We have to hatch out. Watch any insect: metamorphosis is not easy; it may end in death. But in death it must end if it shirks the effort.

We are confined by three main membranes: addictiveness of the body; possessiveness of the person; and pretentiousness of the spirit. Training is to loosen these "egg membranes" lest, like so many a poor chick, we wait too long [and] our energy remains in the ties instead of being drawn and focused in our soul, and we die suffocated, strangled.

Task of the Spiritual Director

It is the task of a spiritual director to judge when the moment has come for the soul to draw itself up, liquidate its resources, and make wholly and intentionally for its goal. There is a time for preparation and there is a time to break through and out. They must not—cannot—enforce action: they can and must indicate the goal and the method. They can watch, and when the travail of mutation comes on, whether at adolescence, [or] at what Jung has called the second adolescence around 40, or at the first shadow of the setting sun—they must be at hand. They must be a true diagnostician: they must judge

267

whether the soul is really seeking the true life of God or is only distressed because it cannot have more of the old. It is far better, the experts all agree, that you come to God when you are clear in your own mind. "Seek the Lord when He may be found" [Isaiah 55:6]—in the great storms thou shalt not come nigh Him.

But concussion of the shell may be the means whereby God causes the torpid to seek Him. Then, diagnosing that the new life has stirred, the spiritual director works unremittingly, though always with equal patience, at the delivery. They watch with unanxious devotion those whom they see God is leading. Some such have not to be left until a crisis, still less a tragedy, intervenes. Crises are not essential; on the other hand, the spiritual lives of the most persistent saints seem to show a series of steps, and some of these, though late in the saints' earthly ascent, as steep, as radically reforming, even as disconcerting as any [rapscallion's] conversion.

The spiritual director is then not merely salvaging derelicts or showing the puzzled how to play life's game. True, they can often save a life of which the standard psychology despairs, and the training they impart is probably the only one that can create the citizenry capable of establishing a living social conscience among the hypertrophied "100-million-nations" of today. But these are byproducts to their main aim and output. That is not to underrate their importance; on the contrary, it serves to show the scale of their task and the value of their main concern. That is to assist in the creation of men and women who are citizens not of another world but of an overworld.

Citizens of an Overworld

We have today an underworld: a middle world of our middling selves, and then a few sporadic outcrops of people as much above us as we are above the persons of persistent ill will. We must help create that overworld if we would ever have a civilization that will balance, let alone progress, by the only true balance of power: psychological power. The spiritual are today hopelessly outweighed by the unspiritual, the moral by the immoral, those who love by those who hate. Humanity, our society, our personal sanities can be salvaged only by a spiritual mutation. That is why the task of the ministry is nodal. That is why, however important the other interests of a church may be, a minister's supreme and supremely urgent task is not serving tables but the spiritual direction of souls.

It is obvious, if that is so and the task is fully to be discharged, that the spiritual director must be in constant training. They must not be outrun by their pupils. No art, no creative act can be taught from a book but by contagion from a proficient. They are the nuclear center around which must crystallize the contemporary spiritual answer to the contemporary challenge. That challenge is startlingly immediate, direct, and brutal. It will not be answered in archaic ecclesiastical terms, but neither can it be answered by economics, by politics, by treaties, or by arms. It is a psychological power and will go out only when it meets its psychological master.

That is the hopeful thing about our crisis: it calls for nothing less than true divinity to meet this true demonism. One policy can match another. One economy balances or clinches its opposite. But a devil attends only to a saint. All else—social workers, sane rationalists, sensible humanists—they brush aside into the [disposal], or, if they will stop crying for the moon, they may actually employ them to do their work for them.

That is why spiritual direction is the supreme need today whether we look at our home tensions, our class conflicts, or our international anarchy. The crisis has burst on us and we may be thankful, for naught else would have driven us to our true base. If we recognize it, then this world disaster is our chance; for crisis is, to those who see deep enough, always the codeword for opportunity.

If the churches turn to producing spiritual directors, it will not be long before in turn there are arising saints, people who are the contemporary equals of Benedict, Francis, Fox, and Wesley. From such a corps will come the new force adequate to the volcanic violences of this age. In a generation, those who have chosen the dedicated life—dedicating soul, mind, body, and estate—may be able to repeat again those words of triumph, "This is our victory which overcometh the world, even our faith" [1 John 5:4].

The Skill of Prayer

Originally published in *The Christian Century*,
Vol. 57, No. 15, April 10, 1940

SOME YEARS AGO, a small book was published called *The Art of Mental Prayer* [by Bede Frost, OSB]. It had a strongly Catholic complexion. Its phraseology and indeed the angle of its outlook had much to daunt undogmatic pray-ers. It gave only such systems of prayer as are approved by Rome. Eckhart and Molinos were shunned. All outside Christianity were slightingly dismissed. Yet it has rightly proved welcome among those who know the need and the difficulties of actual praying. In that subject, the author is a careful authority. His chapters on the special hindrances, problems, and methods are clear, wise, and lucidly practical.

Still, even among those whose desire to learn makes them able to overlook a certain sharp narrowness of outlook, the book is disturbing for a second and quite other reason. The author's occasional intolerance will hurt only souls at much the same level of charity as himself. But what will probably daunt far more of those who would learn more about prayer is the fear of over-definition—a hard precision, not so much about the end addressed as in the means described. "The *art* of prayer." We emotionally restrained, unanalytical northerners and middlers wince at that Italianate word. Is not art just the opposite of nature, and is it not supremely necessary that we should be natural in our approach to utter reality? How can we worship in spirit and in truth if we employ artifices? Is not spontaneity the *sine qua non* of any true worship? Has not one of the chief tasks of Protestantism been to replace the printed responses, the official collects, [and] the formal liturgy by extemporary prayer?

Are We Sincere?

That, it seems, would be an unanswerable objection if only we were as simple and sincere as we imagine we are. If we had the directness of children then, no doubt, we should have direct, unceasing, unreflective access to our Father. But who dare claim for themselves that unselfconscious innocency? It is well recognized that there is no hypocrisy more impossible to erode from the soul, more resistant to the acids of conscience, than the self-assured belief that I am frank, open, sincere, [and] honest in my thought, word, and deed—my life manifest to every person, my soul unshadowed from the light of God. It is because no one can pray for half an hour for three days running without discovering this self-shattering fact—that they are a humbug, a poltroon, a mean fraud. It is because the light of God goes right through my highly glazed mask with which I keep from others and myself the sight of what I am; it is because frank sincerity [and] spontaneous communion with utter Being is a psychological impossibility for a creature such as myself living in such a world, that method is necessary.

Art may be a word too near to artifice and affectation. Science may be too ambitious, though many mystics called their method and technique of [understanding] and of practicing the Presence, a science. Skill at least we must allow. Indeed, any truthful estimate of our situation and our task cannot escape the conclusion that a certain psychophysical athleticism is essential to any success in prayer. We have sentimentalized our relationship with Reality, playing with the notion that we are already fully rehabilitated sons [and daughters], when everyone knows that we are, many of us, still simply prodigals turning over in our minds whether we really like the company of pigs.

Sentimentality is always the taste for words in preference to things, for feelings rather than for fact. Before we talk of constant, unstudied, effortless communion with our Father, we have to ask ourselves where as a matter of fact we actually are. True, as Eckhart says, "He is always ready," but adds, "and we unready." We have to be frank: With how many human beings do we approach true frankness? Are we, really, going to find it easier to be sincere with the spirit of absolute truth and absolute perfection?

Dealing with Mental Indiscipline

We have to confront the fact that we are not merely morally shifty at base, [but that] we are intellectually a sort of mental quagmire. Our minds, let alone our souls, bubble and heave, gutter and slump like a fermenting morass. Quite apart from our spontaneous moral dishonesty—the cramp-like dread that holds us back from seeing and owning what we are—we have first to tackle our mental indiscipline, [which is] our inability to attend to anything save those outward compulsions which, as we say, compel or rivet our attention. Few, until they have practiced skilled silence, know the extent of the hubbub which is going on incessantly within them. We think we can attend, can concentrate, because we can apply ourselves to our business or our pleasure. An insect, shorn of its wings, might as well imagine that it could still fly because it is hanging suspended by its feet caught in the flypaper glue. Our work and our pleasure hold us, not we them. True attention means the power to still the mind by a simple and sheer act of the will, to attend to what at the moment does not attract and even does not seem to be present.

The first essential skill is then to help us to "ready" ourselves, to attain what the teachers of prayer call recollection. "The eyes of a fool are in the ends of the earth," says Wisdom [Prov. 17:24]. Certainly, on that showing, no age has been more foolishly distracted and incapable of recollection than ours. But how are we to focus if we do not know why and where we are focusing? Most people have very little idea as to what prayer really is, and therefore they do not know precisely what to do when at it. "Worship," said the traditionalists. They certainly meant something. Those real, old-fashioned pray-ers could, and often did, adore a Splendor that lifted them out of themselves and sent them back radiant themselves, as today a true artist can "stand moved" before a masterpiece and leave inspired.

But our minds are suspicious of these old phrases. Both the description of the object and of the method confuse us. If there is a Being supreme, can He want our praise? Adulation is a method that postulates anthropomorphism in that which is addressed. So adoration was shelved. Prayer was not worship. What then could it be but asking for favors? Yet that conclusion solved nothing. A little experimentation proved that, though prayers might be answered, prayer is not a really effective method of getting one's way. So "thinking out one's difficulties" became the next explanation of what should be done with the time still leftover, after preaching and church music had filled the main bill. But is that all that prayer may be? That depends, it must be repeated, on the object addressed. The End molds the method. What is God? Certainly not someone who becomes favorable if flattered. Yet the accepted alternative that God is simply my most sensible self does not exhaust the possibilities.

Is Prayer Autosuggestion?

"If prayer is not being given one's way, then it is getting it by autosuggestion"—that has seemed, to many spiritual explorers on the threshold of prayer, the fatal dilemma. But, as is not uncommon with dilemmas, there is a third way, and [that] way lies between the horns. A single question shows that. In "autosuggestion," who is the "auto"? Certainly not I. A power that can remake me when I have failed cannot with any accuracy be called "I." "But certainly not God," comes the counter. Let us remain pure explorers, simple empiricists. What actually happens if instead of petitioning, [if] instead of thinking my problems out, if instead even of complaining or giving myself suggestions, I just stay still—still the mouth, the mind, the will?

Of course I shall at first discover, as noted above, that I just cannot. But if this discovery, that I suffer from an inward *paralysis agitans*, makes me at least determined to see if I can lessen the malady and if, as does happen, the violent trembling of the surface consciousness at length subsides, then something highly remarkable begins to occur. The surface becomes transparent, and I begin to see in. In short, when real stillness is achieved, something reveals itself. Cautious empiricists call it the Light. We need not trouble about names; we are concerned with things and especially with results.

When the Light Shines

Yet Light is a good name, for light has two characteristics: its immediate use is that it shows us things otherwise overlooked. That is necessary, useful, painful: we see ourselves as we are. As the saints point out, because of this no elaborate recitation of our failures is necessary. We see ourselves and know that thus we are; thus, and indeed more searchingly, God sees us. Of course such a focus of disease breeds faults. There is nothing more to say. How can we talk of problem solving, of helping that weakling and checking that evil, when we ourselves, when the one person for whom we are preeminently responsible, have let become such a richly infective center? If then the Light had only one property—to reveal—we should be arrested in our career of escapism; we should be convicted of polluting the water of life, and there would be one spiritual fraud the less—and, quite possibly, [figuratively], one suicide the more. He who meets himself, says the Teutonic folktale, must die.

Light as Healer

But Light, we now know, has a second quality, even more important than its power to reveal: it bears the power of life, growth, and recovery. Exposure to radiation is a therapy. If we stay in the presence of the Light, if we will only take care to prevent our being distracted by any egotism, even concern for our own disgraceful condition, we are altered. A swollen, inflamed joint kept under a sunlamp is reduced. So with us, our ego is reducing so long as we can stay in the Light.

To resolve the ego is far more important than to solve any problems. For all human problems have their final root in the unresolved self. As Eckhart says, there are three things that keep a person from God: their sins, themselves, and time. That great diagnostician of the soul is tracing back our sick condition to its deep source. We need not yet follow him to his third and deepest level. We cannot stop short of his second depth, if we would have any lasting relief from our discontents. To attempt to solve problems or cure faults—even

275

one's own—and to fail to see that all particular problems and faults are only the flowers and fruits of self-will, is like trying to eradicate thistles by plucking off their heads.

Know the Rules!

Prayer, then, can be an empirical science, an experimental therapy. To follow it, we have to know some simple rules. We need to master some skills [so we do] not waste our small store of energy and time. The minimum requirement is that we should understand the necessity and method of recollecting the mind, of holding it in unstraining patience and waiting in the unimaginable Presence.

Those who so practice the Presence, who learn to let themselves be brought into the eternal instancy of the Divine Perfection, do not expect either specific answers to temporary problems or conscious sensations of immediate blessedness. These may come, but they are byproducts. The principal ... is an alteration of mind, a mutation of character below the level of feeling, a change of being rather than an increase in doing. Prayer, in short, is the recovery of the soul's breathing. When breathing has stopped, artificial respiration must be resorted to until, once again, natural breathing resumes. Then the practice of the Presence becomes constant and effortless as with Brother Lawrence. ...

We must not, however, despise even an iron-lung method until we can breathe naturally and without fail. And the humbler we are in noting when our breath is becoming shallow, labored, and even intermittent, and the quicker we then resort to those aids that the Friends of God have wrought for us, the sooner we may hope to be among those who alone dare neglect method, for every moment has become for them spontaneous communion, [and] every act is a prayer because their every breath is drawn in the Eternal Presence.

The Future of Collective Worship

Originally published in *Christendom*,
Vol. 5, No. 2, Spring 1940

WE ARE USED TO SPECULATIONS about the World of Tomorrow. The New York World's Fair had a Temple of Religion, and so had the Fair at San Francisco [i.e., the Golden Gate International Exposition of 1939–40, held at Treasure Island]. Yet no one speculated as to the public worship of tomorrow. Perhaps all futurists took for granted that there would be none, unless as a survival of purely archaeological interest, while the rest of us assumed that, despite all other changes, physical and psychological, worship would remain always as we had known it. Whatever happens, that latter opinion is least likely to be fulfilled. There is progress in worship as in all other human activities—progress, not necessarily advance.

The public worship of Western Christians has gone through three great stages. There was the short springtime of the [early] Church, when the whole heart of worship was, as Alfred Loisy has pointed out, the Agape, that intense fusion of a Communion service and a primitive Quaker meeting. That was followed by the long noon hours of the

Church's ascendancy during which the central act of worship shifted from the Communion to the Mass, an emotional shift from ecstatic spontaneity to solemn formality. As it were, worship split into two peaks, one of private worship [and] personal communion, and another of public worship, the memorializing "sacrifice of the Mass." In this division we see history and immediacy—the worshipper's present and the historic past, traditional dogma and instant religious experience—becoming separated. In the Mass, a deed that decided the future of the Church is symbolically re-enacted and recalled. In the Communion, the individual immediately experiences their timeless union with the Eternal Logos. In the pristine [Catholic] Church, historic fact and instant experience were one. Now they have become complementary.

Whether this division was fatal to ritual's continuance as the central act of worship or not, as a matter of fact we find the next development to be not praise, prayer, or contemplation, but preaching. This is not, as still commonly believed, a Reformation initiative. It had begun—at least, with the Franciscans and their huge auditoria-churches—contemporaneously, and perhaps contemptuously called Preacher's Paradises. St. Bonaventura, one of these missioner spell-binders, actually remarks: "A people grow up far more irreligious who are without preaching than those without sacraments." Protestantism heartily agreed with the dictum of this devout Catholic; and, as organic structure reveals function, we see in the Protestant churches how the pulpit, as it grows to be the central organ, eclipses the altar, as in human evolution we can see in the brain how the nerve center of reasoning—the neopallium—has spread until it occludes that more ancient guide and authority, the olfactory center. So the third stage of Western religion established itself. Preaching, aiming at rational demonstration [and] convincing argument: this was the *raison d'étre* for coming together in God's House.

That epoch ended in our day. The "subjective" discovery of how little our wills are actually affected by apologetics, chimed with the "objective" discovery of how weak the rational proofs are for religious beliefs. Kant's philosophic criticism of the proofs of God's existence was followed by Darwinian undermining much of the foundations of natural theology. In turn, Biblical criticism appeared to make much specific ecclesiastical dogma untenable. This three-fold cumulative attack on apologetics made many people believe that churches could only continue as social centers. When you can no longer go to church to be reminded and convinced that God exists, you go to "to meet old friends and make new ones"—there is no other Being to be met.

This is, however, to go further than the evidence warrants. The churches can have quite another future, for religion's worship is not merely in the pulpit. Nor, as a matter of fact is even the pulpit played out. Instruction and advice are of essential use when given by an authority to students who are sincerely anxious to learn. But the evidence does suggest that we are on the verge of a fourth stage in public worship. It seems that the great spiral of religious development is turning again so as once more to pass from where the center lay in rational demonstration to where its stress lies in direct power to create religious experience. Then the central activity of the group practice of religion will cease to be the exchange of convictions through rational argument. Can we speculate as to what form might be taken by the new psychological functions of public religious exercise?

When we try to study Western religion anthropologically, we see that the acts of Councils do not initiate; rather, they confirm what has already evolved. At best they make a decision between two or quite a few fairly close alternatives. Heresiarchs are, of their nature, far nearer to being one-sidedly orthodox than, after their condemnation, they are allowed to be. Reputable church historians have suggested that the Arians, with better political insight, might have managed to immobilize and perhaps even to expel Athanasius for good, by showing that the position which he had adopted did expose him to the charge of Sabellianism. The real directorate of the [Christian] Church has been certain profound tendencies in Western people, some undoubtably born of intense religious desire—"of God"—and others not at all so easily to be attributed. The primitive church's central experience, in the Agape, crystallized, as we have seen, into the Mass. An experience, perhaps possessed by too high an emotional charge, became a rite, certainly respectable, possibly mechanical.

We may perhaps venture behind the smokescreen of dogmatic controversy and strive to see the actual shifting fires of religious conviction and experience. The Agape was an experience of union with the Risen Lord who was then realized with complete conviction as being present with his servants, both those in the body and those who had passed beyond the body. It was then the obvious triumph over death and time, here and now. This intensity of experience, which perhaps not unnaturally led sometimes to emotional strain, seems to have faded. Perhaps it was tidied out of existence. It is hard for the educated to realize this—but it is quite possible to be too respectable to have much faith in anything but respectability. When the main concern of Christian authorities is that everything be done "decently and in order" [so] that nothing happens which might seem absurd or extravagant to the coldest or the most easily offended onlooker, then certainly, with much that should go, much [also] that is lovely and creative will be lost. If courtship had to be practiced under the eyes of those who thought all lovemaking ridiculous at best and always dangerous, our lives might be more respectable but our lyric literature would perish.

It seems clear that by the fourth century, the Agape is only retained as a funeral feast. This may be highly significant. It may mean that, by that date, the future life was no longer thought of as something to be entered on now, as a something because of which and only because of which Christians were not of all persons the most miserable, but on the contrary, the most blessed. We have considered only two choices to have lain before the [early] Church at that time: either an over-eager Adventism, an Apocalypticism, which, as hope deferred, led to disgruntled idling; or a resigned and finally a hardboiled acceptance of the world as it is, because all hope of heaven must be postponed at least until death. At least, for even then heaven is not to be entered, and only after death begins the real wholehearted preparation for heaven. This view is supported by the fact that the doctrine of Purgatory is late—a sixth-century dogma only admitted, only required when not only is Christ not expected soon to return to earth, but when life here, as an event that has its whole meaning and purpose as a preparation for meeting him in heaven—even that secondary faith degenerates further into a tertiary form.

Yet a third choice did lie before the Christians, and some must have taken it, for the doctrine is present in the Fourth Gospel: the conviction that Eternity is not a great span of time and far away in time, but is quite another condition—the timeless, instantaneous, intensest state of Being. This the early Church knew in the Agape, though maybe, as Lao Tzu says, because they knew they could not say. The fact that the Agape becomes a funeral feast would then be a clear symptom that this faith was gone. There was no longer a customary common experience affirming that there was no death for those "in the Lord"; that those living in the body have already died and their "life is hid with Christ in God," while those out of the body are already raised with him to the "power of endless living"; and that the Gospel is not faith based on a past and ever-receding fact in hope of a distant, undated, postmortem experience, but is an established actuality.

"We know we have passed from death to life" through this experienced "love of the brethren," the love of all the members for each other in their union with their Head. Once that experience becomes rare, the Mass naturally becomes central, because it is essentially an act that assures a safe eternity after death to each individual. It is a promise, a pact, rather than an immediate experience. Hence, as we have seen, Communion breaks from [the] Mass, and Communion itself becomes a preservative act—"preserve thy body and soul unto (a future) eternal life." To the degree that church members had not known direct experience of communion, they must needs be increasingly lectured upon it and reminded about the early times when such experience was common, or about the few (the saints) who continued sporadically to achieve it.

The dominance of the sermon as the center of public worship is then not due to revulsion against sacramentalism but to a realization that if I lack conviction and no one can impart it to me, I had better be given what can still be given: argument.

Yet argument has never been enough. As John Henry Newman, subtlest of apologists, exclaimed: "We are not saved by a smart syllogism." Protestantism was therefore marked by two features that revealed both the extent of its need and its potential power. The one was the phenomenon of Conversion. There were these uprushes from the depths, which, breaking through the limen with agony, not seldom flooded [one's] life—sometimes for years, on occasions until death—with a new, vivid, creative conviction, a new birth. Some churches tried to make this phenomenon part of their procedure and even worked at producing those intense emotional conditions and guilt–stresses that might fire the buried charge. They never succeeded in obtaining clear, permanent results, nor a method beyond grave criticism. As William James established, conversionism does not work with many devout souls. Their natures are not "Dionysian" but "Apollonian." They "go to [God] by inches," to use a Japanese phrase, by a daily self-sacrifice and self-elimination. Nor are the results of conversion, even with those on whom it "takes," generally permanent. Conversionism may then be said to be a spontaneous reaction of the spiritual life when repressed or not, given adequate channels of expression. When semi-suffocated, it bursts to the surface. It cannot be called a method, nor can it be made into one. Rather, it is a reflection on lack of method, on lack of technical religious knowledge. It was and is in the main a frantic "deprivative reaction" against the insufficiency of sermonizing as a spiritual diet.

The other phenomenon of Protestantism is therefore more significant for the future of Christian worship. That is the practice known to us under the form of primitive Quakerism. Quakerism is not an invention of George Fox. It was the rediscovery of an immemorially ancient religious practice—of waiting together in disciplined silence for the Spirit—a practice that led to Pentecost. But, though more a practice and a procedure than conversionism, it was itself not scientifically pursued nor understood. As ever, respectability was embarrassed by the intensity produced. "There is no Quakerism without quaking." This ruling of Robert Barclay, the first Quaker philosopher and historian, was true, if by Quakerism was meant its first manifestations—an uprush of psychic force—but untrue if what was meant was the kindly, wealthy, philanthropic formalism of the generations that succeeded to the first.

Why was the original quality lost? Religious self-assurance chose to be unaware of the achievements of earlier times—that God had always been speaking similarly to the prophets of every tongue. Psychological ignorance failed to observe the connections between size of group and vividness of experience, or even to notice the relation between the preoccupations of the individuals composing the group and the quality of religious "field" that they precipitate. As an anthropological fact, one hundred people—when meeting in silence—do produce a different common mind and conviction (one less intense and more unstable) than do a dozen. People who for six days have been involved even in the most upright handling of growing big business, do, on the seventh, exhale quite a different mental atmosphere [than] a similar number who have no business because they are outlaws for their faith. [These are] people for whom every day and hour has been made endurable only through their breathing in the Presence of God, and who have dared to gather, under threat of losing their worldly all, because in that gathering they would find such a heightened intensity of the Presence that beside this, all else was loss.

In short, Quakerism stumbled upon one of the major phenomena of field or group psychology. But because the pristine Quakers were almost contemptuous of all other religious practice, even that of their own ancestors (dismissing all the strivings and findings of the religious from Jesus Christ to George Fox as "mainly apostasy"), they could not define what they held, still less cultivate it. Its manifestation was therefore largely dependent on temporary conditions: (1) in the constituents—uncritical simplicity; exclusive interest; and, through persecution, profound companionship; [and] (2) in the group—small size; and its complement [of] extemporary, spontaneous procedure. Consequently, as outer conditions changed, the inward state altered. Economics radically modified psychology. The Shaker secession is also not without psychological significance. Here were people resolved not to lose the intensity of experience even at the cost of being outrageously absurd. They "would be fools for Christ's sake" [1 Cor. 4:10].

Again, knowledge of the history of religion, yes, even the knowledge of any full-scale history, might have taught, if not the Shakers or the Quakers, at least those responsible for the attempt to understand religion, or to understand society, that here was a phenomenon not to be dismissed with a snort or a sigh. The high military and political genius Amurath, as readers of Gibbon's *Decline and Fall* well know, time and again forsook the splendor of his triumphant sultanate to flee into the hills and be lost in the ecstatic, kinaesthetic worship of the Sufi mystics. Nor is his record a unique aberration. The force of this enthusiastic appeal upon the shrewdest and most successful intelligences has been known throughout history. Indeed, it is among those who have tasted power to the full that one finds greatest awareness of power's complete pretentiousness. Such persons, therefore, if they can still believe in reality at all, must seek most passionately to force their way through illusion's veil to the Presence.

The real problem, then, that confronts all those today sincerely concerned for the reality of religious worship is not whether there is a Reality to be contacted but whether it is possible to have any procedure—let alone any scientific procedure—without banishing the very thing that we would order, if not command. Must the choice always be either [to] become a confused and scandalous fool whose insanities are streaked and lit by genius and vision, or remain an accurate, worthy, intellectually informed administrator, and know that your Inner Light is a faltering glimmer, your spiritual power a critical tolerance, a hesitant tact? Must all the pitchblende remain the sole property of [native peoples] and all the radium-extracting apparatus be in the hands of those who never can obtain even an ounce of the ore? "Madman" (even though God-intoxicated) "or slave" (even though devoted in their labor), "must man be one?"

That is the supreme problem of actual religion, of the main spring of spiritual devotion today. The future forms of public worship will be dictated by the way or ways in which that problem is solved. May we, in hope of "God's high grace, and Man's endeavor," suggest that there will be a solution? Further, may we propose that, as religious evolution has gone through a great curve of process (from the creation of a profound "field" in which the individual lost their superficial self, to rational argumentation between individuals, and so back again to the "field"), that as religious practice as it stands today seems, at pause, confronted by the dilemma: powerless truth or truth-contemptuous power, the line of advance is one between the horns, is forward, taking both the critical and the creative, the analytical and the integral methods with us? How?

Briefly, by returning again, with a disciplined, skillful, rational approach to the field or group psychology of silence—the pristine pattern of Quakerism, prior to the growth of rank shown by the emergence of the "facing bench," prior also not only to formality but also to size. The work must start, as all seminal work, small. To this must be added specific psychological knowledge—knowledge of the past history of religious experience and practice, and a vivid and self-critical awareness of what is proceeding in oneself and with one's companions. The silence must be real if the field is to form deep and so produce a richly rooted yield of experience.

To be deep, we must understand how deep silence, to be creative, must sink. The silence must be threefold. As Molinos taught, silence of the mouth is not enough. To be profound and fruitful, it must descend to silence of the mind that must cease its vibrant imaginings (which often only increase when the mouth is dumb), and deepest of all, silence of the will, when it ceases its restless demanding that now, without further delay, and as I wish, God shall speak. Then, when such [depths] are sounded, speech may rise *de profundis*—as affirmation, not as argument. Let us, as T. H. Huxley urged, be little children and sit down as such before a fact and not dictate to Spirit how it shall function and why it should follow our use or convenience. Further, each constituent must learn to practice by themselves the deep silence of will-lessness, [of] alert passivity—a quality of the widest and keenest attention. They must not come unpracticed and self-dissonant to take part in helping to create the orchestra of the Spirit. None of these empirical observances of early, powerful procedures, is unscientific. On the contrary, these are the ways to produce the actual data for scientific examination.

That is the second necessary step. A firmly [attained] and well-grounded experience will not be disturbed by critical recollection. Indeed, that is the process which gives us all art and science. After inspiration, after the sudden experiential insight, comes the resultant—the power to work upon the data, the power to reflect on, order, and apply the revelation. Great acting begins with intuition and ends with self-conscious exactitude. First sunk in their part, the actor next succeeds in handling themselves. They find how to render character through themselves with the conscious detached technique with which a master painter holds and plies their brush. The surer the vision, the more precise, the more conscious the rendering. Recollected observation is therefore essential.

Still again, we must learn all we [can] (and it is an immense literature) about the body–mind—how the absolute degree of attention is mobilized, ordered, [and] focused. Here time and place have a contribution to make. Some hours are better than others. Diet, exercise, livelihood—study of these all yield knowledge that we shall be inexcusably negligent if we do not [absorb]. There must be no casualness today. The epoch of happy accidents and hardly [understood] "openings" is over. We must be as precise in preparing for the Infinite as we are carefully guarded against limiting it by premature definition. High [understanding] of what may not be spoken can often be helped and largely induced by arrangements which, deliberately dispensing with words, employ form and sound. Music and symbol can often engage the surface analytical attention and prevent distraction—the dreadful capacity for noticing the irrelevant—so as to permit the deeper, integral attention to emerge beyond these arrestors and dissipators. We must all the more know what we are doing in order to allow what is done to us when we have prepared to remain in profound, unhindered mystery.

Such then is the briefest suggestion of what the pattern of creative worship might be in the future. Those who are fully alive to their contemporary moment (the only people who deserve the description "this worldly") must realize that our psychology, our social crisis, and our present religious revolution all call for the creative synthesis of the trends in dynamic group religion—collective contemplation—with a critical understanding and practice of its rules, disciplines, and powers. Only thus will religion once again recreate that essential condition that can cause the human spirit to mutate, to be born again, to begin a new evolution, and so can contribute—and it alone contribute—those inspired characters who alone can save humankind.

I Believe in Peace (abridged)

Originally published in *Religion in Life,*
Vol. 9, No. 3, Summer 1940

I HAVE BEEN ASKED to state the roots and ramifications of the philosophy of life that led me to the pacifist position. This, I need hardly say, is no light requirement, and anyone who is aware of the complexities of human motivation and the obscurity of their own mental and moral growth might well decline such an attempt. What person dare say they can give a truthful account of the causes of their convictions? Is it not a person as sincere, as daring, and as profound as Paul of Tarsus who maintains, "Yea, I judge not mine own self" [1 Cor. 4:3]? Yet this self-examination before a critical and interested audience is a valuable exercise, and not merely for the speaker in search of more self-knowledge.

I am not suggesting that such comments and speculations as have occurred to me could be used toward a further development of sociology, but it does seem possible that if anyone has for some time been driven to ask questions about the basic drives in society, though his conclusions may be insignificant and his answers inapplicable, some of the problems that his search has uncovered may stimulate minds, more free and more penetrating, to find the real reply. This account must therefore have in it an autobiographic element.

The approach to the problem of peace and war came for most of us, born as the nineteenth century aged in the English-speaking world, from two sides: the religious and the political. It was clear that in Christianity, peace was advocated and perhaps even required. The Sermon on the Mount was hard to explain away. A series of great Church Doctors from Clement of Alexandria, Origen, and Tertullian right down to Lactantius, who lived to see the Church about to be established, maintained there could be no doubt as to Christ's words. Those later, such as Augustine, who defended any coercion, did so with obvious discomfort; and finally Aquinas so hedged round his definition of a just war (which is the only war not to be adjudged as murder), that some Catholic theologians maintain that the only war capable of coming within that definition would be a war launched by the Pope—all national wars are *ipso facto* criminal.

Nor did the extension of our knowledge of other religions shake this conclusion, whether or not that extension might seem to infringe on the absolute sway of other dogmas. It was clear that the only other world faiths that had an ethic at all comparable with Christianity's, were equally emphatic in their condemnation of all violence and their advocacy of peace. It was not merely that Christ's teaching and that of Gautama and of the Taoist original, Lao Tzu, pointed to peace as an admirable end. They stressed with equal force that peaceful methods were the only effective means of attaining a peaceful end, and that violent means, used for whatever purpose, even to achieve peace, could only, because of their nature, lead to more violence.

Operate with septic instruments and it matters not however noble your intentions, the patient must die. However seriously ill the patient may be, however anxious you in your wish to help may be, however much, for the moment, you may seem to attain your objective and to disclose and eradicate the apparent focus of trouble, the patient will not, cannot recover. The apparent triumph of using Beelzebub to cast out Beelzebub is most perfectly and succinctly described by those laconic technical descriptions you will find in journals of surgery where new experimental operative techniques are recounted. After much specialized detail giving the procedure, there come two concluding phrases, the first in bold type, [and] the second, the last word of all, in italics and in brackets. The first is "Operation Successful." The second, "Patient Succumbed."

Religious authority—the establishment of moral laws by citing texts and commentators—underwent severe restriction during the years I am reviewing. The lower and the higher criticism reduced the credit that our fathers had given to original documents and official commentaries. The shift from the religion of authority to that of experience did not, however, weaken the pacifist position. It was clear, from the early Christians, through such a medieval example as Saint Francis, down to the Quakers and many contemporary missionaries, that when the power of dynamic "interest–affection" was employed, when all people were treated as children of a loving Father, a contact was possible even with the most [undeveloped], and the lowest could be raised to trust, confidence, and co-operation. ...

It is clear that peace is essential for humanity. War is the compendium of vices. War is cancer in humankind. It must be cured, or the patient must die. That is the clear diagnosis. But diagnosis, alas, is not cure. Because war is deadly, that does not ensure that peace will [succeed]—far from it. Indeed, if war is social cancer, then all our ordinary hopes are vain, for we are an old species, as mammals go, unstable, and so to be expected to show the specific derangements of senescence. The essential morbid manifestation of an elderly organism is precisely the emergence of autonomous malignant growths. Nearly all our arguments in favor of hoping that we shall outgrow war, [show], therefore, in precisely the opposite sense. That "one increasing purpose runs, / And the thoughts of men are widened with the circling of the suns" is to extrapolate, as a straight ascending line, a process that is a curve of ascent and decline. Advance in early life foreruns retreat in age.

"Natural amelioration"; "the inevitable improvement in the spirit of the age"—these civil slogans are expressions of the same mistake. The growth of specialization in our intellectual interests and social concerns and the growth of sensibility in our emotional range and tension—these characteristics of the more advanced members of our communities have also been taken to be reassuring, but, on examination, show themselves as confirming the deeper diagnosis. Specialization means greater power but equally less coordinative purpose and less responsibility among the experts, technicians, and specialists. They cannot help this; the vast disintegrative process is (so long as they stay in it) beyond their control; private virtues result in public vices. Sensibility means greater feeling but, equally, [without] any power to [stop] the world's misery or to understand its source, [resulting in] a greater tendency therefore to be shocked into despair. We are all reduced to the status of the chorus in a Greek play. We can foresee the doom of the protagonists and wring our hands. By our position as onlookers, we are helpless effectively to intervene.

Therefore, we have only to continue as we are going, growing in ever finer and more special skills, feeling for ever wider and more complex ills, and the giant organism, of which we are the cells, will die. Lacking a profound mutation in consciousness [and lacking] our recovery of an instant sense of our actual solidarity, even the most upright specialist is only that simple vigorous cell that has returned to the simple, reproductive, uncoordinated level—in other words, a cancer cell. Nor can we hope to put the clock back and force people to live in societies so simple that, in such, the individuals who compose them must see the consequences of their acts and must be joined and held in a comprehensive coordination in and of the whole unit. The desire for complex societies, for a life of distraction, for ever-heightened excitement, risk, gamble, and the spectacle of disaster—this frame of mind ... causes our present dying society. The disease can only be cured by curing the infected cells. Our giant states with their increasing accelerated instability are the projection of our late, complex, and fissiparating psyche.

Here, however, we arrive at the dividing of the ways. The growth of self-consciousness, which has been fatal to tradition and has exhausted intuition, not only gives the individual a new capacity for freedom, but through the collapse of the old, a new opportunity to pioneer. The economic explanation of (or excuse for) things can be cut through right down to the real cause: human nature. Setting ourselves to the understanding of ourselves, we realize that we have never been free, and that the way we have lived has never permitted freedom, intention, or any peace, save an accidental deflection of conflict, and also, that we can be free and at peace as soon as we really so desire. The age of the avowed intentional Orders can always succeed the ages of Disorder. So we may begin at once to build up a New Force for humanity. Nothing can be done with the monster states; they are too anchylosed to be molded into a fresh movement; they are too massive for their huge momentum to be checked. The "specious present," that period during which no change can be made in time, extends in proportion to each community's size. The specious present of the "one-hundred-million" bureaucracy is probably nearer ten than five years. Probably, too, in such a hypertrophy, any intention, any plan, whether wise or mistaken, can never catch up with unforeseen, unintended, unpreventable change—which makes hay of all past planning.

We are driven, then, to deal with small units that can be affected and that we can affect. And it is from such small defined sources, from such "radiated seed," that a really new stock may spring. [Through] the realism of pacifism—this dealing by good and not evil means with individuals to bring about good ends through them—people [attain] to goodness so that they can live the good life of true communion with each other. This [is] the only policy that produces the results it claims and intends; [it] is also the noblest idealism. For it asserts that the end and purpose of the universe is nothing less than the free act of each individual whereby they choose to serve and give themselves to a God infinitely powerful, infinitely kind, and infinitely patient.

God does not coerce this consent or it [would be] no consent. Utopia is not the aim of the world—though it might be a byproduct of this surrender to God and can only be achieved by such an act. Hence to coerce people is to delay and do one's best to frustrate the universe's meaning. The task, and it is a heroic task, of pacifism, is to win people by example and inspiration to the immense effort required for the soul to surrender itself to God and freely to choose His will. Because this power of freedom is given to each soul, it cannot be extorted, and no one can say when it will be employed. But each of us can come to the full knowledge of God's will and become so that we live perfectly transparent to, perfectly transmittant of His love, His understanding, and His patience. Then we are not disturbed about success or whether we shall live to see an earthly Utopia. In the great imagery of Mahayana Buddhism, it is described how every perfected soul, as it attains to the light of full understanding and enters into complete Liberation, turns back and stands incandescent with the Divine Compassion to wait in perfect patience, illuminating the way until the last creature, the most degraded, the most [ignorant], the most malignant, awakens to the realization that it, too, is not outside God's pity and, waking, sees the whole of the creation awaiting perfection, a perfection only possible when the unity is completed by this last and lowest's willing assent.

That as far as I can see is the faith and practice of pacifism, and it is in such a faith and practice, and only in such a faith and practice, that I can see hope and meaning for humankind.

A Rationale of Ritual
(abridged)
Originally published in *Christendom*,
Vol. 5, No. 3, Summer 1940

RITUAL, SYMBOLISM, AND SIMILE put off some people. They say these flourishes prevent clear and simple understanding and comprehension. They resent what they call obfuscations of superstition. They know these antics only stand in the way of their clear-eyed and single-hearted [perception] of the One. But it is dangerous to be too sure. It is the mistake, not of a subtle mind, but of one that has prematurely concluded the problem to be simple, to say that Ultimate Reality can be easily and rationally grasped. We have to ask every method to help us, every illustration to raise us from our common concerns to the state of Pure Being. Reason is good, but [if] depended upon wholly, it may end in arresting our growth because it cannot go beyond the premises given it by the senses. When so used, it tends to make us fall into two rudimentary [misconceptions]: the first is that what we are seeking is to be rendered completely in logical terms when in fact it lies almost wholly in the realm of the antinomies. The second mistake is to assume that what we are seeking is completely clear, objective, external to ourselves; that we can approach it with a casual and, in a way, a superior detachment; that it must wait on our judgment as to whether it has any right to our attention or worth for humanity.

We have then to employ methods not merely to help us understand the nature of the experience with which we are surrounded. The methods also have to act so as to prevent—screen out—our almost instantaneous, unquestioningly assured [misunderstanding]. When the reason has discovered that there is no reason why there should not be an Ultimate Reality, when we have discovered as a fact that even to [perceive] the common-sense world as it is, and not as we with our useful-or-not-useful "filter" strain it, we have to be very watchful. We have not reached the end of our quest but [have] only begun it. We have only had a glimpse of Reality. Now we must see whether we may command and develop a faculty of [perception], of integral thought. For this is needed to carry us on from the point at which analytic thought [admits] that it has finished ordering the [perceptions] given by the customary range, area, and focus of consciousness. ...

We cannot do without form; we cannot leave any part of the vast front of the body–mind behind us when we would shift the level of consciousness and rise into unhindered worship. The whole of the individual being, from clearest thought, through feeling and mood, down past habit and reflex, even to function and organ, must be shifted toward its goal. The entire being must mount in a vast well-ordered sweep. Otherwise, [as can happen to] a [young woman] for the first time wearing a [long, flowing] dress, we shall trip over our train and find ourselves unable to rise.

As, then, a good [scribe] "addresses" themselves to the sheet on which they are about to write (as a good golfer "addresses the ball") and will not make a stroke until the whole procession of their many linked selves give notice that they are ready, ... so too with right ritual. It does not scramble and plunge, but "recollects" [our many linked] selves, assembles the whole spirit, mind, and body "as a reasonable, holy and lively (or vital) sacrifice" ready to be wholly sublimated by the descending Universal Spirit. So, all wise teachers and spiritual directors repeatedly warn against precipitancy in worship, a hastiness in wishing to plunge in without order, and counsel always both a preliminary preparation and an epilogic quiet. All sane ritual provides these things. Nor does it merely help us to get under the glittering surface of *maya,* parting the flashing mesh, holding back the tentacles of customary attachment that coil round us as we would pass through. It does us two further services. When we are through "the magic casement," when we have been able to uncoil our self-centered, vicious-circled self until we can touch the rock behind the mist, sane ritual—scientific spiritual exercises of the body-mind—can help us from falling back through fatigue before we have gathered all we may, and can help us to bring back through the guarding gates without loss all we have gathered.

First to consider is the power of sustaining our attention of the Unreflected, the Incomparable. This needs all aid; for our mind is always shuttling and shimmering, dipping and fluctuating between what it notices and what it thinks of the thing noticed. We are always wavering between seeing things and losing sight of them in the mist that rises the moment we see, the mist which springs as any gleam of reality falls on our foggy selves and we instantaneously reflect: "How will this aid me, how may this harm me?" Fatigue is largely due to lack of right interest and the rise of wrong interest; pure interest in what is perceived lapsing into interest at ourselves in being interested and admiration at our part. Our first step then is to see that the body—that residue and sediment of the ego-centered self—shall not start the relapse. ...

Reason, through exact and detailed psychophysical knowledge, can and must help ritual's development. Reason only objects and hinders when it is not seized of all the facts that are involved in worship and the practices of contemplation.

We have seen that ritual has to help us to do two things. The first is to shift our focus as quickly as may be, for in that highest quality of attention—contemplation—we have only a little time to attain the moment of full awareness. It is for us always a race with time, a race to assemble our powers of concentration, to gather our scattered interests into one focus and so attain utterly undistracted realization before fatigue begins again to dissipate us. Ritual can be a quick method of calling in all our resources, of marshalling body, mind, and spirit in one salient alignment without hitch or delay.

Most of us are like the impotent man at the pool of Bethesda. We spend all our prayer time in just crawling down to the water's edge only to find when we have done so that we have [taken] so long that the water itself has already subsided by the time we have reached the brink. It needs great skill to cull these moments of clarity. We are stepping from one frame of reference to another, and we must do so without getting ourselves caught in passing from one form of concentration—the attention that is held by outer interest, as when at a task—to another, the inner undistracted look. We must leave the outer without stirring up a train of associations which, like a dust cloud, will follow us into the other atmosphere—that other atmosphere which is so still that it has not, as have the outer worldly attentions, the windy power to blow away alien dusts. When the body and the mind can do something to back up the spirit in its turn of attention, then they cease to be liabilities, loiterers like Lot's wife, and become assets.

Secondly, ritual, having helped us over the threshold, can keep us in the room we have [gained]. It aids us to maintain our extended vision and clarity by sweeping aside uprising interferences, as dross can be skimmed off the bright surface of molten metal.

But it has also [another] vital service to render: it has to make it possible for us to return to the outer world with something of the atmosphere we have breathed in the inner. The light must not fade when we leave the Presence. We must learn to see its complete and utter whiteness in the spectrum–band of the temporal rainbow. In time it is present under these divided forms. Ritual attempts to render this fact. Unless we have some method, there is no doubt that our vision will be brushed off us as we pass back into the ordinary world. It is not that it is fairy gold, a vain emotion. It is because we have no vehicle in which to carry into our thick air an essence that must otherwise evanesce.

We can remedy this great loss and constant disappointment by full psychophysical knowledge. We must remember that we are a tripartite being, a threefold creature, and even in the intensest concentration, even in the moments of most sublime self-forgetfulness, we are nonetheless a breathing, heart-beating, secreting animal. Unless the body also worships, the soul's and the mind's worship are by so much the less. So it is that in real and full worship, the body learns to be as rapt as the soul; and when the creature returns from such an audience, not only the psyche but the physique is for some time resonant with the harmony it has heard and the harmonizing with which it has responded to that music. We must then remember that the rational mind thinks in propositions, by argument, and with illustrations. The subconscious mind [understands] through symbols. Full attention begins to be possible when the object of notice seems intellectually interesting, absorbing, emotionally moving, [and] appealing. Both of these attractions must, then, be commanded.

Thirdly, there is the body. It worships kinesthetically. That means that its attention is through a change of rhythm. We know its spontaneous salute to the Adored: bated breath, the heartbeat that rises with the lark's flutter and then pauses like the lark's hover. The body needs to take up its position, its posture, to stand at attention, to move in its obeisance before that bodyless Rhythm, that soundless unceasing creative Word, of which flesh and blood are a momentary utterance. The body is not only less apt to interrupt; it can act as an able acolyte if it is permitted to adopt certain postures and is called upon to lend its attention at times in which its own diurnal rhythm brings it up in a crest of upward reaching physical release and aspiration. Time of day and posture, the hour of office, and the placed position can all, then, be basic helps.

Worship must, in short, always combine, if it is to attain to any intensity that may leave a lasting impression, a rationale—a technique intelligently followed to attain a certain desired state of mind, [and] a behavior pattern, a psychophysical carriage or presentation—if it be no more than sitting in alert openness [that] sustains the rationally directed attention. ... Worship must be a rhythmic cresting in the wave-motion of living; the periods of contemplation must regularly and precisely balance the times of action. As the heart muscle rests between each beat, so must the consciousness pass in constant systole and diastole, from the contemplation of Reality as the One and as the Manifold.

The whole day is thus found to proceed in a patterned sequence. For as the twenty-four hours are divided between sleep and waking even among animals, for even they are double-natured, so with

297

humans as a spiritual creature, as they are tripartite, a third beat must of necessity be present in their rhythm. Between sleep and waking, between the detensioning relaxedness of slumber and the exclusive engrossment of work, a third opening presents itself and must be taken if the soul would live. Then it is that the spirit practices an awareness that is more unrestricted than sleep and more absorbed than any mental work. Therefore, besides ritual methods, there should also be ritual times, until the whole of life is ordered into a single art of worship—each timed spell of meditation setting the theme that will be modulated and orchestrated through the intercalated spell of action. Such seem to be the rudiments of ritual development. Along such lines may develop an art of worshipful living, a science of practical religion.

The Practice of the Presence

Originally published in *The Christian Century*,
Vol. 59, No. 17, April 29, 1942

"THE PRACTICE OF THE PRESENCE" is again a popular phrase. It is being recommended as a palliative if not a cure for many of our internal and external troubles. But if we are to put any weight on it, we ... must understand what it is and how it is done. It is a recipe that has had a long popularity. During the seventeenth century, it was almost the sovereign specific for spiritual distress of every sort. Perhaps nothing could show its universal appeal better than the fact that [Cardinal] Richelieu, that arch power-politician, wrote a little book on it, advocating its extraordinary efficacy. At the other end, we have the extreme Quietists saying the same thing. That Richelieu with all the active [Roman] Church persecuted the Quietists while they on their part declared that most of the practices of the Church were unnecessary and even obstacles, shows that there must have been considerable confusion of terms.

Nor when we come to the book to which the phrase owes most of its popularity with most moderns—Brother Lawrence's *Practice of the Presence of God*—is the difficulty elucidated. Lawrence, it is clear, did not think of himself as a precise teacher, and he took for granted that all he said would be taken in the framework of Catholic theology. It is necessary to stress this, for study will show that two standards are recommended in the book—the one is easy; the other produces the extraordinary results that made people want to consult Lawrence. These two standards present no difficulty to a Catholic. They are familiar with the doctrine of the two lives: the lower life of action and the higher of contemplation, the lower of life in the world and the higher of life "dead to the world."

Life on Two Levels

The Lawrence letter ["Third Letter"] where he says that the young soldier will be able to make a satisfactory practice if now and then on the march he remembers God and makes a motion of the will toward Him, is written with this, the lower life, in view. The young man will be doing enough, with confession, absolution, and the sacraments, to [ensure] that he will not go to hell. But he will go to purgatory and will have a stiff time of it there. For all that he might have done in this life—which, as St. John of the Cross teaches, he might have done with far greater ease in this life by giving up his days wholly to religion—must then be done. God is not mocked.

The remainder of the letters are written for those who intend to do their utmost in this life to attain to the Presence of God, for they realize it was for that they were created and are in the world. The instruction, or at least the practice, here indicated is very severe.

Still, again, careless reading may make one unaware of this. If, however, we turn to an authority who is not writing a few brief letters, mainly of encouragement to people who have fully equipped spiritual directors, but is issuing a careful manual on prayer, then we cannot escape seeing something quite startling. The practice of the Presence is indeed commended as an admirable and necessary practice. But it is said to be of great difficulty and to come late in the spiritual life. Let anyone seriously try it and they will discover this is so.

Spiritual Discipline Not Easy

Augustine Baker, O.S.B., in his manual of prayer called *Holy Wisdom*, states that until the mind has long been trained by careful practices in the actual hours of prayer, ... to keep the mind on God during the time when one is occupied with other things is almost impossible. He says that for any beginner to claim that he or she can so do is either for them to deceive themselves or for them utterly to confuse their thought and action. What then is to be done? St. Teresa's advice is quoted, "We cannot become perfect in a day." We must begin by making "virtual" acts or resolutions when we come out of prayer that we will preserve the frame of mind [and] the scale of values which we had in prayer.

That is the advice of a famous [spiritual] director of the nineteenth century, Pére Libermann. Both he and Baker, however, note that this frame of mind will be undergoing a steady distortion while we are occupied in worldly things, even if those things be not spiritually harmful. We should, therefore, be with other people who are trying to do the same thing. We must remember that the vast mass of people thinks such behavior odd and irrational. [This] suggestion works in our minds and gradually destroys our conviction of the reality of the spiritual world. We are like the man in Jack London's famous story, "To Build a Fire." We are out in a subzero temperature, and if we travel alone, we may be spiritually frostbitten before we know it. We become numb, and in a little while our whole spiritual life may be in acute danger. We lack the power to rekindle our faith by ourselves.

To Carry the Glow

The only way, then, that these experts recommend for attaining to that constant circulation between God and the soul is for the beginner never to leave themselves too far from a time of definite prayer. They cannot yet carry the flame with themselves; but from one fire to another, if not too far apart, they can carry a glow. It is for this reason that those who attained to this Practice warn us of a temptation that the thought of the Practice may hold for us. We may think of it as an alternative to regular prayer. They hold this to be deadly. We shall think we can practice the Presence; we shall stop therefore our careful prayer times and quite quickly we shall find that we have stopped our feeble attempt to practice [the] Presence. We are then in deadly danger.

How then are we to carry over from one time of prayer to the next? François de Sales makes a recommendation that he found to work when he was attaining this state. He took from his prayer some thought or phrase, and, like a tuning fork, he kept ringing this in his mind. With the help of this, he was able to judge whether he was "going off key." When this practice has become fairly regular, it is found that, though it seems mechanical, something living is being sown in the depth of the mind. The real task would seem to be to find a method whereby the reverie level of the mind, instead of day-dreaming about [things], will be directed to God.

Studies in industrial psychology have shown that this level of the mind continues its line of thought even when the surface mind is outwardly occupied in skilled work. Probably this background of thinking, this climate of the mind, is present, [though] following its own currents whatever our surface minds are doing. This type of thought does not get in the way of practical action. Indeed, it has been shown that, provided this reverie is content about its own business, the critical intelligence can be directed with greater force and freedom onto the outer world. For this happy basic feeling–tone leaves the person free from self-concern to throw themselves into their work.

Industrial psychology has also shown this basic feeling–tone is less and less often found to be cheerful. We are most of us distracted by self-pity and ego-commiseration. There would be very practical value, therefore, if we could make this undertow of the mind less of a drain upon our energy. It is precisely this that the practice of the Presence yields as its preliminary benefit.

Still, even to gain that state is difficult. How are we to influence this willful, powerful, and childish level? There is only one way. It is deaf to argument but open to reiteration. Further, certain times are more favorable than others. It pays to reserve some time in the very early morning when first waking and late at night just before falling to sleep, to expose that level, which is then near the surface, to the light of God. The method is slow, but it is unfailing. It can be greatly hastened by modifying our habits of life so that in every way they will be in accord with that Presence which we wish to keep consciously with us. For in the end, Ruysbroeck has the last word, "Ye can be as holy as ye will."

Little Used Keys to Religion

Originally published in *Christendom*,
Vol. 8, No. 1, Winter 1943

NEARLY FIFTEEN YEARS AGO, a remarkable film was widely shown. It was called *World Melody*. It was actually a clever development of the silent travelogue, taking the onlooker round the world. Its originality, however, lay in the fact that by skilled shooting, it showed how strangely alike our varied world actually is, if we don't see the label or hear the accent. One tracing shot swept the eye up Chartres' western front, but halfway up the façade, dissolved into the temple at Puri. Another began with the Neapolitan procession on the Feast of St. Januarius, but changed into the car of [the Hindu deity] Juggernaut. The architectural sculpture, though inspired by widely different dogmas, coalesced [into] the dancing figures in religious ecstasy—one could not help feeling that their religions, though creedally opposed, were fundamentally similar in their level of devotion.

Such a film raises the question whether there is not a third way of estimating religious associations. The first way of judging whether religions could unite was whether they used the same formularies. Then, mainly with the rise of the Modern age, came the realization that creeds were not enough. Christ's teaching, at least in this respect, began to be put in practice among the liberal Christians—the tree was to be judged less by its label and more by its fruits. The ethical life that a creed produced, and not the creed's cosmological accuracy, was to be the test whether it was true and whether it would combine with other creeds. Such an attempt—simply to judge a creed by its associated morality—though a considerable advance on the judgment formed solely on the logic of definitions, was still insufficient.

A third way therefore should be sought. Judging trees by their fruit is certainly a sound method, but with two provisos: first, you must be prepared to wait till the tree fruits. Fruiting is an end process, and if you are choosing trees to plant, you have to choose them before they have fruit or even flower. Secondly, a tree may fruit well because it is of such good stock that it can flourish on soil which would starve a less robust growth. Some people seem so naturally good that they can produce lives of great sanctity while practicing a religion which is not of the highest type. ... What then is needed is a test somewhere between the creedal test and the moral, some description that would tell us of the essential process or praxis whereby the fruit, the moral life, is produced. "We are not saved by a smart syllogism," remarked J. H. Newman, that remarkable convert to the great church of dogma. What then saves us [and] makes us capable of the new life? It is not intellectual belief—that does not change conduct. It is not ethical practice—that is to put the cart before the horse. The answer to this vital question would seem to lie in this third way of estimating religion. This third way is by the actual religious practices that a religion inculcates.

This third test should be more familiar than it is. Why we have not used it more decisively is because of an accident, or a chapter of accidents, in our own religious past. The ancient [Christian] Church—Orthodox and Catholic—certainly attached the greatest importance to such practices, but the practices themselves were identified with the creeds. Hence, for example, when the early Fathers and later the Jesuits had to recognize sacramentalism being practiced by the "heathen," instead of seeing that here might be the same thing as theirs expressing itself with another accent, their reaction was to dismiss it as Satanic mimicry of their own most sacred mysteries. And when Protestantism triumphed, it continued to make that identification: it destroyed all such practices as had only "Catholic" explanations, only retaining those which had "warranty in Scripture." Yet we now know that a practice may have high therapeutic value while the explanation given for it can be demonstrably false. John of Gaddesden, the famous physician of Edward II of England, prescribed red hangings for the rooms in which smallpox patients lay. The current explanation that red was a "noble colour" associated with the sign of Jupiter, a very favorable planet, was false and led to the practice being abandoned. The fact that screening out the actinic rays by the red curtains saved the infected skin from scarring could not then be known. A mistaken explanation should not compel us to abandon a working practice. Are we then to welcome every superstition? No: there is the third test, besides the dogmatic, which may be false, and the ethical, which may come too late and be too partial.

In the early days of vitamin research, when the actual vitamins could not be isolated, they were called accessory food factors, and their presence could only be detected by [an] indirect and delayed test as to whether the animal flourished when fed on the diet. So, too, has it been with religion. We have known that certain elements essential to the life of the soul were present in the rich complexes of all the great religions. But we could not isolate the working elements from the useless, and sometimes harmful, accretions. We have known that something essential has been lacking in a church or teaching which was only ethical. The awkward choice then seemed to be either the [coarse, earthy] whole-meal loaf or the completely aseptic, completely unnourishing [white] bread.

That dilemma is no longer absolute. We can now begin to extract the religious vitamins. Though religion is the richest field in which to search for such social vitamins, the religious have not as yet contributed much to this important study. Partly because of the high specialization among all scholars, religious scholars found no faculty ready to study this borderland subject; while the person with "clinical experience," the minister, felt such a reverence for their study that they were apt to shrink from an empirical attitude. As a consequence, it is from outside sources that most of our information has to be brought.

In this study, there are two lines of approach. The first, most evident, but least welcome to actual practitioners of any religion, is the estimating of the psychological equivalent, the actual working element, in any specific cult or dogma. For example, though without scriptural warranty and therefore rejected by Protestants, two great cult–dogmas have grown steadily in the Roman Church: the development of Mariolatry, and the purgatorial doctrines. It is clear that both of these cult–dogmas meet a human need of which the psychologist is aware but the rationalist ethicist [is] ignorant. We can see, through the last two thousand years, the mother of Jesus being brought out from the modest position assigned to her in the Gospels to that of the *Theotokos* and finally to that of "joint mediator" with Christ himself. As the Father, [as] taught by Jesus, becomes too lofty, Jesus becomes the Forgiver. In turn, as the Christ becomes wholly the Judge, someone must be found to intercede with him. The idea of all-forgiving motherhood has threatened to supersede that of the Father and the Good Shepherd. So, too, with the doctrine of purgatory. Not fit for hell and uninclined to qualify for heaven, the average sensual person feels that provision must be made hereafter for them to make the moral grade they refuse to make now. And after four centuries, the Church bowed to the popular demand and has been developing so complex a theme ever since.

This line of research is now generally familiar to most students of religion. The second line, though it promises results more valuable for religion (because [it is] more likely to be accepted by the religious than the psychological explaining away of their devotions) has nevertheless till now aroused less interest. This is the study, not of the evolving *mythos* in which a psychological need expresses itself, but of the actual social pattern that such a need precipitates, and in which, far more than in the *mythos*, the need expresses itself. For example, the actual development of the rosary is closely associated with the Mother worship in Catholicism. But the use of beads, *mantra*, and the group of fifteen [people] saying the rosary together at stated times are the actual psychophysical and psychosocial factors that give us insight into an essential [element] of religion, link us up with other religions such as Mahayana Buddhism and Vedanta (from which in all probability the rosary was derived), and suggest lines of practical research in the development of group prayer. What is true of the rosary is true also of the rites that have grown round the concept of purgatory—specific prayers and masses for the dead, the "month's mind" when the bereaved family meets for a service of recollection, and so forth.

Anthropology today is increasingly interested with this branch of religious enquiry, with what is now generally called "patterns of culture." It is recognized more and more that these actualized rhythms of social behavior are the permissive concomitants (and indeed not infrequently the causes) of codes and dogmas. Further, as ethnology finds ever less evidence of physiological race as the cause of different and conflicting ethics, it becomes of increasing importance to study those "social heredities," those millennia-long currents of culture and standards of taste that give rise to nationalisms and super-nationalisms.

It is this study that the science of comparative religions now needs to [perform] in its own field. From it, there may be hoped something far more than a new detached tolerance toward people of another dogma than one's own. It might be possible by this new method to discover the essential praxis in each religion and, with that extracted, to find not a method toward what some Catholics call, with some contempt, "union all round," but the recognition of groups, in whatsoever religion they may be, as in fact practicing, though with different definitions, the same character-modifying exercises.

The subject is, however, so new and large that here only a few tentative suggestions can be given as to the lines which might [warrant] investigation. Its difficulty and the kind of "convergent evolution" that it might detect may be illustrated by the fact that, though dogmas in the more conservative churches may not change for centuries (and so the superficial enquirer may consider such churches unalterable and rigid), the actual practices may be continually evolving. As Dr. G. G. Coulton, the medievalist, has proved, many of the actual practices of pre-Trentine Catholicism often bore as little likeness to the present Roman Catholic pattern as that pattern does to its contemporary Protestantism. Two people of the same generation are often more in basic agreement, though each assert that the other is wrong, than either would be with their own medieval ancestor. As Dr. Percival Dearmer, the liturgiologist, has shown in the Mass—that conservative heart of the Roman Church, that body of conservatism—an evolution [that] has continued through the centuries, and indeed sometimes has become a devolution. Modern Low Mass, as he shows, is an actual "social decadence" [i.e., in decline]; a rite which was once a culmination and creative focus of sociality [has] now become a private business, a priest and one server being all that are required.

If then in the Roman Catholic Church social evolution does go on in response to certain subconscious shifts of need and interest, how much more should we expect this in freer churches? For example, anyone who has studied the social patterns of the Quaker meeting as it has continued for nearly three centuries will see not only that it is moving, but that it has almost finished one process and is turning into another. From a "free-moving" and generalized organism, it is tending toward becoming specialized and more fixed. At the beginning, the "free group" generated sufficient energy to produce an intensity of conviction, a *metanoia*, which felt all forms, other than occasional unpremeditated outbursts of speech, to be limiting. Speech, even, may have been rather a collapse than a culmination, a failure to "hold one's spiritual breath"—the need, not to heighten conviction but to release a pressure of unspoken realization that was becoming unbearable in its intensity.

So the "ministerial" pattern begins to appear and is now followed by more people than ... the original Quaker practice. The Sufi practice would also seem to have begun by being a spontaneous kinaesthetic response—or detensioning—of a spiritual experience of acute intensity. Later it developed into the stately "sun and planet" ritual–dance. The Holy Communion in the early Church—it, too, would seem largely to have derived its pattern from an overflow of psychic energy. This first compelled an unpremeditated expression. Then regulation channeled such outbursts and made them seemly. And, finally, when that flow was failing, [it] kept the last drops from being lost in the sands of indifference.

If one generalization may be permitted in this vital but undeveloped subject, it would be [the following]. Up to the present, intelligence has not known how to produce this sense of unity. All that rational, conscientious social humans have been able to do has been to provide reservoirs in which these outbursts might be conserved, kept against drought, and not permitted during flood to inundate the surrounding countryside. Indeed, there is not a little truth in the re-mark regarding the periodic socioreligious revivals of the Middle Ages that "to set an enthusiast to catch an enthusiast was the moral of me-dieval monasticism." Yet at best it is a half-truth, and our practical concern today is with the further part of this problem: Cannot the ded-icated intelligence go on and learn how, not merely to control a "gusher" from the spiritual deep, but also how to drill down to such depths and to release this power constantly and adequately?

As a matter of fact, the traditional common method used by the Protestant churches to bring about individual metanoia—the revivi-fied sense of the Beloved, and eternal community and of the soul's part in it—was by conversion. Conversion is under a cloud; but it will of course come back with all its problems unanswered, all its disad-vantages unremedied, unless the religious sociologist can show us a more excellent way. At present we reject conversionism for fair rea-sons, individual and social: too often it does not endure with the individual, too often it holds them only with the rudimentary appeal of private salvation. But it is not enough to reject, not enough just to be "Protest-ants." And though this research is still in embryo [form], here again a few hints as to possible practical discovery are to be had.

Though granted little significance, the fact is well known to all stu-dents of religious patterns that in such groupings there is a clear relationship to be detected between quantity and quality, between size and effectiveness. The small Quaker worship group "works" bet-ter than the large. That this has nothing to do with rational convenience is shown by the fact that a silent meeting which is small nearly always achieves a greater intensity, a greater awareness of in-tegration, than a large one. The basic unit for Jewish [communal] worship is ten. There is some evidence that in primitive Christianity the dozen was considered as the ideal number for the Agape. The multiplication of altars may have had its origin not in a growing hag-iolatry, but in the intuitive feeling that, when a group exceeded the dozen, ... another [group] should be formed.

In exploring a subject in which detailed research is still to [dis-cover], no hint should be neglected. It is therefore worth adding to the above slight evidence from recognized religious practices, two from religion's penumbra. Work such as Dr. Margaret Murray's on the witch cult in Europe has shown that this cult was a denigrated survival of the old fertility religion, arrested at the totemistic level of its development. Its relevance to this enquiry lies in the fact that the "coven," the unit of meeting, was confined to twelve. That the sense of unison and degree of group suggestibility was at its maximum at such a number we need to recognize, even though such a unison was employed for antisocial purposes.

So, too, with respect to another almost excommunicate cult, spiritualism. Though when successful, a spiritualist church may attempt to copy the manners and proportions of standard churches, yet no enquirer into psychical research can doubt that the strange, still unclassified phenomenon of the séance is at its maximum when the sitting includes about a dozen members. In such a grouping, circularly arranged, the optimum conditions seem present for creating a field of energy beyond the capacities of any one individual; and, on the other hand, this field seems only to grow weaker if the group is enlarged. In social experimentation, there is also a little further confirmatory evidence. John S. Hoyland, the British Quaker who between the two Wars made a number of fruitful efforts to initiate decentralized economic enterprises for persons permanently unemployed, discovered that the optimum unit for individuals working at an agricultural project was about thirty. But for a worship unit, he had to lower the number. He had thought that twenty was satisfactory, but it is probable that further experimentation, especially as the group became more integrated, would show that at the traditional dozen the best results would be obtainable.

There is a natural unwillingness to reduce groups and compel secondary groups to form (thus disrupting the original), especially when this seems at the behest of some psychological and self-conscious whim. Such evidence as given above regarding the basic, essential [elements] in religious social patterning is of course very slight. Nevertheless, though scanty, it is sufficient to suggest a possible line of research. Religious experience is now considered essential religion. That means, if it is to be real, religious exploration. But religious experimentation is still, if not frowned upon, viewed with apprehension. And there is reason for that. Even if nothing but our superconscious were involved, to try and be too scientific

310

about that, too self-conscious, is not that enough to bring its processes to a standstill? Here then we seem [to be] facing a dilemma.
Accurate knowledge is necessary if religion is to go on serving modern, self-conscious people. Père Poulain, the Jesuit authority on
prayer, could hardly be charged with rash empiricism. Yet he begins
his classic study, *Des Grâces d'Oraison*, by pointing out the necessity
of modernizing traditional knowledge and making the approach
conscious, systematic, scientific. And this intention of his was chosen for express approval by Pius X when commending the book.
There is then no doubt a necessity that we should understand and
even analyze the elements that go to making a living religious group-
praxis. Superstition is simply the accretion of waste products that
the living religion of the day was not vital enough to eliminate.

There seems no more hopeful point of approach to this necessary but
difficult study than through the study and testing out of the social patterns that are found to be the invariable concomitant of high and
"recharging" worship. The first and simplest opening—already suggested—is the study of number. As numbers may easily be too high,
so, on the other hand, when religion is intensive, especially Protestant
religion with its stress on the individual and their individual approach
to the One, the value of number may be neglected. Mental prayer—
rising from meditation to contemplation—has now become an active
interest of many who, till this [time] have been outside any church.
There is a danger that such explorers will lose much help and guidance through their shrinking from group worship. The demonstration
that in organized group worship—provided that each constituent is indeed devoutly worshipping—there is a value for the individual not to
be obtained in solitary prayer, however necessary that, too, is—such a
demonstration will yield remarkable results for working religion.

Today there are tens of thousands of enquirers who have already found answers to their first questions: Is religion worthwhile;
does it work; is it essential? The next questions are these: Can [com-
munal] worship be shown to be a necessity; are churches an
essential armature (as modelers say) to give support and [founda-
tion] to the religious life, or are they simply a crust and patina that
confines and corrodes a religious life that has become too weak to
continue to burgeon?

The answer of history is that churches have been both. The challenge of the future is that they should decide which they will be. But the new Protestantism, as we may perhaps call this new individual interest in, and exploration of, the life of prayer, cannot be indifferent as to this issue. Its own progress depends on the churches' power to become armatures and to break with any suggestion that they are patinas. And the churches' power to do that will depend not a little on the help that such exploring individuals are ready to give in sharing in the exploration of joint patterns of worship. It may well be that if the churches can decide to use such explorers as liaisons, rather than as one-hundred percent converts, if they will agree on a concordat of worship pattern rather than on a uniformity of creed, a new age may be dawning for religion through this evolution of further integrations of actual communion.

Suffering

Originally published in *Christendom*,
Vol. 12, No. 2, Spring 1947

FEW PROBLEMS CONCERN US MORE than the problem of suffering. But, as matter of fact, we really seldom face up to it. This may seem a strange statement to make about a people that spends probably more than any other nation has ever spent on hospitals and medicine, and that, when it invented a religion all of its own, called it "Science," and devoted it to the elimination of human pain. Yet the truth of the above fact is confirmed, not disproved, by these two observations [i.e., we are concerned with the problem of suffering; we seldom face up to it]. These two reactions of the richest society the world has ever seen, proved—by their contradictoriness—that modern humans were not putting any real thought into the problem of pain. For not only was America refusing to think deeply, to diagnose, on pain. The same was true of all Western peoples. No research was being undertaken into pain itself.

Some dozen years ago, the present writer was asked to address the junior faculty at one of the largest London hospitals. He asked for such an investigation—that pain should no longer be dismissed as a symptom, but studied in itself. One of the senior members wrote to him saying that he had tried for years to get any foundation interested in the problem. He had failed. And it was clear that he had failed because of the whole climate and prejudice of medical research. The physiological or materialistic assumption so ruled all thinking that pain was regarded as something that of course would yield and disappear when physiological knowledge was complete.

And there was much to support the notion, at the beginning. Even today there is a constant stream of analgesics and anesthetics pouring out from the chemical and biochemical laboratories. The hope that it will be possible to render people painless, and so incapable of suffering, is still held by most researches in the nervous system. And, on the other hand, there is the work in hypnosis which shows that when drugs fail, there may yet be another path to painlessness by direct access to the deep mind that registers suffering. Yet, even on these findings, there would be grounds for further enquiry, for that disquiet which leads to radical discovery.

For we know, well enough, three things: first, that there are physical pains that manage to elude all defenses; secondly, that when they are defeated in one attack, they may return in a worse and more overwhelming form; and, thirdly, that there is some strange relationship between physical pain and mental suffering, and between all suffering and the sense of the worth of life. But though we know these things, we don't like facing them. For the conclusions that they suggest might be very unpalatable. Ever since the close of the Ages of Religion—when this world was considered as a bridge to another and this life as a training for that—we have felt that we must, can, and will make heaven here. And as we have become more materialistic, we have tended to make out that Utopia to be one of healthy animals enjoying their sense life ever more fully, ever more exclusively. Hence, we hold, in spite of the facts, that physical pain is the supreme misery, the one thing that stands in the way of our enjoying ourselves perfectly, and that mental pain can only be a resultant or shadow thrown by some disarrangement in the body.

This conclusion, which we see rises from our determination to enjoy ourselves here and now and with the use of all our senses, has led to some equally mistaken views about physical life. Naturally, if we were determined to be sensualists, we had to make out that nature, when left without the fussiness and limitations of moral law, was healthy. We said, "It is natural to be healthy and happy and to be well because you are doing as you please." But as a matter-of-fact, natural history does nothing to bear this out. It is clean assumption, wishful thinking to help us make the case we want. All wild animals seem to be infested with parasites. The great London Zoo showed that every animal in captivity improved in health because it was possible to rid the poor victim of some of his devouring "guests." Dr. William Swinton, the keeper of the Mesozoic Reptiles in the British Museum, is one of the greatest authorities on disease as shown in fossil bones. He has proved that back to the giant Saurians, such diseases as arthritis, cancer, rodent ulcers, [and] osteomyelitis were quite common. Whether these creatures suffered we can't say. That they were often terribly diseased is certain, and it is certain that they did not owe their infections to humans. The animals we see are generally active, because as soon as they become exhausted, they either fail to get their food or another animal eats them. Wildlife is then full of suffering, passive suffering. But it is quite as full of active suffering.

For when we look into the question of pain, we find that there are two kinds of suffering. This is the first important discovery we make, and it is from this point that we can pursue our problem and possibly find a new insight. These two kinds of suffering, passive and active, are certainly found in all wildlife. For besides the death penalty exacted on all wild creatures if they fail to keep well, there is also a price of suffering exacted for every one of the vital activities. Most animals have to work themselves, literally, to death to get enough to live. They are worn out long before they have lived as long as they do live, [even] if their food is found for them. The social animals are no exception. A bee could live a whole season. As a matter of fact, it lives about six weeks. Its wings wear out with the incessant work for the hive, and then it is left to die. The raising of young exacts a heavy toll from all animals. Nor does the cost the parents pay excuse the young from even greater effort. [Many] creatures never succeed in getting out of the egg. Birth is the very first of every creature's agonies. Microscopic dental research has discovered the scar of that struggle marked, as is the track of a major illness, on the teeth of all dentine animals. In the nest there is struggle. The weaker are pushed to the wall. Once its siblings have pushed it over that frontier, the parent birds are utterly deaf to their starving chick's cry.

Yet there appears no way out of this agony. For, if left with so much food that they need make no effort, all animals seem to degenerate. Birds lose their wings—they do not change them back into hands. Grazing animals lose their lower forefeet. The right whale, the most powerful animal that has ever evolved, is now so helpless, owing to the fact that it simply has to swim through a thin soup of food to feed itself, that a shark, the *orca gladiator* ... can swim into its mouth and eat out its tongue. All animals, when free to breed without restraint, seem to multiply until a virus plague suddenly gains on them and wipes out all or nearly all the species.

In wildlife, then, not only is there suffering, but also suffering seems necessary to life. Unless the creature will make a painful effort to live, it must fall back into the clutch of destruction and death. The fish that will not swim against the stream must drown.

And yet none of us can feel, when watching creatures at the height of their effortful living, that life is simply a cruel trap. Nor, indeed, when that effort begins to fail in them—which is nearly always as soon as reproduction ceases—can anyone but a sentimentalist wish to delay death, since the power to reply to life's service is gone. Can we then fail to see, even at animal level, [the] two kinds of suffering, [passive and active], and, even at this dimly conscious depth, is it not already clear that pain and pleasure are not the two standards whereby life's value is to be gauged?

All through the history of living things, must we not recognize another, a different, a completely opposed principle, a law of being that disregards the pleasure–pain principle as an utter misconception of life's purpose? Indeed, before we go on to consider humans, we must ask a larger question: whether we have not up to the present, at least in the Modern Age, completely [misunderstood] the life process through an unconscious mistake in our premises. Increasingly, it becomes difficult to account for any living process unless we recognize the presence of *connation*, the element of striving that is the specific sign of the life process in contrast to the entropic character of all non-living processes. Indeed as Nikolai Lossky has pointed out (*The World as an Organic Whole*), it may well be that all life is "*ectropic*" and is a process of reversing, or at least arresting, entropy. (See also Dr. J. A. V. Butler, "Life and the Second Law of Thermodynamics," *Nature*, Aug. 3, 1946.) If then the character of life is connation—a striving toward an end, even if that end be no more than stabilization—a pleasure–pain [explanation] is an inadequate and misleading description of the process, because comfort and dis-comfort—at least here and now—do not enter in. The pleasure of the moment is disregarded and [the] risk of pain [is] undertaken in order to reach another state than that in which the creature finds itself. Probably wherever there is reproduction, there is a departure from comfort toward the attainment of another condition in which en-larged experience, rather than the removal of discomfort, will prove to be the criterion of success.

Those, however, who have sentimentalized over the animal have said that its tragedy is, though it is true that it is thrust by the life of the race toward ends for which it will through its instincts sac-rifice itself, it cannot know these ends. But as it cannot know the end, neither can it see the painful length of the way. It is saved from hav-ing to "look before and after, / And pine for what is not,"[76] from counting the cost and shrinking from what lies before it. It goes from moment to moment, and the more animal psychology is studied (see Eliot Howard's *The Nature of a Bird's World*), the clearer it becomes that each crisis brings with it not only the appropriate reaction, but even the additional access of strength and willingness to face that issue (animal grace). The fact seems to be that animals in their wild state—when domesticated, their psyche has been radically altered by making it dependent on a human and not on the race—are not individuals but units of their species and that it is in the linear psyche of the entire species that we must look for that stream of conscious-ness that is striving to a goal and which counts the cost. What we do know now without a doubt is that as soon as in any individual wild animal the effort of full activity becomes impossible, and passive suffering might begin, that individual is swept out of the effort-stream into oblivion.

Now it is clear that though this element can be recognized in ani-mals—the teleological striving—yet in humans alone does it become explicit. In humans there is evident a personal choice and individual responsibility. Their chief characteristic [is that] they can choose, and their primal and basic choice is the construction that they decide to put upon life. Will they see it as a private concern out of which they are to get as much pleasure with as little cost as they can, or will they put meaning first and subordinate their feelings to that? Humans are not fallen because they have obtained intense and detached consciousness. Their fall is becoming *self*-conscious, engrossed with self. (Recall Dr. William Inge's remark on Plotinus: "*Self*-consciousness is a kind of inattention.") Then, as Eckhart has said, in an ever-more confined shrinking, humans draw themselves in. First, they falsely identify themselves with one moment ("temporality"). Next, with one place ("multiplicity"). And finally, with their separate body ("corporeality" or sensuality), the ultimate entropic goal of materialism.

This is, of course, a failure of vitality. And the symptom that humans are so failing is that they become increasingly passive, failing to take the initiative, afraid of cost, effort, and painstaking. Creative ages, we can see clearly, are marked by the adoption of meaning as the criterion of the worth of life. Hence there is great increase in profound art, philosophy, and radical discovery. Decadent ages have as their sole criteria comfort and pleasure, the accumulation of wealth to protect that comfort, and the only pursuit, amusement, which means the absence of the Muses because they are the names for all the creative interests of humanity.

The view of life that says that life is only to be understood teleologically, does not say that humankind does not suffer or that suffering is an illusion or even that it may not be necessary. What it does say is that to judge things by the pleasure–pain principle is irrelevant and is only attempted when people have lost the true criterion: meaning. Pain does exist, and if people will not find out what it means and solve it in the meaning of the whole, then [pain] itself will become the end of existence—as the thing to be avoided at any cost. What has been called "the hedonistic paradox" is the facing of the fact that the way to find happiness is not to seek it but to find that it has come of itself as a byproduct of striving for ends and meanings greater than individual happiness. So too with pain. To strive to avoid it is to set up against oneself unconsciously the infinite growth in hypersensitiveness. So luxuries are always turning themselves into necessities. The way to escape pain is neither to attempt to soothe it away with comforts nor with analgesics. A life without feeling is hated by the life within us more than keen pain. The way out from pain is not by escape and rest but by effort.

So we come back to the two aspects of pain. They will remain fatally confused as long as we think of pain–pleasure as the meaning of life, instead, were that true, as the proof that life has no meaning. There is, no doubt, the possibility of passive pain, indeed the certainty, unless we will do what we should about it. For humans are free to choose passive pain if they will and to prolong it in a way that an animal mercifully cannot. As we have seen, the time that an animal is permitted to stay in passive pain is only so long as it may pause and summon all its powers to see whether it can recover, return to the attack, [and] regain the power of positive effort. Even while it is doing that, it is not truly passive and therefore is not suffering in the deep, frustrant, and tragic sense of that word. Humans, because they have become individualized, and so can ... identify themselves with their bodies, try to prolong the state of passive suffering because they do not wish to recover the power of active effort and painstaking expression. Having wanted only comfort, pleasure, and sensual ease, when these are over, people can only keep on retreating from pain, hoping in the dregs to find clean drink. They are skulking where the chances of recovery are least, living in pain where they can never throw it off. This is the tragedy of a vast part of human invalidism.

We must then distinguish with the utmost sharpness two things that our sensualism and defeatism—our refusal to concede that meaning is the secret of life—have made us confuse and take as one. To do that, we must borrow two words from the Greek. The low sensual suffering is rightly called *patheia*, and with that word goes for us its various senses of decay, collapse and failure, infection and defeat. But there is its opposite pole—the other word for the other kind of pain. That is *agonia*—a word taken from the wrestling match, its primary meaning. No doubt when a man is wrestling, striving to win a race, climbing a peak at the very limit of breath and muscle endurance, he is in pain. His face shows it, [as] contorted as the woman's face [is often seen] in childbirth. But to tell a person that they are in pain is irrelevant—indeed they are probably unaware of it. For supreme effort banishes that kind of self-conscious introspective shrinking sensitiveness.

The same, too, is true of things of the mind—mental effort. The eighteenth century's highest praise for the supreme workmanship of the time, and the master that produced it, was that it showed its maker to be "a very painful man." This certainly did not mean that they were a person always full of aches and pains, but that they were one who could *take* any amount of pains and was never content until they had. It might look exhausting to the onlooker, but to the worker—what engrossment, what absorbed delight. So Carlyle could rightly say that genius is the infinite capacity for taking pains. Such indeed that supreme artist Michelangelo proved himself to be when he came down from the Sistine [ceiling] with crippled back and boots that stuck to the flesh.

Nor is patience itself a passive word. It can be the supreme activity. The word "suffer" in English is a strong word. For when we say, "Suffer this man to do something he desires," we mean that we ask the stronger of the two, one who has [surplus] self-control and masterly patience, out of their excess of such strength, to allow a weaker, less-controlled creature, the tolerance, the time, and the room in which they may, through that generosity, display themselves and "give way." To grant suffrage [i.e., certain leniencies and liberties] is for the strong who have power to be so strong that they will permit others to express themselves.

Passion, too, is a strong word, in the light of what suffering and passion are endured for. We use passion for the strongest feeling an ordinary young healthy person can feel: the feeling that will take them out of themselves, make them want to give their life for [another], make them feel unworthy of this other creature, and which will impose on them a series of animal denials—from putting them off their food when they are first in love right on to the life of long self-denial to give happiness to their family. Right up to the supreme Symbol of Sacrifice, the act is called The Passion, for though there is in it supreme suffering, the suffering is wholly transmuted by the purpose for which it is being undergone—"Who for the joy that was set before him, endured the Cross, despising the shame" [Hebrews 12:2].

We must not then think of suffering as something that can be treated as a materialistic concept. After all, on the grounds of true and valid materialism, there can be no such thing as suffering—it is purely subjective, private, personal. It is possible to see another body writhe; not one tang of its suffering is felt a millimeter from the surface of its skin. There is no material proof of pain, only of some of the correlates that at times seem to accompany it. Suffering as we may have it—the negative pole round which, and its complement, pleasure, all life then revolves in the vicious circle—is not the normal experience of life or humanity. Indeed, this picture of things only appears in those short phases when a society is going to pieces because it has lost all true sense of meaning and values and the real worth of living. Whenever there is meaning, then people know that suffering does exist but that its quality depends entirely on how it is taken.

If one has vitality and one's group has the sense to know what meaning is, then all that is asked of anything pleasurable or painful is whether it will lead to meaning. Once we have discovered that it makes for meaning, "makes sense," [and] results in ever fuller understanding, in purpose and design, then creative effort is roused. Then, however much the worker suffers, suffering becomes something that only matters as a gauge to the further capacity the sufferer has in them to give. The actual physical pain is transformed into a power of stimulant allowing the agonist to release more effort. And at the end, when they are at full capacity and feel that they have released their full effort, they are then above pain. Indeed we know as a physiological fact that they have won complete freedom from the pain. It is not that the pain is not present in the nerve impulses transmitting it, but that it cannot be registered by the consciousness through which alone it could become real. This is because with total attention, total interest in a goal and end, no more room is left in the field of consciousness to notice what is going on short of that goal. The complete anaesthesia of hypnosis is nothing more than a striking example of how, when attention can be completely commanded, there is no room left in consciousness for any general feeling or any intruded impulse of pain. The entire capacity for feeling has been mobilized and transferred toward the object of supreme attainment.

Such is the state which everyone, which humanity at large, might attain if only it chose. But the choice means giving up the pleasure–pain principle as the director and explanation of human behavior and putting in its stead the doctrine of meaning. Those who have found the meaning of the whole and so live that [this] meaning may be the sole purpose of their lives are headed for this release. They are not trying to avoid pain. But one of the other "things that are added" when the Kingdom of Heaven is put first and made dominant in a person's life, is freedom from pain as the world knows it and dreads it, and by its dread enlarges it.

Wanted: Spiritual Muscle Builders

Originally published in *Faith and Freedom*,
Vol. 6, No. 5, January 1955

A church which becomes a gymnasium for spiritual muscles will keep us fit. It can make religion so inspiring and exacting that the church will hold the loyalty of its members out of their awareness of its necessity for themselves.

–Original Editor's Note

AS RELIGION DESIRES to meet contemporary needs, we should no longer look upon the churches as clinics, still less relief institutions. A clinic means a place for beds, where, as the word shows, the inmates recline and, in many cases, decline.

It has been said, with bitter point, that churches began by being power stations: they then declined into hospitals. Today they seem little more than almshouses for the [unskilled] and incurable who are looking out for someone to keep their consciences, to keep them comfortable, and to keep them for good at the expense of the charitable.

The church of today faces an immense opportunity, but only if it closes as an almshouse to be reopened a gymnasium. A gymnasium means a place where people go, not to wrap up but to strip; to work, not to doze; to lose fat, not to gain it; to gain muscle—not sympathy; to pay to be fit, not to be paid for being incompetent, flaccid complainants! But how to rouse people even to wish to lose their sloth?

Psychiatry today has kept busy just salvaging people, just returning them to what is still called "normalcy." But normalcy really means, at present, and can only be, that state of neurosis in which every society must land if it thinks only of means and neglects ends. As a consequence, a psychiatrist generally knows little of mental and spiritual growth. They are concerned only with arresting decay. They are a repairperson, not an architect.

Humans Are Still Growing

Religion today can and must create a concept of a goal, a vision of humanity, even at its present best, as an uncompleted temple. And this concept must be put in forms that people can understand and desire.

In the Fourth Gospel, Christ states it succinctly: "that they may have life and have it more abundantly" [John 10:10]. There we see our creative alternative. We have seen that besides the familiar threat and promise, "Either go back to barbarism or on to socialism," (impossible regress or false progress), beckons this far more energizing and inspiring offer of Egress. Egress simply means to cooperate with Evolution. Let it continue in you.

[Upon] reviewing the whole of life and scanning all the surviving species, biology notes that humans and humans alone seem to be unfinished. Humans alone seem to have, unspent within them, great energy. This energy can transform them and release in them the still-untapped capacities that are locked inside them. Further, medicine and hygiene, taking stock of the human unit, have discovered that if these creative capacities are not employed, they become the fruitful source of psychosomatic illness. A balked disposition, a timidly or lazily neglected talent—such a condition, research has shown, is found to be the fountainhead of what in the end becomes crippling and agonizing physical disease.

Muscles for Spiritual Adventure

The Power of Life is determined that humans shall never retreat into anaesthetic comfort and become a creature incapable of adventure and only content to be kept. If the churches do not awake to this fact, they will find themselves stranded. The two facts stated above compel a decision:

(1) If we are to tackle the growing neurosis and psychosis (ten percent of the population is, on a conservative estimate, in acute need of psychiatric help), we must show how to live fully. We can prove how our miseries spring from our cowardly sloth that refuses to live fully. We must try to communicate a new vision of life's worth—a demonstration of how rich life might be when it is lived to its full demand.

(2) This goal is attained and can only be attained by skilled, strenuous exercise of the mind, the emotions, and the physique. That is why it was said above that the church of today should be, and the church of tomorrow will have to be, much more of a gymnasium than an almshouse—or a museum.

In the churches that have survived, we still see the vestigial remnant of the original energy-arousing disciplines. But initiations that were experienced, when they worked, as real rebirths (and so ordeals, for ordeal means test, examination) have now been reduced to mere formalities.

The church that is worth joining, the church that is fit to retake the moral leadership of humanity, should be hard to join. It should be at least as morally difficult to become a full member of it as it is intellectually strenuous to become a member of Phi Beta Kappa. True, it should offer salvage to those of us who wish to recover, but, as a good psychiatrist does today, it should search our conscience [and] ask us: Is it our intention to become fit for strenuous growth, or do we wish only to [attract] further debilitating sympathy?

A church that becomes a gymnasium for spiritual muscles will keep us fit. It can make religion so inspiring and exacting that the church will hold the loyalty of its members, not out of their sense of duty to others, but out of their awareness of its necessity for themselves. If the church will not so reorient and restyle its service and find this new contemporary focus, well then, other organizations will take its opportunity. Already the writing is on the wall.

The reaction of collectivism, fascism, communism, [and] socialism has nothing to offer. But a number of "spiritual seedlings" are starting up under the stress of human need. They have nothing to do with the "crank churches," the "fancy religions" or revived "revivalism," or the heated-over hot-gospeller. They do not call themselves churches. They possess no [administrative offices] or endowment. Each of them is stripped, stark, streamlined to an exact, exacting, specific, and desperate human need.

Ad Hoc Witnessing

Examples of these functional groups are shown by Alcoholics Anonymous, Narcotics Anonymous, and Recovery Incorporated (the latter grew specifically for the mentally troubled as the other two developed to combat dipsomania and drug addiction). We can find a number more. Each was forged by desperate people who, through a terrific ordeal and with the help of others who had gone through the same experience, came to an initiation, a new fellowship with fellow initiates and a new life of helping fellow sufferers to help themselves.

But that service gives no [handouts]. It rouses the patient to work out their own salvation and insists that a principal part of that work lies in holding down a job. These *ad hoc* churches make a wonderful witness to the human need and to what can be done in specific desperate crises. They point to what the [Christian] Church can and must do—not for particular cases, not as a last resort—but for *everyone*, in time, preventively, and as the gate to full living.

When the great pandemic of smallpox spread across Europe two hundred and fifty years ago, an intelligent woman accompanied her husband who was going as an ambassador to Constantinople. Smallpox had spread out from these Turkish territories. The Turks told the lady that if she would save her children, she must first feed them well and then expose them to a mild case of smallpox infection.

Two generations later, Edward Jenner found that cowpox would give an equally good resistance with much less danger. And so we have worked with increasingly skilled and more accurately adjusted inoculations. In psychology and the therapy of people's soul, we are stopped still at the stage which the medicine of the body reached five or six generations ago. We leave people to fall into disaster. Some survive and are stronger. Many succumb.

We know that general resistance cannot be preserved by protection and isolation. That is now called "false immunity." As soon as such "soft health" is exposed to infection, it is swept away.

This means if we wish to salvage ourselves, we must take preventive inoculations in the realm of the psyche precisely as we do in that of the physique. Such preventive inoculations can be given in the form of specific exercises, initiations, and ordeals. The churches once practiced these exercises, and for this, therefore, the output of the churches (i.e., their fully trained membership) was respected throughout the world and recognized as the Salt of the Earth, the Light of the World.

But, it will be asked, what contribution could such a therapy make to the social situation, the political crisis? Psychological salvage can solve many social problems. The direction in which our society is heading is marked out by the fact that one bed out of every five is occupied by the inscrutable disease schizophrenia and its abject patient [is] schizophrenic. The Church was meant as a "cure of souls"—its original title, a bearer of good news to individuals, setting them free from anxiety, delusion, and sin. Would the Church not be fulfilling its social function if it could prevent any of its members [from] swelling this inundating tide and recover those who have already sunken?

Yet we know people do require of a church not merely that it yield salvage and preventive work, but that it set before the world a dynamic way of thinking, a creative approach to the social problems of humankind. And in fact, this is what has been one of the outstanding features of each of the successive Christianities. The Apostolic Church taught, "Let your light so shine before men that they may see your good works, and glorify your Father which is in heaven" [Matt. 5:16].

Glossary of Sanskrit Terms

-*Advaitist*: A follower of nondual Vedanta.

-*Ananda*: Supernal bliss, which is the nature of God and can be experienced by a spiritual aspirant.

-*Atman*: A person's innermost nonmaterial spiritual essence; akin to one's soul, though the Atman is devoid of ego and personality.

-*Avatar*: An incarnation of God in human form.

-*Bhakti*: Devotion to God.

-*Brahmachari*: One who practices continence.

-*Brahmaloka*: A blissful, nonmaterial celestial plane; heaven.

-*Brahman*: The limitless, nondual essence of existence; God.

-*Dhyana*: A state of unbroken concentration; one-pointed meditation.

-*Ishtam*: An aspirant's spiritual ideal.

-*Japam*: Repetition of a mantra.

-*Jiva*: The individual self, bound in time and space.

-*Jnana*: The conceptual or abstract approach to God for intellectually inclined aspirants.

-*Karma*: The theory of cause and effect; predetermination.

-*Karma yoga*: The path of realizing God by serving the divine in all creatures and performing all actions selflessly.

-*Lila*: The concept that this universe is merely a divine play, a joyful pastime of God.

-*Mantra*: A short word or phrase conferred by a capable, qualified spiritual teacher that is infused with immense spiritual power.

-*Maya*: The illusion that this three-dimensional universe is the true reality.

-*Sadhu*: A Hindu ascetic renunciate, though not necessarily a hermit.

-*Samadhi*: The deepest state of nondual contemplation.

-*Samsara*: The cycle of birth, death, and rebirth, to which all creatures are subject until they attain to enlightenment.

-*Sat-Chit-Ananda*: "Existence, Consciousness, Bliss," which is the inherent nature of God.

-*Sattvic*: Pure, harmonious, balanced.

-*Siddhis*: Psychic powers.

-*Tat Twam Asi*: "Thou Art That," which means that a person's spiritual essence ("Thou") is one with God ("That").

-*Vedanta*: A school of Hindu philosophy, teaching that a person's innermost nature is divine and the goal of life is to manifest this divinity.

Additional Nonfiction Titles by Gerald Heard

The Code of Christ
(Wipf and Stock Publishers, 2007 edition)

The Creed of Christ
(Wipf and Stock Publishers, 2007 edition)

Prayers and Meditations (edited by Gerald Heard)
(with a new foreword by Marvin Barrett)
(Wipf and Stock Publishers, 2008 edition)

The Five Ages of Humanity
(Sky Parlor Publications, 2023 edition)

The Source of Civilization
(Wipf and Stock Publishers, 2019 edition)

Training for the Life of the Spirit
(Wipf and Stock Publishers, 2007 edition)

Notes

1 John Roger Barrie, "Spiritual Legacy of Gerald Heard," edited version of website post from johnrogerbarrie.com, October 6, 2021.

2 John Roger Barrie, "Gerald Heard and Vedanta," a talk given at the Vedanta Society of Southern California on May 1, 2005, later published in the July–Aug. 2008 issue of *Vedanta For East and West*. The present version has been expanded in many sections. This version also specifies the sources of various references and quotations, and it incorporates corrections as warranted, the principal of which is pegging Gerald Heard's date of initiation by Swami Prabhavananda as occurring in 1939, as is now substantiated by two sources.

3 Gerald Heard, "What Vedanta Means to Me" in *Vedanta and the West*, Jan.–Feb. 1951, pp. 26–27.

4 Gerald Heard, "First Pilgrimage," a lecture given at the First Congregational Church in Akron, Ohio, April 1953.

5 "First Pilgrimage."

6 "First Pilgrimage."

7 "First Pilgrimage."

8 Christopher Isherwood, *My Guru and His Disciple* (New York: Farrar, Straus & Giroux, 1980), p. 68.

9 *My Guru and His Disciple*, p. 310.

10 Jay Michael Barrie, letter to Swami Yogeshananda, May 14, 1981, excerpts of which are posted on https://www.geraldheard.com/writings-and-recollections/2017/8/2/trabuco-college-tryout, accessed July 2024.

11 Jay Michael Barrie, "Introduction," *Training for the Life of the Spirit* by Gerald Heard (New York: Strength Books, 1975), p. 28.

12 Jay Michael Barrie, "Introduction," p. 28.

13 "Trabuco College," https://www.geraldheard.com/blog/2017/7/22/trabuco, accessed July 2024.

14 "Trabuco College," accessed July 2024.

15 Huxley began researching his *Perennial Philosophy*, a classic anthology of mystical texts, by around May 1944 [Sybille Bedford, *Aldous Huxley: A Biography* (New York: Alfred A. Knopf, Inc. and Harper & Row, Publishers, Inc., 1974), p. 427], and he completed it in April 1945 [*Aldous Huxley: A Biography*, p. 437]. However, in contrast to conventional accounts which contend that he wrote *The Perennial Philosophy*

at Trabuco College or that he primarily used Trabuco's library for the book's source material, two reports present different narratives.

Firsthand witness Prof. William H. Forthman—a Trabuco College resident from June 16, 1944, when he had just graduated from high school, until May 5, 1945, when he was called up by his local draft board—wrote in a 2005 letter to the Vedanta Society of Southern California (VSSC), "It is false to say that Aldous penned *The Perennial Philosophy* using the Trabuco College library. He and Maria were living in the desert at that time (where he had a fine collection of books), and he brought page proofs of his book to Trabuco when it was ready for publication. But Trabuco played no significant role in its composition" [William H. Forthman, letter to the VSSC, June 7, 2005].

In addition, in his *Dawn and the Darkest Hour*, George Woodcock writes of Huxley's *Perennial Philosophy*: "an assiduously dispersed legend asserts that he actually wrote the book at Trabuco College, but there is no evidence of this in his published letters" [George Woodcock, *Dawn and the Darkest Hour—A Study of Aldous Huxley* (New York: The Viking Press, Inc., 1972), p. 239].

[16] William H. Forthman, letter to the VSSC, June 7, 2005.

[17] Jay Michael Barrie, "Introduction," p. 28.

[18] Jay Michael Barrie, "Introduction," p. 29.

[19] For the purpose of this collection, I have included Gerald Heard's published talk "On Ramakrishna" as one of these thirty-nine articles.

[20] See https://www.geraldheard.com/recollections for accounts posted by Swami Yogeshananda—"Trabuco College Tryout"; William Stafford—"We Built a Bridge"; Franklin Zahn—"Temporary Monk"; and Miriam King—"Life at Trabuco."

[21] *My Guru and His Disciple*, pp. 11, 14, 16.

[22] Marvin Barrett, personal reminiscence, from 2002, posted on https://www.geraldheard.com/blog/2017/7/22/later-years#r6, accessed July 2024.

[23] *My Guru and His Disciple*, p. 19.

[24] Gerald Heard, *The Creed of Christ* (Eugene: Wipf and Stock Publishers, 2007 edition), p. 32.

[25] Gerald Heard, *Training for the Life of the Spirit*, (Eugene: Wipf and Stock Publishers, 2007 edition), p. 14.

[26] *Training for the Life of the Spirit*, p. 13.

[27] Gerald Heard, *The Code of Christ* (Eugene: Wipf and Stock Publishers, 2007 edition), p. 123.

[28] *The Code of Christ*, p. 168.

[29] *The Creed of Christ*, p. 26.

[30] *Training for the Life of the Spirit*, p. 61.

[31] *Training for the Life of the Spirit*, p. 82.

[32] *Training for the Life of the Spirit*, p. 48.

[33] *The Creed of Christ*, p. 28.

[34] *The Creed of Christ*, p. 92.

[35] *The Creed of Christ*, p. 142.

[36] *The Creed of Christ*, p. 13.

[37] *The Creed of Christ*, p. 130.

[38] *The Code of Christ*, pp. 24–26.

[39] *The Creed of Christ*, pp. 64–65.

[40] *The Creed of Christ*, p. 63.

[41] *Training for the Life of the Spirit*, p. 40.

[42] *The Code of Christ*, pp. 7–8.

[43] *The Creed of Christ*, p. 31.

[44] *The Creed of Christ*, p. 61.

[45] *The Creed of Christ*, p. 100.

[46] *Training for the Life of the Spirit*, pp. 20–21.

[47] *The Creed of Christ*, p. 103.

[48] *The Creed of Christ*, pp. 108–109.

[49] Alfred, Lord Tennyson, "The Higher Pantheism," 1867. Heard cites this line three times in this collection, although he omits the words "is He," and he twice substitutes "or" for the last instance of "and," and he once omits the first "and." The complete, correct line reads as follows: "Closer is He than breathing, and nearer than hands and feet."

[50] *The Creed of Christ*, p. 168.

[51] *The Creed of Christ*, p. 119.

[52] *The Creed of Christ*, p. 71.

[53] *The Creed of Christ*, p. 79.

[54] *The Creed of Christ*, pp. 79–80.

[55] *The Creed of Christ*, p. 78.

[56] *The Creed of Christ*, pp. 73–74.

[57] *The Creed of Christ*, p. 83.

[58] *The Creed of Christ*, p. 98.

[59] *Training for the Life of the Spirit,* p. 17.

[60] *Training for the Life of the Spirit,* pp. 19–20.

[61] *Training for the Life of the Spirit,* pp. 41–44.

[62] *The Code of Christ,* pp. 111–112.

[63] *The Code of Christ,* p. 118.

[64] *The Code of Christ,* p. 122.

[65] *The Creed of Christ,* p. 68.

[66] *The Code of Christ,* p. 103.

[67] *Training for the Life of the Spirit,* pp. 94–95.

[68] Alfred, Lord Tennyson, "Locksley Hall," 1835. Heard misquotes the word "process" and instead uses—possibly intentionally—the more imaginative, less clinical word "circling." Heard cites this line four times in this collection. Tennyson's correct line reads as follows: "And the thoughts of men are widen'd with the process of the suns."

[69] *Voice of India,* May 1939.

[70] G.K. Chesterton, "The Ballade of a Strange Town" from *Tremendous Trifles* (1909).

[71] Robert S. Lynd and Helen Merrell Lynd, *Middletown: A Study in Modern American Culture* (New York: Harcourt, Brace and Company, Inc., 1929).

[72] Robert Browning, "Rabbi ben Ezra," 1864.

[73] Alice Meynell, "I Am the Way," 1921.

[74] William Ernest Henley, "Invictus," 1875.

[75] Matthew Arnold, "A Summer Night," 1852.

[76] Percy Bysshe Shelley, "To a Skylark," 1820.

About the Author

BORN IN LONDON on October 6, 1889, Henry FitzGerald "Gerald" Heard lived a life that would take many fascinating and fateful turns. Heard spent his university years at Cambridge University's Gonville & Caius College. There, in 1911, he was conferred a Bachelor of Arts degree with Honours in history.

Following Cambridge, Heard worked for Lord Robson of Jesmond, then for Sir Horace Plunkett, founder of the influential Irish Agricultural [later "Co-operative"] Organisation Society. Heard published his first book, *Narcissus*, in 1924, which advanced the revolutionary idea that fashion and architecture provide clues to the evolutionary stages of humankind. In 1929, he produced his second book, *The Ascent of Humanity*, a brilliant, groundbreaking essay on the philosophy of history that was awarded the British Academy's prestigious Hertz Prize.

Heard began his career as a public speaker in 1926, lecturing for three years under the auspices of Oxford University. In 1929, he became literary editor of *The Realist*, a short-lived but significant monthly journal of scientific humanism. There he worked with a distinguished editorial board that included Aldous Huxley, Julian Huxley, and H. G. Wells. Pacifists Heard and Aldous Huxley, associated with the Peace Movement, gave lectures in England in support of their cause during the mid-1930s.

From 1930 to 1934, Heard served as the BBC's first science commentator, commanding a large and regular listening audience with his sparkling fortnightly broadcasts. H. G. Wells said of him, "Heard is the only man I ever listen to on the wireless. He makes human life come alive." The prolific Heard published ten books during the 1930s.

Gerald Heard moved to America, arriving in New York City in April 1937 on the *S.S. Normandie*, accompanied by Aldous Huxley. He traveled throughout the United States, taught for a term at Duke University, and embarked on a lecture tour with Huxley before settling in Southern California in early 1938. The next year he met Swami Prabhavananda, founder of the Vedanta Society of Southern California. Heard subsequently introduced the ecumenical Vedanta philosophy to Huxley, Christopher Isherwood, and other Western notables, which prompted mystery writer Ellery Queen to write, "Gerald Heard is the spiritual godfather of this Western movement."

In 1941, Heard put the larger part of his personal financial resources into building and endowing the pioneering Trabuco College, which advanced comparative religion studies and interfaith practices in a coeducational, semi-monastic setting. Under the spiritual direction of Heard, and 30 years ahead of its time, Trabuco College was discontinued in 1947 and later donated to the Vedanta Society of Southern California. In addition to writing essays, articles, short stories, and delivering more than a hundred lectures, Heard published an astonishing eighteen books during the 1940s.

Alongside his nonfiction, Heard wrote several acclaimed mysteries and supernatural fantasies under the pen name H. F. Heard, including *Reply Paid* and *Doppelgangers*. He published two fiction anthologies, *The Great Fog* and *The Lost Cavern*. His bestselling 1941 novel, *A Taste for Honey*, praised by Christopher Morley and Boris Karloff, and listed among the exclusive Haycraft-Queen Cornerstones, was loosely adapted into a movie, 1967's *The Deadly Bees*, the first in the killer-bees genre. (Karloff played Mr. Mycroft in the ABC-TV adaptation of *A Taste for Honey*, titled "The Sting of Death," which aired in 1955.) His 1947 whodunit masterpiece, "The President of the United States, Detective" won first prize in the second-annual *Ellery Queen's Mystery Magazine*'s prestigious short-story contest.

For the remaining fifteen years of his active life, Heard spent his time and energy in writing, lecturing, research, travel, and making numerous radio and television appearances. He moderated an eight-part series, *Focus on Sanity*, which appeared on CBS television in 1957. He lectured at many of the major colleges and universities in the United States, including Harvard, Cornell, Princeton, and UCLA. He spoke at religious venues as diverse as the Vedanta Society, the First Congregational Church in Akron, Temple Sinai in Beverly Hills, and the Soto Zen Temple in Honolulu. Heard was a behind-the-scenes inspiration and catalyst who spurred many individuals to pivotal accomplishments in their careers. His last book was his 1964 magnum opus *The Five Ages of [Humanity]*, which Robert R. Kirsch, literary critic of the *Los Angeles Times*, praised as "the most important work to date of this challenging and brilliant philosopher, a volume which in scope and daring might be the 'Novum Organum' of the 20th century."

Gerald Heard, influential author, historian, lecturer, and philosopher, whom Rabbi Zalman Schachter-Shalomi referred to as "the repository of the most encompassing cosmology of his generation," succumbed peacefully on August 14, 1971, at his home in Santa Monica, California, at the age of eighty-one. For more information, visit www.geraldheard.com.

www.ingramcontent.com/pod-product-compliance
Lightning Source LLC
Chambersburg PA
CBHW060856120626
46553CB00001B/104